LEATHERCRAFT

LEATHERCRAFT

SID LATHAM

WINCHESTER PRESS

Designed by Fred Samperi
Photos by the Author

Published by Winchester Press
205 East 42nd Street
New York, N.Y. 10017

Printed in the United States of America

Library of Congress Cataloging in Publication Data

Latham, Sidney.
Leathercraft.

Bibliography: p.
Includes index.
1. Leather work. I. Title.
TT290.L36 1977 745.53'1 76-52410
ISBN 0-87691-227-7

CONTENTS

Acknowledgments

It was difficult, with all the fine leathercraftsmen in our country, to settle on those few represented in this book; many fine artisans have been left out because of time or distance.

For those who did work with me, my thanks are due: To Pete Gerber and Al Mar of Gerber Legendary Blades who allowed me to roam their factory freely and work with Doug Hutchins, head of the Gerber leather department; Sam Lucchese of the famed boot company in San Antonio, who gave much of his time for research on exotic leathers; Walter Kneubuhler, one of our premier knife craftsmen, who favors the knives and leatherwork of the Mountain Men; and Denverites Jerry Ashton and Jack Barnett whose meticulous work is shown in these pages.

One of the oldest leather companies in our short history is represented by S. D. Myres Saddle Company of El Paso, Texas, whose Jim Spurrier and Bill Wootres opened their workshop to my camera and recorder. In Savannah, Georgia, it was young Sam Lynah who represents the skills of the modern craftsman, and, finally, Jerry Rush and Gaile Bachand, who undertook the task of crafting a real Western-style fringed jacket.

To all these friends—some new and most old—who took the time to explain the intricate and involved methods of crafting leather, go my thanks and appreciation.

To Lilyan

Foreword

After spending some six months traveling around the country to visit leathercraftsmen and spend time in their workshops I can only attest that the crafting of leather has come a very long way since I first tried my hand at it many years ago.

While the hides remain the same, and improvements in tanning notwithstanding, skills in carving, stamping, and all the other tasks still require tremendous patience, especially during the learning process.

Anyone wishing to attain the high degree of skills shown in this book will learn that patience is the one primary asset required to do clean, artful work. There are no shortcuts in crafting with leather.

If there be one rule in leathercraft, it is: take your time. Don't try to hurry any process, but allow sufficient time to understand completely and exactly how the next step is to be taken. Leather is expensive, and becoming more so each day; move slowly before commencing expensive cuts on a piece of it until you fully understand what is to be done.

So read carefully, know your tools, and think about the first step. Good luck.

Sid Latham

CHAPTER ONE

An Introduction to Leathercraft

Leather is one of nature's most exciting materials. It appeals to the senses with both texture and scent—roll your fingers over a piece of finely tanned calf and it feels like a chunk of soft butter. Good leather is sensuous, exotic, and practically anything else you want to call it.

As a craft material, leather is unparalleled. It may be sewn, stamped, tooled, carved, molded, dyed, laminated, painted, and even burned with an electric pencil. It can be decorated with porcupine quills (if the craftsman is ambitious), covered with beadwork or silver conchas, laced, fringed, and even have bits of braided horsehair worked into the design for a Western or Mexican motif. Leather may be glued, hammered, formed, or molded. Any item that is woven or tied, either utilitarian or decorative, may be crafted from leather and will last for a hundred years or more, or—without care—dry and crack within a very short time.

Leather comes in all shapes, sizes, and finishes. It can be scaly like snake, lizard, or alligator skin, thick or thin, have hair on one side, or be smooth and silky, with the feel of a rare fabric.

The History of Leather

The history of leather is truly the history of mankind itself. Man has used leather from earliest times and its uses were passed from one culture to another. In fact, the earliest recorded examples are in the form of pictographs in caves—probably from around 20,000 BC—depicting hunters with skins about their bodies, and petroglyphs in ancient Egyptian tombs showing leather offerings to various gods and kings. Legend has it that

The Frontier Leather Company of Sherwood, Oregon, inspects all hides on arrival.

the ancient Greeks slept in deerskin beds so as to be protected from reptiles. In our own West, many of the Plains Indians wore shirts of skin that were considered to hold great powers in battle. And how about modern slang? We "skin" a man in a deal and there are those who play a "skin game." Some people are "thick skinned" and youngsters are frequently known to have their "hides tanned."

Incidentally, the tanning of leather is a measure of man's ability to improve and develop his skills as time goes on. Tanning removes impurities and makes the hides strong as well as pliable. It prevents the absorption of water and keeps the hide from drying out.

Oak tanning is still practiced today as it was thousands of years ago; it was first attributed to the ancient Hebrews. The Greeks knew chamois and opened the pores of a hide by continual washing and by rubbing oil into the pores while stretching the hide on a frame. This type of leather was used for much of the clothing of the upper class. It was soft and pliable and, more importantly, it was waterproof. Later, the Romans again improved upon known skills. Not only did they make softer leather for clothing, they also turned out exceptionally hard leather for wear in battle. In fact, they even crafted leather armor for their horses and chariots. This type of leather was molded to fit the wearer's body while still wet from the tanning "pickle." Then it was heat-treated or tempered until it was hard enough to deflect war arrows, the slash of a sword, or the thrust of a lance.

The Moors were probably the finest leatherworkers of their time and learned their skills when the Phoenicians invaded North Africa in 1600 BC. The Moors, like others, added their own unique skills, improved upon the tanning process, and introduced an exceptionally fine and supple leather made from goat. It became known as Moroccan goat and even today is used for the finest and most expensive bookbindings.

Time and conquest wait for no man and when the Moors moved across the Straits of Gibraltar to Spain in the eighth century AD, they took their traditions of fine leathercrafting with them. The Spanish combined their own techniques of leatherwork along with those of the far Sahara, and Cordova became for a time the most civilized city in the world and a center of the arts, not the least of which was leathercraft.

In those early days the secrets of tanning were passed down in families and through various tanners' and leatherworkers' guilds. Even today, leathercrafters' workshops can be found in the same locales in the cities of Fez, Meknes, or Marrakech where the ancient guilds operated. The traveler to North Africa may still see beautiful craftsmanship in knife sheaths, saddlebags, and all those other exceptional objects crafted by the leatherworkers of Morocco.

Tanning had a different history in the United States, particularly as it evolved among the American Indians. The Indians were the first craftsmen of our land. They might also be called our first ecology-minded society, since what they hunted was not only consumed for food, used for shelter, clothing, and weapons, but also supplied material for entertainment and even medicine.

Take the buffalo for example. A partial list of the uses of the buffalo is staggering: The hide, turned into soft buckskin, was used for cradles, moccasin tops, robes, bedding, belts, leggings, shirts, pouches, quivers, gun cases, dolls, and lance covers; the rawhide was used for shields, buckets, moccasin soles, drums and drumsticks, ropes, thongs, saddles, knife cases, quirts, bullet pouches, and a dozen more items; the tail was turned into fly brushes, decorations, and whips; the horns were used for cups, powder horns, spoons, ladles, and other objects; the hooves and feet were used for glue and rattles; muscles for sinew, bowstrings, thread, and cinches; bones were made into knives, arrowheads, saddletrees, and quirts; the scrotum was used for rattles; the paunch for bucket linings, cups, basins, and dishes; bladders were turned into sinew pouches, quill pouches, and small medicine bags; the tongue was considered a great delicacy and eaten immediately; other meats were converted into pemmican or jerky; the buffalo chips were burned for fuel or for smoke signals; the beard was used for ornamentation of clothing and weapons; the four-chambered stomach as containers for carrying and storing water, and the contents of the first stomach were used to treat frostbite and skin diseases; and, most important of all, the brains were used to tan the animal hide.

As can be seen, a single buffalo was really the department store of the Old West. Out of the buffalo came everything that was necessary to daily life; and, as the Sioux Indians used to say, every animal had enough brains to tan itself.

Brain tanning was unique to the American Plains Indians and provided the finest and most delicate buckskins for shirts, leggings, and other articles of clothing. The technique was explained to me by Blaine Beal, an oil-company executive and keen student of the Plains Indians.

Modern Tanning Methods

The success of any tanning operation begins with the safe handling of the hide after skinning the animal. Too many hides are ruined by being rolled up and tossed into a corner of the garage for weeks or months. The Sioux had no salt and simply tossed the hide over a branch to allow it to air dry; but for the modern tanner, the best method of preserving a green hide is to apply a generous amount of salt before rolling it up for storage. It will keep at least a year this way and be ready at the tanner's convenience. There are ten steps to produce quality buckskin. Some take only a few minutes and the longest about an hour, depending upon the individual's skill. Here are the ten steps in the order in which they should be performed:

Soaking. If the hide has been salted or even air-dried, it will probably have become quite stiff. Soaking in water will soften the hide and help remove the remaining blood from the skin. The water should be cool, not cold, and weighting the hide down with rocks will keep it wet and not allow it to float to the surface. Change the water if it becomes discolored or dirty and don't in any case let the skin soak more than twelve hours without a change of water. The limit of soaking is three days, but less than that will give more durability to the skin.

Stretching. While the skin is supple from soaking, it must be stretched and fleshed. A frame can be made from four 2 by 4s, about a foot larger than might seem necessary to allow for stretching. Spike the frame well, or better still, use angle irons, for many hides will bow a frame during the drying process.

Cut holes around the hide three or four inches apart with a sharp knife, then lace the hide to the frame using sturdy nylon rope. Once the skin is on the frame, being careful not to lace too tightly in the beginning, place the frame at a slant (a sawhorse would be fine) and begin the next operation.

Fleshing. This procedure will remove fats and tissue which would keep the brain solution from getting into the skin. This should take about an hour, the first time at least, provided the scraper blade is sharp.

Since few modern men will have access to an elk horn scraper, a long-bladed sharp knife may be used. Hold it at about a 45° angle to the hide and scrape the hide thoroughly.

When the hide is scraped, the tissues and fat and scraps of meat should come off in fairly good layers. When the job is completed, the hide will be white or have a slightly pinkish cast. Now is the time to retighten the lacing and set the hide aside to dry. In five or six hours the skin should be dried and the hardworking craftsman will have a skin of rawhide with hair on one side. Should there be a desire to make a robe or other item with hair, go directly to the braining process and skip the next step.

Dehairing. To obtain soft, pliable buckskin, the hair must be removed. Sharpen your knife well before beginning and then scrape clear a section of hide beginning at the top. Make long strokes in the direction in which the hair lies. The first layer of skin will come off with the hair. You will hit areas where it is difficult to remove the hair, and in getting through these areas it will usually help if you resharpen the knife. Use caution to prevent cutting through the hide and take extreme care when working near the edges of the skin, where the hide might be thinner. Any remaining small pockets of hair can be cut off with scissors after the laces are removed.

Braining. This is the crux of the operation and fresh animal brains are preferred. The brains should be cooked in water in a small pan over a low flame for about fifteen or twenty minutes. As they turn white, remove them from the fire and set them aside to cool. Use the mixture while it is warm (not hot or cold) and apply it to both sides of the skin. Rub it in as you would a cake of soap and cover every exposed area. Brush on the broth remaining in the pan to thin this pasty, soapy mixture, a procedure that will help the absorption of the brains. Now set it aside for at least half a day. (Naturally, if the skin is to be used with hair remaining on one side, the brains are used only on the clean or non-hair side.)

Second Soaking. This work is done the day before the hide is ready for finishing. Dampen the hide with a sponge, then unlace it and put it in a container filled with luke-warm water. Let it soak until the next day. Should the hair still remain on the hide DON'T remove the hide from the frame. Instead, dampen the hide part with wet rags, covering the entire surface, and let the hide set for several hours until it becomes soft.

Second Stretching. This is done if the hair has been removed in the previous steps. The hide is relaced on the frame after soaking.

Graining. Use a six-inch blade of metal or wood as a squeegee to remove water from the hide. Both sides of the hide must be worked to remove all moisture thoroughly. Naturally, if the hair still remains on one side, squeegee the inside of the skin only. Continue to use the squeegee since it will stretch the fibers and also help remove any dirt that will ooze out with the water. The hide will have a tendency to shrink while drying. To prevent this, keep the fibers stretched and work steadily on both sides of the skin while it is drying. Long, overlapping strokes are best and must be done over all

Large machines remove hair in seconds.

parts of the hide. To speed up the drying, use an electric fan. For another forty-five minutes at least, the skin should be continually stretched and worked between the hands. Again a fan will help in the drying. It should be constantly moved from one section to another to ensure that the hide dries evenly.

While the hide is still pliable and still slightly damp, cut it from the frame. Don't worry about the lacing holes since there will be a waste area of roughly one inch that can't be used. Once several hides are tanned, experience will show the novice tanner the proper time to cut the hide from the frame. If it is cut down too early, it will need to be rubbed for a longer time; if removed too late, it will be more difficult to work across the rubbing rope.

Rubbing. A good length of rope tied off tightly to a couple of beams or trees about six feet off the ground will do the trick. Woven rope is the best since it won't turn or unwind during use. The rope will sag during use and must constantly be retightened.

First take the hide and throw it across the rope. Grasp both ends of the skin and pull as hard as your strength will allow. The hide should visibly stretch. Do this in all directions.

Next comes the actual rubbing process. Toss the hide across the rope. Hold both sides of the hide and pull down first one side and then the other. Work the hide from top to bottom and from side to side. The heat generated by the pulling helps dry the skin and contact with the rope will give it a fine texture.

Continue to work the hide. Then, to cut down on the day's labor, wrap it in dry towels on both sides of the skin, and place it in a plastic bag. Store it in a cool place. Now all that is necessary is to continue to rub the skin for about ten minutes a day until it is completely dry and soft to the user's satisfaction.

Smoking. This is a method used to waterproof a hide. It is also an old Indian technique for adding color at the same time.

Should smoke-tanned skins become wet, they will still dry out soft. Regular buckskin will become stiff and hard and will require rubbing to soften it again.

If hickory wood is available, it will give a medium-brown tone. For Westerners, sage is excellent; in the old days, dried manure was probably the most common. Actually, any type of wood may be used but it should be either rotten, green, or wet so it will give off a good smoke rather than flames which will endanger the skin. The bag used for smoking is sewn up one side with the bottom open. It may be suspended from a tripod made of branches. The fire pit should be fairly small, usually no more than six to eight inches deep and no more than a foot in diameter. Make a fire to produce good hot coals. Then place wood over the coals and suspend the hide. Be careful to watch the fire pit constantly to make certain the wood doesn't suddenly catch and send flames shooting upward that will burn the skin. Look into the bag every ten or fifteen minutes to check the color. When it reaches the desired shade of brown, turn the bag inside out and repeat the operation. When both sides acquire the proper tone, roll the skin up and place it in a bag for a few days to allow the color to set.

While we're on the subject of tanning, let's examine some other methods. Early tanning vats were usually just holes dug in the ground. They were lined with planks and the hides soaked in limewater to loosen or remove the hair. Afterward they were thoroughly scraped until most vestiges of hair and fat were removed, then placed layer upon layer in these huge earthen vats. Between each layer was a goodly sprinkling of oak bark. The vats were then filled with water and the hides soaked for an unbelievable six months until tanned.

Although small developments in tanning evolved, it wasn't until a 19th century English scientist, Sir Humphry Davy, discovered other various barks and nuts which contained *tannin*—the astringent chemical that does the tanning. These experiments soon led to more discoveries and chemists found chromium salts would do the same job in a few days. Although the leathers were stiff, at least in the original process, they could be softened for use. The time thus saved in the tanning process, rather than taking half a year, spoke for itself. Another improvement in this type of tanning was the additional treating of leather with soap and oil. This made it stronger, more workable, water resistant, and easier to use.

In modern times, the tanning of leather has become a more complicated and technically involved process. Chrome tanning is probably the most widely used method and the leather produced by it is preferred by many craftsmen. In fact, chrome-tanned leathers can also be vegetable-tanned after the initial tanning process and this adds other favorable properties to the leather.

While it may impart more technical information than the reader desires or needs, some background on modern tanning methods may be of interest.

Hides are invariably shipped to the tanner in a cured condition that preserves the hides (wet salting is one way). Incoming hides are first soaked with water and wetting agents, plus disinfectants to take out various impurities. The hides are then fleshed by machine. To remove the hair, modern tanners use a chemical depilatory process. This completely destroys the hair and prevents any bacterial decay that could ruin the leather at a later stage. Again a special dehairing machine is used and the leather is ready for the next process called *bating*. Bating neutralizes the chemicals used in the previous process. The hides are washed to remove all the excess fibers. Ammonium sulfate or ammonium chloride is then added to convert any remaining lime into a soluble solution that can be washed away.

The methods of tanning we have discussed so far—except for the addition of modern chemicals—have been fairly traditional. But tanning becomes much more involved with chemicals and controls of the leather. Hides must be transformed into an acid environment by a process known as *pickling*. This is a prime step and calls for an electronic pH meter to control the acidity and alkalinity of the solution. Absolute control is of utmost importance here because the chrome-tanning chemicals are not soluble under these alkaline conditions. The pickling adds salt and acid to the leather and is in itself an excellent preserving method. The tanning agents convert the raw hides and fibers into a usable product. They also add abrasion resistance, stability, make the hide more flexible, and ensure that the hide will take continual wetting and drying.

Chrome tanning can be considered the foremost method because it can be done in a short time and turns a raw hide into the finest piece of leather a user could desire. But the process isn't finished yet. All hides are of different thickness and must be cut and shaved. Certain portions will have one use and, if the hide is thick enough, it can be split and used for suede.

At this point, the leather may be retanned to obtain other properties, or dyed and then fat liquored. The latter process involves using oils and other fat substances—either animal, vegetable, or mineral—that puts back into the leather the oils and lubricants required for flexibility. Excess moisture is then removed and, at the same time, the hides are smoothed and stretched. The leather is then set out to dry. When this stage is completed, the hides must be conditioned for various uses since some leathers require great suppleness and others need hardness of various degrees. This stage is called *tempering* and is done by wetting with water, using a capillary action. *Staking* is a mechanical flexing and rolling of the skin. It is one in a series of steps that controls the final softness. The leather is then *buffed* to remove minor scratches and other surface damage. Incidentally, leathers that are not buffed are referred to as *full grain* leathers and the process may stop at this point for some hides that may be used by leathercraftsmen.

At this point, the leathers are ready for the finishing stage. Some leathers may even have a grain pattern embossed in them, which sends leathercraft purists into fits of despair. The only way to eliminate this is to be selective when buying leathers for craftwork and pick those that have a natural finish. All that now remains is for the tanner to grade his leather. It is selected for thickness, softness, uniformity of color and size, and the number of defects in the skins.

Classifying Leathers

Classification of leathers can sometimes be confusing, even to the so-called expert, and imitation leathers that take the name of the real thing only add to the confusion. The term Morocco should indicate that the leather came from goatskin and Cordovan from horsehide. Carrying this a bit farther, kidskin would imply it is from kid and chamois from the small antelope-like animal that lives in the high country of Europe and the Caucasus. However, both of these leathers really come from lamb, although they undergo different treatments. In actuality, modern terminology and technology, particularly in the leather business, have made the classification of leathers rather imprecise. In general, however, very fine leathers come from the small animals such as sheep, goat, young deer, and calves. Larger animals such as elk, moose, horses, cows, buffalo, and the trunks or ears of elephants provide greater areas for selection of "skins," although the thickness of the finished leather is no indication of quality since very thick hides may be split to provide thinner leather.

The quality of an animal's leather is, of course, dependent upon its natural environment—what kind of food it ate, the climate it lived in, and how many times it got caught, say, on a barbed-wire fence. The proper slaughter of animals is also important to the well-being of the finished hide or skin. Careless cutting or skinning by sportsmen, as well as improper treatment of the hides before tanning, can result in leather of poor quality.

A good example of such mishandling is related by Sam Lucchese, President of the Lucchese Boot Company. Sharkskin, he says, is one of the most popular skins his firm has ever used to craft a fine pair of boots, but it is difficult to get good skins because of careless handling. When they catch a shark, most fishermen don't skin it properly and do even less to preserve it. Sharkskin, incidentally, is one of those unusual skins that begin to rot from the center out and a finished boot may not show rot spots until months after it's made and sold. Although X-raying of skins will help locate some of these areas before cutting, frequently only a few belt strips may be obtained from a large hide. "This is a real pity," Lucchese says, "because sharkskin makes a wonderful boot for both comfort and wear."

The Properties of Leather

What are some of the physical properties of leather? First and foremost, it "breathes" because it contains millions of tiny air spaces that provide for the circulation of air. Leather will protect against wind when worn as a garment and, to a lesser degree, keep out a certain amount of cold air. Leather will, on the other hand, pick up a fair lot of moisture and, depending upon the control in tanning, absorb a lot of water or a little. That is why the proper selection of leather for a craft project is important. Leather is flexible and certain weights of it make excellent garments. Leather is strong and under tensile tests is one of the strongest sheet-like materials known. Elongation is also one of the important properties of leather since it will allow flexing during movement. Gloves and moccasins are a good example of this.

It is important to understand the various properties of leather since it will acquaint the

Splitting hides is done with machinery in order to obtain more "splits" from one hide.

craftsman with what can or cannot be done with certain types of leather. The wrong choice of leather can lead to failure in any project, whereas the correct type will certainly guarantee success.

Leather with fur on it can be used for many items. It may be cut, sewn, or glued like any other piece of leather, but care must be taken to ensure that the small hairs are not caught while sewing. When cut, it should only be cut from the hide or flesh side and, of course, cemented from the hide side as well.

Buying Leather

When buying leather, some initial confusion may set in because there are so many types of leathers and tanning processes. An understanding of how leather is sold will help. Although it is possible to purchase an entire hide (and many tanneries will insist on this since they don't have the time to cut it into smaller sections), the wholesaler may—but not always—have it cut into smaller sections and the retailer may often sell it another way. Sam Lucchese offers some expert advice on buying leather. "Do business with an old, established firm," he says. "Don't buy by price alone—that can be the most expensive. Stay away from small jobbers and junk dealers. Whenever possible, go direct to the tannery. A good tannery will give competent advice on the proper leather for the project at hand. They will guide the inexperienced craftsman and sell him the exact leather for his needs." Lucchese also adds, "Tanneries are busy places and buying hides there takes time and patience, plus a fair amount of perseverance, but once the contact is made, good hides or skins will be made available." The Lucchese Boot Company will occasionally sell leather to an aspiring craftsman. Although they aren't in the leather business itself, they will sometimes make certain pieces of unusual skins available.

One of the problems with the more exotic anteater, lizard, or reptile skins is that nature really didn't grow the animal in the right shape and, in remote areas of the world, the native skinners don't always remove the skin correctly. Often the specimen will be cut down the back rather than the belly and there are holes in the wrong places. Moreover, the poor care these skins often receive during transport and shipping can render them useless for tanning.

Leather is usually priced by the square foot and it comes in various thicknesses, usually from one ounce up to twelve ounces. What this means is that one ounce of leather tips the scales at one ounce per square foot and is roughly 1/64" thick. Six-ounce leather would run about 3/32" and ten or twelve ounce about 3/16" in thickness. Once leather goes over ten ounces, it is usually sold by the pound rather than the square foot. As to price, we shall avoid giving actual dollar costs in this book. Leather prices have been constantly moving upward and any quotation at this writing may soon be out of date.

Naturally, the better leathers like fine Morocco or calfskin, or rare lizard, reptile, or fine elephant trunk can be very expensive indeed. The beginning craftsman should give serious consideration to their use, or wait until he has become more skilled before starting a project with expensive skins.

Knowing about leather is just as important as knowing what leather to use for a particular project. The following list will give the newcomer some idea of different kinds of leathers and their usage.

Craft and Lining Leathers

Tooling calfskin. This is considered by many experts to be the best leather for quality tooled work and comes in a variety of modern colors. The weight should be about three or four ounces per square foot and is an excellent thickness.

Pigskin. This is a modestly expensive leather, but its natural grain will help set off some rather special effects. Although it has an attractive grain it may also be tooled.

Steerhide. This hide, used in light weight of course, is excellent for things like billfolds and other small items. It will tool well and offers a good pattern because of its grain. Three to four ounces per square foot is best.

Sheepskin. This can be an excellent substitute for the more costly run of fine tooling leathers. It also lends itself to both tooling and dyeing and makes an excellent lining leather. It is not so expensive that an entire skin, usually five by eight feet, could not be purchased and set aside for future use.

Suede. Suede, either of lamb or sheep's skin, is excellent and makes fine camera or lens pouches and fringed jackets. It comes in many colors and is also excellent as a lining leather.

Alligator, lizard, snake. These can all be fairly expensive leathers but make excellent hat bands, belts (properly lined), and other high-grade items. Because of their natural scales, they can't be tooled.

Carving and Tooling Leathers

"The best leather for tooling and fine carving must be vegetable-tanned," says Billy Wootres of the S. D. Myres Saddle Company, El Paso, Texas. Wootres has been in leatherwork for almost forty years and he speaks from experience.

Fine quality leather is necessary for tooling and carving and the experienced craftsman is especially particular about his choice of leathers for any article. Belts, gun holsters, spur straps, or knife sheaths should be made from nine- to ten-ounce cowhide such as strap or skirting leather. Incidentally, a meticulous craftsman will always avoid using the leg, belly, neck, or flank of the hide.

There may come a time when the craftsman finds it necessary to purchase sole leather for moccasins or sandals. This is sold by another term called "irons"; one "iron" is about $^{1}/_{48}$" thick. Most sandal soles are equivalent to about ten-iron leather which comes out to twelve- to thirteen-ounce hide.

Although Sam Lucchese's advice regarding the purchase of leather is sound, not everyone, particularly people in small towns, may have access to a tannery. For the new leatherworker Tandy Leather Company shops will probably be an excellent source of supply for all those items so necessary for leatherwork. With over three hundred stores around the United States, Tandy sells hides, tools, finishes, dyes, conchas, lacing strips, and patterns to make everything and anything. I can recommend them for all those little bits and pieces so necessary to any project.

Gauging leather to obtain exact measurements of square feet to each hide. Note dial above operator's head that will give correct readout.

CHAPTER TWO

The Decor of Leather

Modern leatherworkers have brought their skills to a high degree of perfection with carving, inlaying, stamping, molding, and dyeing of leathers. Yet centuries ago, even before trade beads were brought into our country, the Indians did magnificent decorative work with porcupine quills.

This work was done by the women of those tribes which ran from the Eastern woodlands and ranged throughout the West and upward into Canada. Oddly enough, the porcupine wasn't always found in the country inhabited by many of these tribes, indicating that the Indian, like many others, wanted things that weren't always easy to get. In Alaska, for example, some Alaskan Indians used bird quills and wove them into designs for belts, but it was the Indian of North America who brought these skills into the realm of art. Moccasins, belts, arrow quivers, pouch bags, knife sheaths, and clothing were highly decorated with intricate geometric patterns in brilliant colors.

Considering the primitive life of these early peoples, who wandered through the great plains in freezing cold winters and hot dusty summers, it seems hardly possible they would have had either the time or inclination to devote to such elaborate decor. Nevertheless, they trapped for or traded porcupine quills, sorted quills, and frequently made long journeys to obtain their dye material. They also spent many hours working with buffalo berries and squaw currants just to produce a red dye. Wild sunflowers and coneflowers were used to make the yellow color and certain wild grapes were used for black dye. Although the modern craftworker has a wide array of tools and implements, usually made by someone else, the Indian made his own. And, surprisingly enough for the involved designs he created, he used relatively few tools. These included a pouch for the quills, a bone marker for tracing the design, a few awls, a couple of strands of

A combination of braided horsehair and leather for belts.

sinew, and a knife. It is thought among experts that a quill-flattener was used, and a few specimens of these do exist. However, they were fairly large and cumbersome and probably required so much time and energy that they were not used very often. The usual method of flattening quills was to hold one end in the teeth and draw a tightly pressed thumbnail down the length of the quill.

With the introduction of beads in the early 1800s quillwork slowly died out, although there are a few old women still alive who can do this magnificent artwork. Even before modern trade beads came along, the Indians made crude native beads of shell, bone, teeth, seeds, and worked deer hoofs and toes into their decorations. These were used to adorn articles of clothing as well as saddle blankets, pipe stems, various sized pouches, and many other objects.

The Spanish influence in the Southwest brought silver work and silver conchas to both the settlers and Indians. The agents of Hernando Cortez who first headed north out of Mexico introduced silver coins that were soon hammered into trimmings for saddles, bridles, holsters, hat bands, and belts. The Navajos, who knew and practiced silver work in the 1860s, adapted the techniques of the Spaniards and carved out small sections in the ends of cottonwood logs as forms for their conchas.

Horsehair, or Pelo del Caballo, was done in certain areas of Mexico and introduced to the southwestern Indians as well as to the early cowboys who took up horsehair braiding to while away long hours on trail rides. This skill never reached the popularity that it did in Mexico and has slowly died out due to the lengthy time required to work with horsehair. It is still popular in Mexico and those who journey below the border may still find braided horsehair hat bands, belts, and an occasional bridle and reins, particularly in many of the border towns where Western accoutrements are still popular.

Horsehair can be inlaid into leather and often a long belt can be attached to leather strips for longer wear. Smaller strips of braided horsehair may be used for hat bands and is usually laid onto a piece of tooling calf and sewn down for added strength. It is often possible to find a completed hat band of hair and these rare items, usually with a sliding knot and tassels, may be used without the addition of leather backing.

With the current popularity of silver work, silver conchas are now in vogue. They may be obtained from many of the Indian shops in the Southwest or can even be made by the craftsman. They make excellent decor, particularly against black leather, and can be used for belts, hat bands, and gun holsters. A line of gleaming silver conchas down the side of chaps will proclaim the wearer, if not a man of wealth, certainly a man of impeccable taste.

There are indeed many ways of changing the appearance of leather. Some include carving, stamping, inlaying, burning, and various other methods. Lacing is one simple way of adding decor to a belt and it requires nothing more than punching holes along the edges and lacing them with a contrasting thong. Others which are more intricate may require greater time and skill. All of these techniques will embellish leather and some are particularly effective. Others, if done by unskilled hands, can be inferior examples of the leathercrafter's art and accomplish little except to ruin a fine piece of leather. Taste, of course, is a very personal thing. Fashion constantly changes, and with leather, as with anything else, good design characteristics should be considered.

When in doubt, it may be best not to try to embellish the leather at all. Just let the

Highly decorative beaded Plains Indian moccasins.

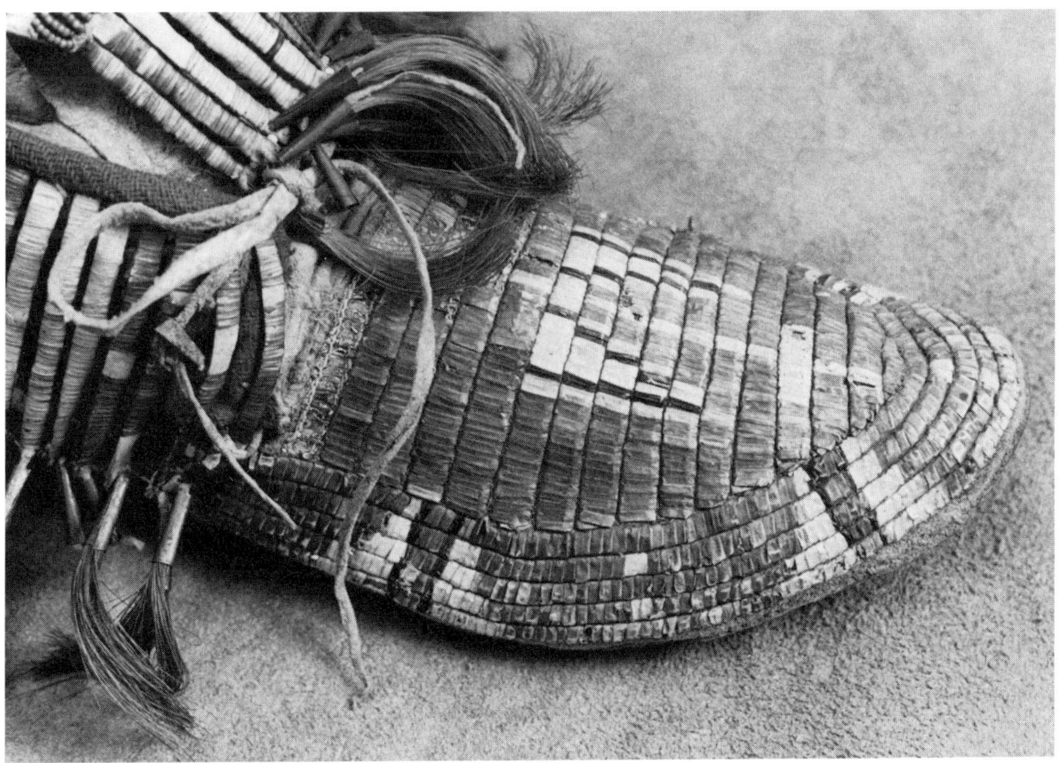
Before trade beads came to the West, porcupine quills were used to enhance many objects of clothing.

pure form of the leather and its texture be the star. At other times, say with a western or ranger belt, well-executed ornamental tooling may be just the touch required. Gun holsters are a good example. Some men prefer plain holsters while others want a modest amount of decoration, say basket stamping or Mexican-edged lacing. Quite a few law enforcement officers in the Southwest, especially the Texas Rangers, New Mexico State Police, and some Border Patrolmen, go all out in decor. Some examples are fancy Navajo grips of silver inlaid with turquoise or coral, flower carved holsters and matching belts (many of the latter done by the S. D. Myres Saddle Company), and occasionally a fancy hat band. Such elaborate work may not be for everyone, but a craftsman who acquires reasonable skill will be able to do such fancy work within a very short time. Let's look at some other ways you can improve your leather decor.

Coloring leathers. There are a number of ways of doing this but perhaps the easiest is to use the new indelible marking pens. The felt tips come in various sizes and, with the wide range of colors available, it is fairly simple to apply colorfast inks to plain leather. This calls for no special skills and is only limited by the artistic ability of the craftsman. Add a wax coating when the work is completed.

Batik. This is a Far Eastern technique that is basically a wax resistant way of dyeing. Whatever is covered with wax will, of course, resist dye. In batik, the design is drawn into the wax and then the dyes are applied with small sponges. The design may be as intricate or as simple as desired. Once the job is completed, a thick layer of newspaper is placed over the leather. Then a medium-hot iron is run over it until the wax melts and is absorbed by the paper. The trick here is not to overheat the iron or burn the leather. Specialized batik dyes may be used, which are usually found in any craftshop. But Tintex, available in a rainbow of colors, works just as well.

Tooling. There are two important things to remember in tooling. First, the correct leather must be used and it should be a proper "tooling" leather. This means it should be a full-grained, vegetable-tanned steerhide, cowhide, or calfskin of uniform thickness. Second, the leather to be tooled properly must be damp, NOT WET. Forget about the Boy Scout craft shop days when leather strips were soaked for hours in a pail of water—no wonder that carefully stamped belt for Dad never turned out right! The correct way is to rub the grain surface with a damp sponge, set it aside for a few moments until the surface begins to dry slightly, and then it is ready for tooling. What happens when the leather becomes too wet is that all those nicely placed cuts and stamps will swell back almost to normal as the leather drys out. Conversely, of course, if the leather is too dry it will be difficult to work. It will drag the knife, prevent a good impression, and sometimes there is even a danger of ripping the hide. When working with large areas, such as a gun case, it may be necessary to apply more moisture occasionally, so a pail of water with sponge or rags are handy items to have nearby.

Tooling covers a multitude of techniques but all result in depressions or raised areas on the leather. This can be done by carving, stamping with various dies, or incising. The latter is a method of lifting out tiny slivers of leather or modeling with a hand-pressure tool. Some absolutely magnificent work is being done using these techniques.

Burning. An electric pencil will burn a slight brown line into leather that can either become a design in itself or a basis for other designs that may be colored or dyed. These pencils don't become overly hot and no annoying smoke is produced.

L An inlay of contrasting bits of leather. This work was done at Lucchese Boot Company in San Antonio, Texas.

R Finely carved example of quality leather work by modern craftsman Bill Wootres.

Stamping. Carving and stamping can be combined. Quite frequently it is necessary to stamp the background of carved portions to make them stand out. Stamping requires metal dies and a fairly heavy hammer to strike the dies firmly enough to make an indent in the dampened leather. Practice on scraps first to find the right amount of pressure required. Since stamping does require repeated taps of the hammer it can't be emphasized too strongly that each tap of the die should be of equal pressure if a consistent pattern is to be achieved.

Carving. The most important item here is the swivel cutter or knife. It is exactly what the name implies—a U-shaped top upon which the forefinger rests and a swiveling knife on the bottom that is turned by thumb and finger. The better models come with interchangeable blades and enable the user to do almost any type of carving from basic designs to the most delicate and intricate work. Most amateurs hesitate to try carving because they are afraid of making a mistake and ruining the leather. Granted, carving is certainly more difficult than stamping, but once it is learned the work done with this old technique will give great satisfaction.

Styles of leather carving and tooling from the S. D. Myres Saddle Co. of El Paso, Texas.

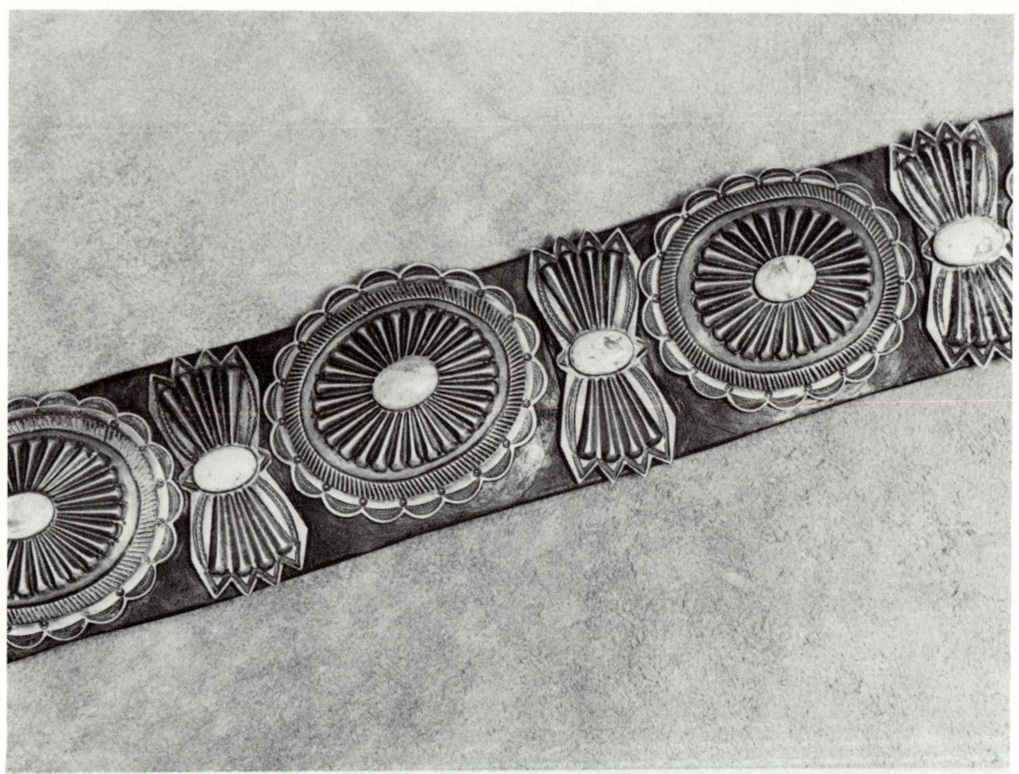

Very old Indian-made silver conchas strung onto a black leather belt.

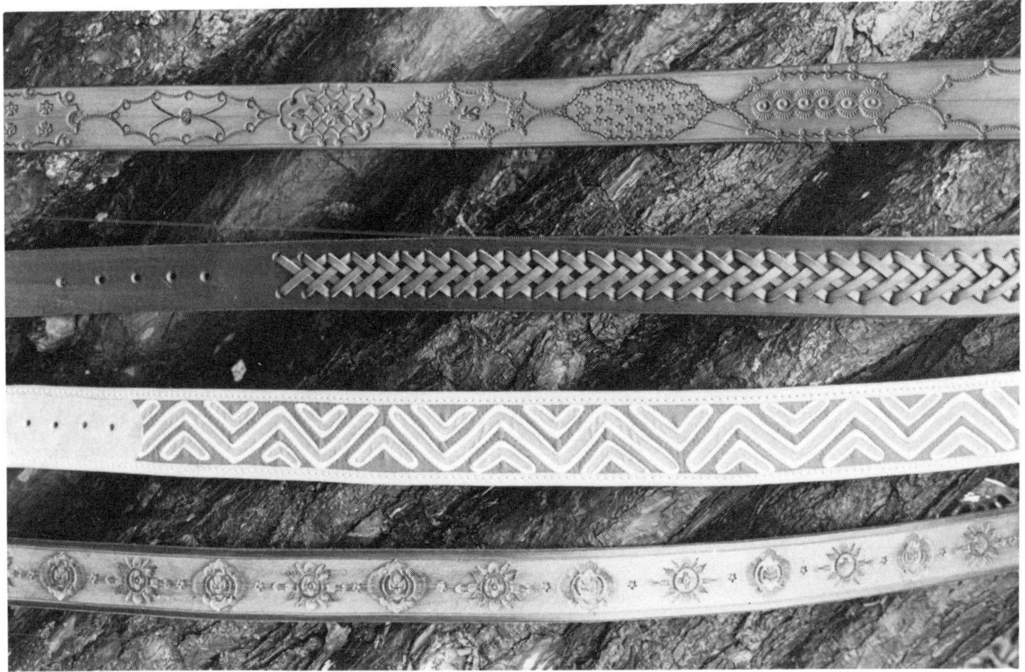

The modern trend in leather belts by the Sweetfield Leather Company.

Incising. Incising cuts away tiny pieces or slivers of leather and the area left may be dyed in color. The swivel knife is used here and we would suggest lots of practice before attempting this technique.

Camouflaging. This is a technique for going over the background, or the plain parts of the design, after various stems, petals, or other designs have been carved into the leather.

Laminating. Leather comes in limited thicknesses; however it can be laminated to other pieces with cement and built up to any form or height. Once the cement has hardened, these pieces may then be carved (with wood carving tools), drilled, or even sawed. Laminating is a favorite method of making boxes and getting enough big chunks for sculpting some unusual art objects.

Forming. This is really a way of shaping wet leather over molds or free-forming various designs. Vegetable-tanned leather should be used because it will absorb water better. Nails or staples are used to stretch and hold the leather while it dries. Some objects made in this style are pots, bowls, masks, gun cases, and even replicas of Indian shields.

It should be remembered that leather can be decorated with almost any object. Tufts of fur, bits of bone, shells, and odd-looking stones have all been used both to enhance the leather itself as well as to add a decorative touch. Indeed, there is little new about leather (except, perhaps, modern tanning) and the craftsman may be as traditional as he desires or as avant-garde. Leather chess or backgammon boards may be crafted with contrasting colors and leather wine racks add a highly decorative touch to the home. There are few items that cannot be crafted of leather.

CHAPTER THREE

Leathercrafting Tools

Leathercrafting can be done on the kitchen table with a good slab of marble or granite for stamping and a piece of pine for cutting. Or it can be done in a fully equipped leather shop where there are hundreds of tools and every convenience at hand.

Many leather shops I have visited have been well-equipped models of efficiency, while others have had only the basic necessities for stamping and pounding. The beginning leatherworker need not rush out and purchase many expensive tools. For example, a good sharp knife will do many jobs and eliminate a draw knife, a head knife, and a skiving machine. A solid block of wood or a hammer from the home tool chest will eliminate purchasing a special leatherworker's mallet for stamping dies or pounding pieces of leather that have been glued together.

There are, of course, some basic tools that are necessary for any type of leatherwork and the beginner is well advised to acquire these slowly and as the need arises. The aforementioned sharp knife is a prime necessity and an X-Acto knife is used by many leathercraftsmen. A steel ruler or square is a must since it will permit straight and angle cuts and allow accurate measurements. Other basic tools are a sturdy pair of shears, an awl for making holes and stitching, and some beeswax for rubbing both awl and needles. Even a razor blade can be used for cutting and skiving edges. A small brush can be used for applying edge coatings of dyes. Soft pieces of flannel will come in handy for polishing and rags for applying dyes. And an ordinary table fork can be used for marking stitch holes or drawing parallel lines for sewing or decoration. The latter will make it unnecessary to purchase assorted thonging chisels, which are also used for marking various stitch or punch holes.

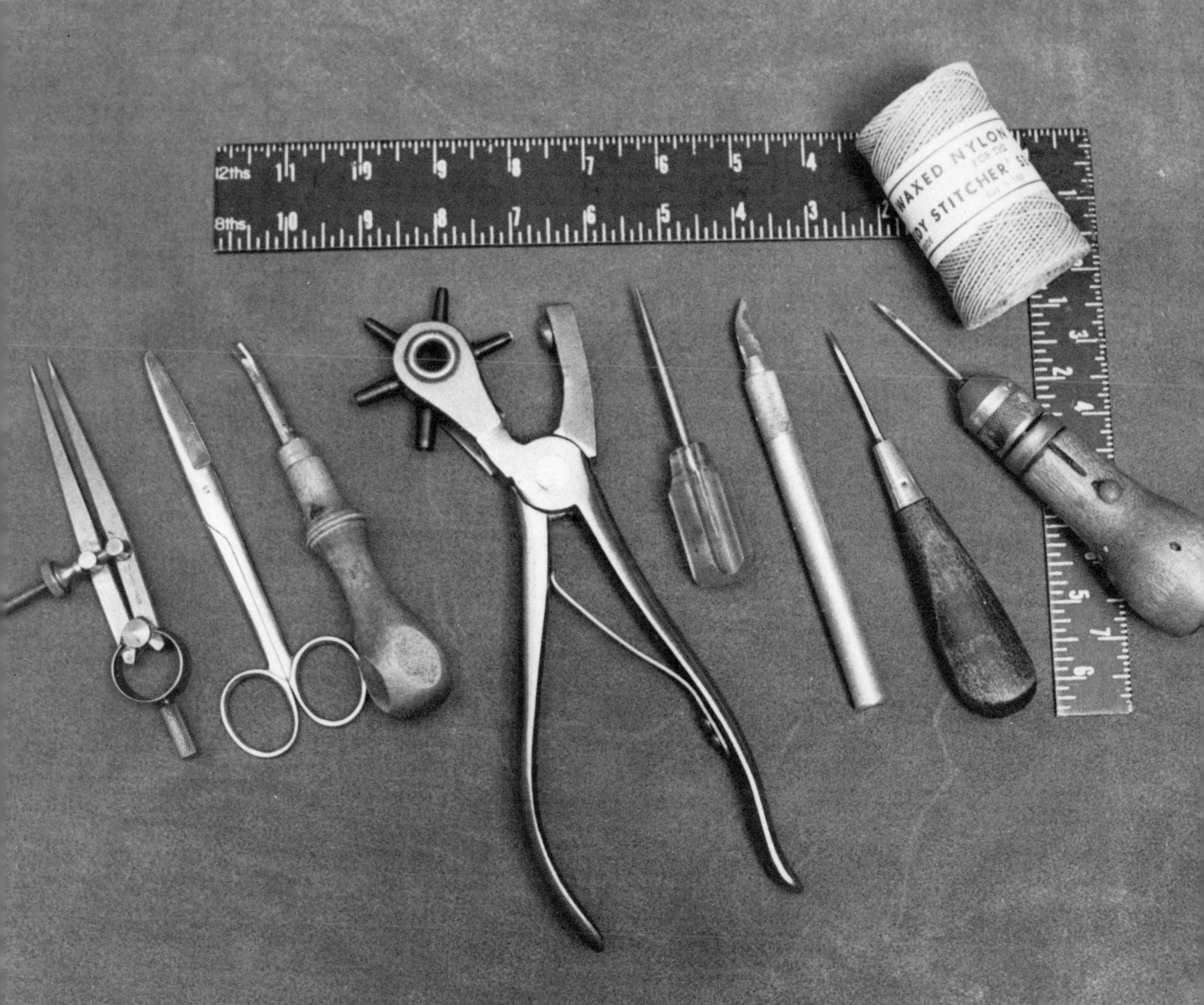

A selection of tools that is sufficient to start a beginning craftsman on simple projects.

There are some leatherworking tools, however, that can't be improvised and these include a revolving punch used for punching holes for lacing, eyelets, holes in belts, and for applying rivets. You'll also need snap-button tools for fastening rivets and edge-bevelers which come in various sizes to strip the edges of belts and holsters. A rampart gouger is used for making creases so the leather will fold easier. In addition, you'll want lacing needles, assorted harness needles, a fid (it looks like an awl) which is used for enlarging holes and is an excellent aid in lacing, and a stitching awl that allows the user to sew a lockstitch with the aplomb of a professional. Dividers are important since they are used for marking spaces for stitching holes as well as drawing parallel lines along the edge of a belt or marking lacing holes. An edge-slicker is a wheel-like device with a groove that is run back and forth along the edges. You'll need it for softening angle cuts in leather as well as putting a burnished finish on the edge.

Fringe can be cut by hand with either scissors or a knife. But this can be a long and

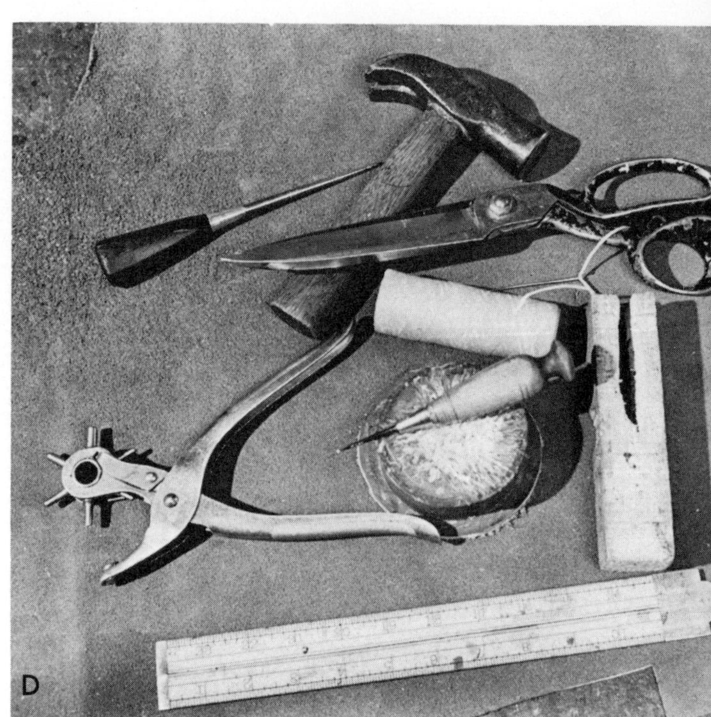

A Pinking machine used for making fancy edges. Pinking shears can also be used for garment-weight leathers.

B Jerry's Leather Stripper, shown here being used to cut fringe.

C Stamping dies made of nails. Files or grinders are used to make the design.

D The tools of Walter Kneubuhler. The odd-shaped piece of wood is used when forcing needles through leather. It will allow the needle to come through without sticking in the table.

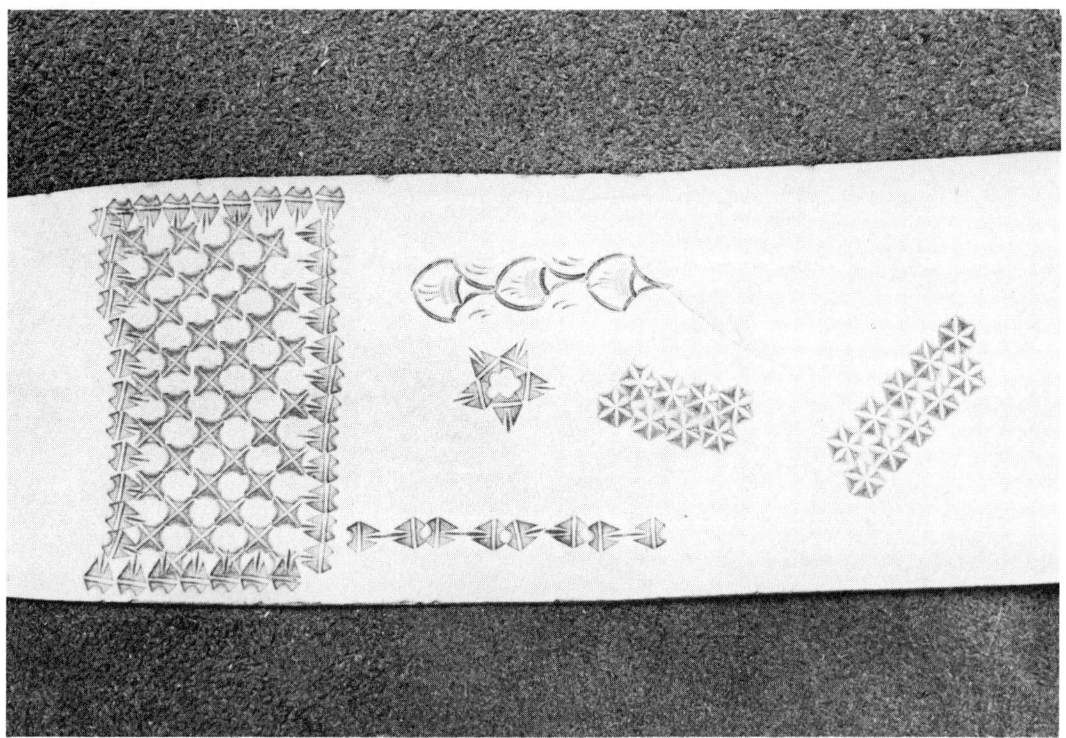

Some of the designs created from the homemade stamping dies.

A tooled gun holster with a professional mallet for hitting the leather stamps and the swivel knife for cutting the design.

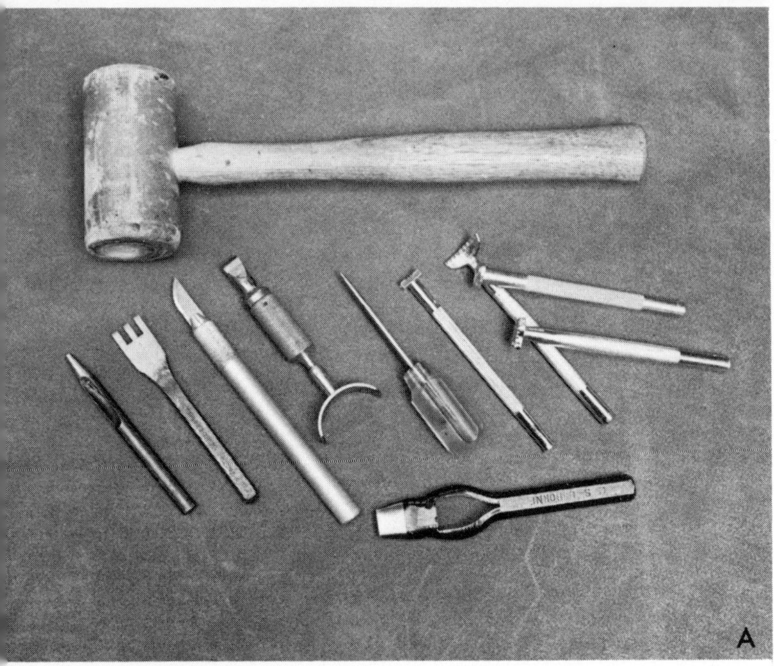

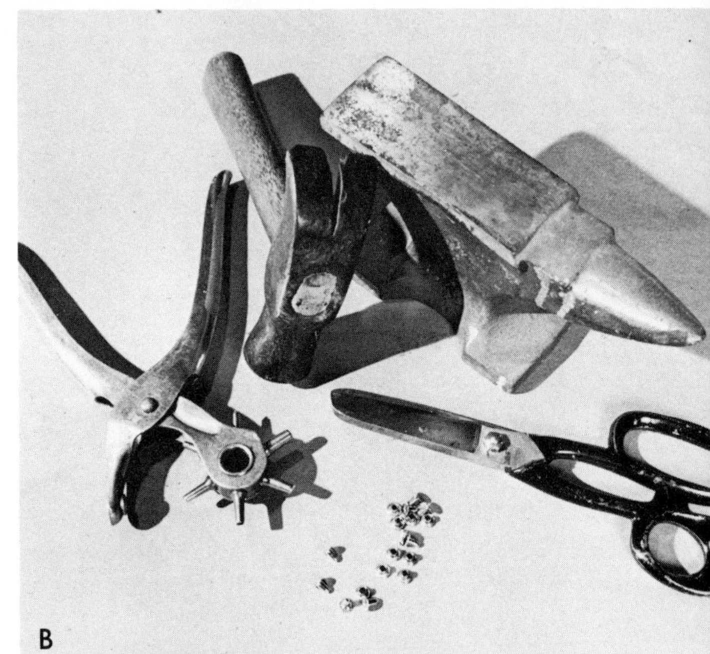

A A leather mallet and various punches, awl, and knives. The fork-shaped tool, second from left, is a thonging chisel. They come in various sizes and are used to form slits in leather for leather thongs.

B Left to right, a revolving thong punch for making holes in leather for thonging, lacing, and rivets. It is also used for belt holes for a buckle. Also shown are a regular hammer, small anvil for hammering rivets, and leather shears.

C A skiving machine used for thinning the edges of leather, so that a fold may be made for buckles or snaps.

D Skiving done with a sharp knife will give the same results.

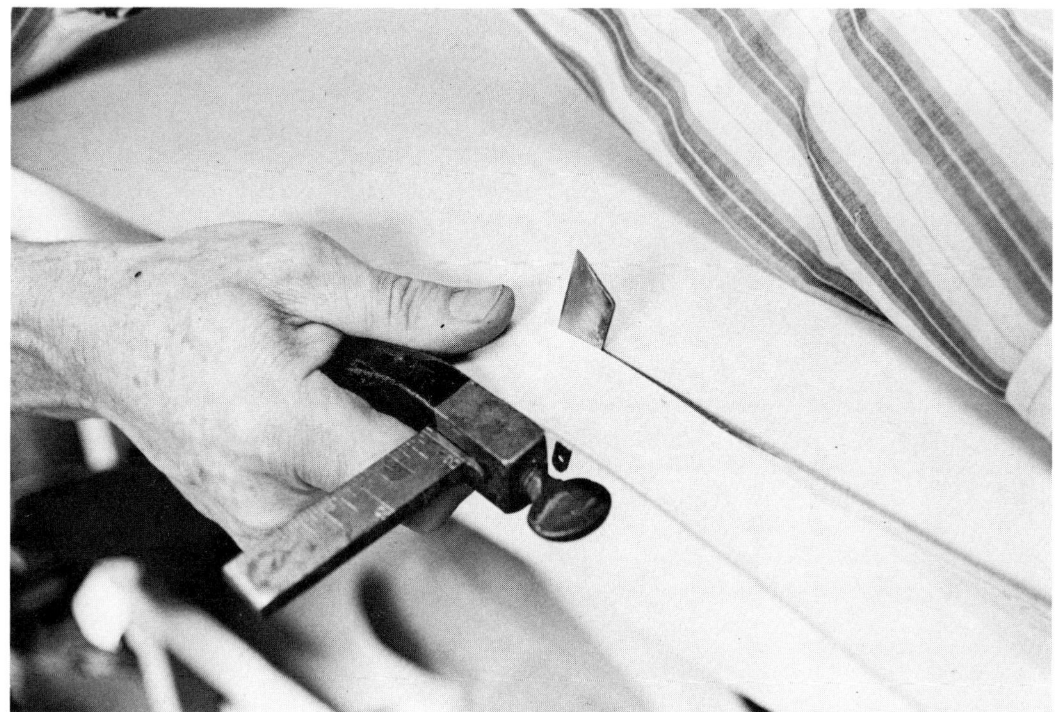

A draw knife being used to cut a belt strip. The width of the cut made can be adjusted by a thumbscrew.

The head knife being used to cut a pattern. Some craftsmen find the head knife difficult to use and a straight-bladed knife will give nearly the same results. However, the head knife will cut curves easier.

An edge-beveler being used to finish the edge of a belt.

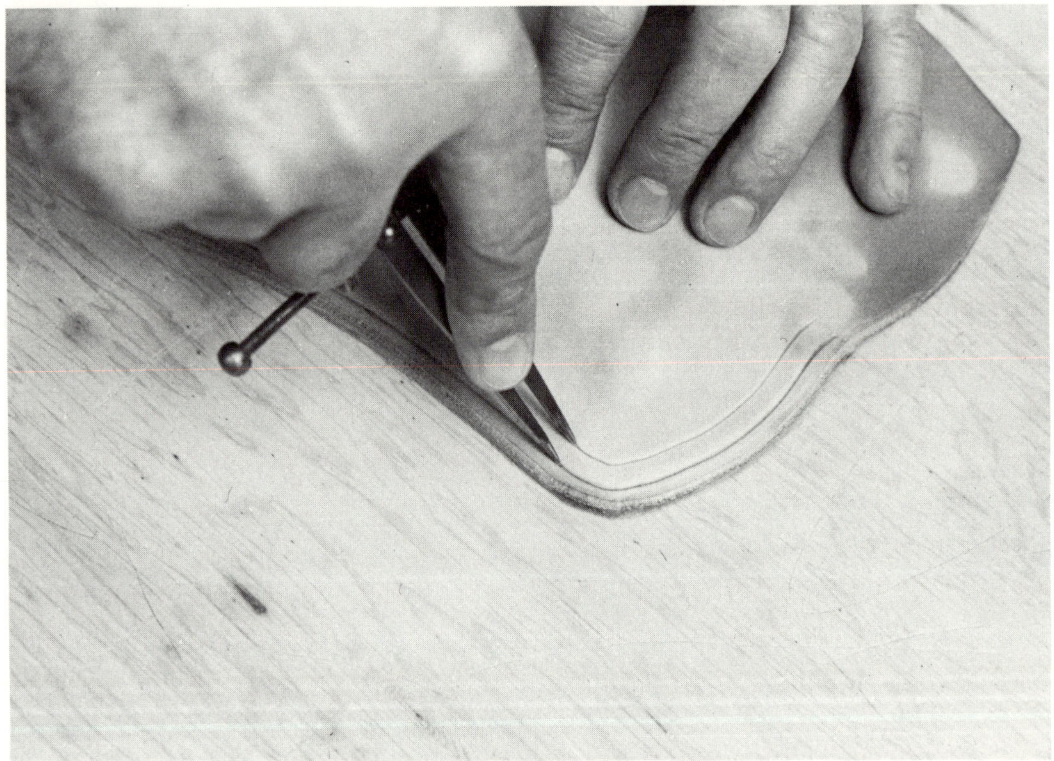

Dividers are used for marking stitch lines, decorative trim, or thong holes.

A A stitching awl for sewing a saddle stitch.

B A swivel knife for cutting designs in leather.

C A hardwood edge-slicker.

D Punches come in various sizes and shapes and are used for punching holes for straps or thongs.

An awl may be used for enlarging stitching holes.

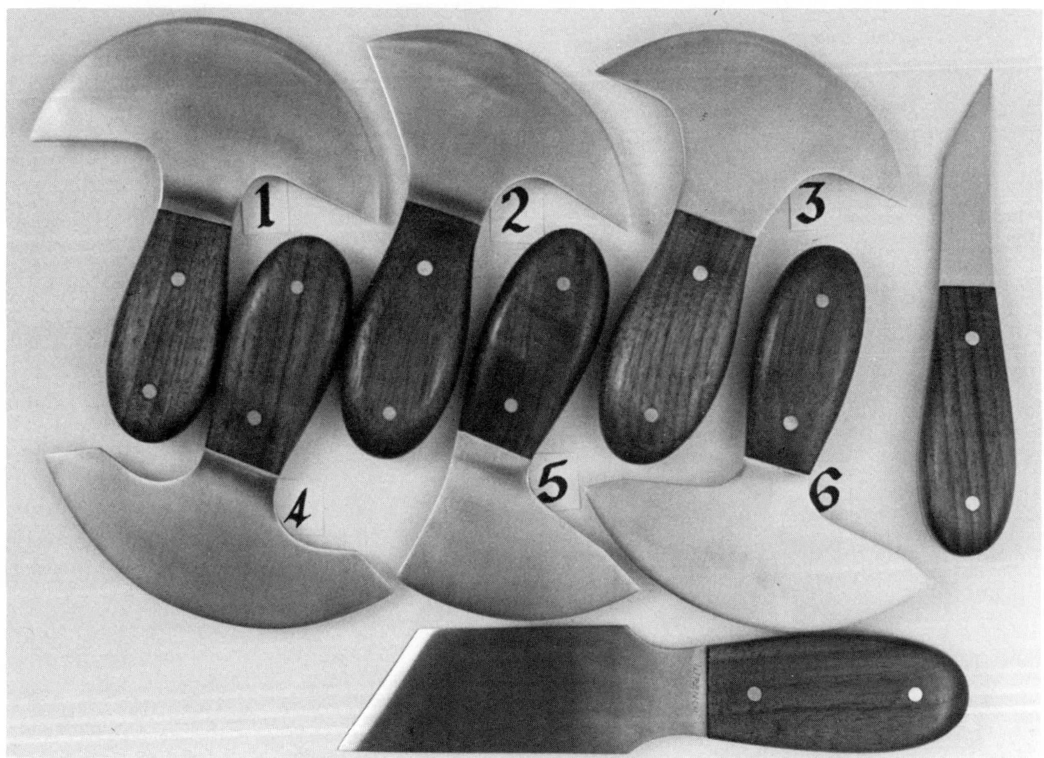

A selection of custom-crafted leather knives made by Bob Wrench.

tedious job especially if there is a great amount of fringe to be cut. Jerry Rush of Jerry's Leather Goods in Englewood, Colorado, has invented a device he calls Jerry's Stripper. Although it sells for the modest price of $19.95, it isn't just a gadget but a well-constructed tool for cutting suede, leather, cloth, and even balsa wood for model airplanes. With it, up to twenty-three strips may be cut at one time in ⅛" multiples, or the blades may be moved about and strips as wide as three inches may be cut. The Stripper is also an excellent method of obtaining lace and braided belts. Finally, it eliminates the boring task of fringing by hand.

If the craftsman decides he really wants to get into leatherwork full time, there are a number of machine tools that will certainly make life easier. There are, for example, skiving machines that will skive or thin down leather and electric drills that will take sanders, buffing wheels, and drill holes for sewing or lacing. A sewing machine with a special heavy-duty motor will be a delight in sewing heavy thicknesses of leather and a cutter, a revolving wheel that cuts heavy leather, is a pleasure for those who want to trim sole leather or patterns of sandals drawn on leather. While all these will cut down on time and will do the task in minutes, an imaginative leathercraftsman will be able to improvise and double up on the basic tools he has. For example, sharp knives will still do much of the cutting and trimming.

Bear in mind that while many hand operations can be done by these machines more quickly, they need not necessarily do a better job than a craftsman with a modest amount of skill. Also, the more machinery that is used, the fewer hand operations there will be in the finished product. And that is really what leathercraft is all about—hand craftwork.

One tool the craftsman must get used to using may come as a surprise. It is cement. Pieces of leather are cemented together for lacing, punching holes, and many other tasks in crafting leather. One excellent product used by many leatherworkers is Barge Cement made by the National Starch & Chemical Company in Towaco, New Jersey. It resembles rubber cement and, in fact, may be even stronger. It is a miracle-worker in leather and holds pieces together with a grip of steel. Naturally the inside of the leather is coated with cement; however, Barge won't stain (I've seen it used on chamois) and it doesn't soak through the skin. It is a superb all-use "tool" that makes leathercrafting easier today.

For the craftsman who wants the best, there is a knifemaker named Bob Wrench who custom crafts leatherworking tools. His address is P.O. Box 10904, Eugene, Ore. 97401. His blades are 1095 high-carbon steel hardened to a Rockwell of 58. He will also use D-2 tool steel, but considers this a special order. The handles are of walnut and he has everything from six sizes of head knives to skiving knives, a pattern knife, two different silver lacing awls, 3/32" and 5/32", plus custom-made draw-gauge blades. Of course it is possible to do leatherwork without such finely made tools, but it's nice to know there is one custom knifemaker who appreciates the scarcity of fine leathercrafting tools and takes the trouble to use proper steels and woods in making them.

Again, price won't be mentioned here because the price of material keeps rising constantly, but the interested reader is assured of a quick reply and the latest price list by sending $1.00 to Bob Wrench at the above address.

CHAPTER FOUR

The Care of Leather

Like the weather, everyone talks about caring for leather properly, but few really know how to go about it. Sam Lucchese gives this expert advice: "Remember, leather is skin and it will react in many cases just as your own skin does. Drying means cracking and peeling and while we don't suggest ChapStick there are several good leather conditioners that will keep boots and other leather articles soft and smooth. Leather care is just like caring for your own skin—first you wash your face with soap and water, then you dry your face. If it is tight, a good moisturizer is used not only for protection but comfort." Lucchese and Jim Spurrier of S. D. Myres Saddle Company both agree that saddle soap is probably one of the worst things that can be put on leather. First, most saddle soaps are too caustic and strong; second, most people don't know how to use them. Even so, one excellent saddle soap is Belvoir Glycerine Saddle Soap. In fact, any glycerine-based soap will do wonders for shoes and boots.

The trick is to work up a good lather *without too much water*, then wipe it off *immediately*. Let's take the care of boots one step at a time:

1. Remove loose dirt and dust with a brush or rag.
2. Wash thoroughly with Belvoir Glycerine Saddle Soap, a soap which cleans and preserves.
3. Apply a thin coat of Properts or Meltonian Cream, then brush or rub with an English chamois cloth until luster is obtained.
4. For a higher luster, apply a thin coat of Kiwi paste or Meltonian Wax and brush and rub again.

For a completely thorough cleaning, follow Steps 1 and 2. Then clean with Whittemore's Cleanall to remove all old polish. Remember, don't allow polish to build

Some of the fine leather-care products on the market today.

up on leather. It will act as floor wax does on linoleum; that is, it will discolor, build up layers, prevent the leather from breathing, and eventually cause cracking. When you use a leather cleaner, don't rub the cleaner into the leather but rather wipe off the old polish with the cleaner. Once this is done, apply a coat of Lexol leather conditioner, especially where the sole is sewn to the boot, and allow to dry. And never, repeat NEVER, place wet leather near heat for drying. Wet leather, especially shoes and boots, should be treated with Lexol and allowed to dry naturally, no matter how long it takes.

Lexol in thinner coats should be used more frequently on reptile and elephant since these leathers are drier than most and can use a little extra conditioning. In fact, all leathers require attention about every six months. As for grease or oil spots, most can be removed with Goddard's Spot Remover. Follow the manufacturer's instructions.

Most water stains or sugar spots can be removed by covering the whole area with a mixture of one-half white vinegar and one-half clear water. Alcohol stains will often respond to the same treatment.

Suedes are probably the most troublesome to care for and should be taken to an experienced leather cleaner for treatment. For example, Jerry's Leather Goods in Englewood, Colorado, tumbles sheepskin coats in sawdust and the results are amazing. Another excellent product is Rain & Stain, not as a cleaner but as a protector of leather. I could scarcely believe it when I tried it on a piece of cream-colored suede. Just spray on and water will bead up and roll off. It won't affect the color of the material and doesn't stain. Caution, however: It should only be used on new or unworn garments or those freshly returned from the cleaner. Once garments are cleaned, Rain & Stain will come off and the garment must be resprayed.

Meltonian Suede Cleaner is another excellent product for suede or chamois. First, a stiff wire brush should be used to remove loose dust and dirt. Any shiny or matted spots can be brought to life with an emery board. The surface is then lightly sprayed with the cleaner, using care not to saturate the suede. After a few moments, a clean cloth is used to gently wipe and remove any remaining dirt.

Many leather shops have their own concoctions for the care and preservation of leathers and Jerry's Leather Goods is no exception. Known as Jerry's Spot Remover Powder, it will take out grease, oil, food, and dirt. Jerry Rush won't say what it contains—after all, it's his formula and he's entitled to a couple of trade secrets—but I've tried it on a thoroughly soiled suede camera bag. While I must honestly admit it didn't make it new looking, it did remove much of the grime and I'm sure that a second treatment would improve it even more. The remover is a white, chalky powder that's sprinkled on the suede. Left on for ten or more minutes and then brushed off with a sponge, it will certainly improve the appearance of any leather. For grain leathers, a soft cloth is used. Furthermore, it won't harm colors and leaves no odor or ring.

An old Boy Scout treatment for cleaning leather—and it was the only method recommended by Dan Beard—was to spread a bed sheet on the floor, put a fringed Indian jacket and leggings on the sheet, and sprinkle them with cornmeal. If you try this, rub the dry meal in thoroughly with your hand and then brush off with a stiff brush. Surprisingly, it has always worked very well indeed and removes enough grime and dirt to give a modestly new appearance to such leather articles.

Another excellent preparation for the care of smooth leathers is Meltonian Leather Balm. It should *not* be used on suede, buck, or any type of nappy leather, but it is fine for shoes, luggage, gun cases, belts, and all those items crafted of smooth leather. It's simple to use and while it does remove surface dirt, it's a good idea to give a treatment of saddle soap first. Once the leather has dried, apply Meltonian Balm with a clean cloth, rubbing well into the leather. It's best to work small areas at a time. Once the entire item has been covered it can be rubbed to a rich luster with a piece of flannel.

Leather does require care and should be given a thorough treatment about every six months or so. Leathers also have an affinity for moisture; they can even pick it up from the air. While a small amount of moisture is good, too much will cause leather to stretch.

Should leather tear or rip, don't attempt to sew it because the stitches will be too obvious. Instead, a small piece of thin leather can be glued on the back of the tear with Barge Cement and then hammered down. The cement won't discolor the material and the tear can be carefully worked down with a slight pressure of a fingernail to make the damage almost invisible. Since leathers don't have any directional pattern, a rip won't run far. Most damage is caused by catching a jacket on nails or other protrusions. This simple method works best and I've seen a number of handsome suede jackets fixed in this manner and the result is amazing.

Simple maintenance of leather garments and other leather items will give them long life. Properly cared for, a favorite gun case or piece of luggage will continue to be a favored companion on many trips for many years.

CHAPTER FIVE

Lucchese "Handcrafted Hat Bands and Belts"

Although the Lucchese Boot Company of San Antonio, Texas, is famed for the quality of their boots, they are less known for the superb hat bands and belts crafted in a special department. Known as the Ferrari of bootmakers, Sam Lucchese has a family tradition of eight hundred years of fine Italian leathercraftsmanship. His is the third generation of the famous San Antonio firm.

What makes Lucchese boots so expensive? The answer is exotic leathers and the demands of his clients. The Lucchese Company has made boots for such people as Theodore Roosevelt, Paul Anka, John Wayne, the late President Lyndon Johnson, and the Baron de Rothschild. The highest priced pair of boots Sam ever made ran about $1200; they were crafted from anteater and hornback lizard. "That's not counting the gold tips with jewels on the toes," laughed Lucchese. "I suppose something with diamonds would be more expensive."

In the old days, when his grandfather arrived in San Antonio around 1880, he would make any boot as long as it was black. Originally the firm crafted boots for the cavalry and artillery at Fort Sam Houston. Since San Antonio was a railhead for the cattle industry it naturally became a focal point for bootmakers. Asked if he thought his family settled in San Antonio because of the lure of the West and cowboys, Sam replied, "No, I feel sure my granddad was pushed more by the pangs of hunger than the romance of the cowboys."

Many of Lucchese's customers use a fine pair of boots as a working tool. Before a man enters the show ring with his prize bull he will carefully tuck his trousers inside the boots just to show off the fancy boot tops. As one customer said, "My bull may not win,

Jorge Abrego of the Lucchese Boot Company selects leather for belts and hat bands from the firm's huge stock of leathers.

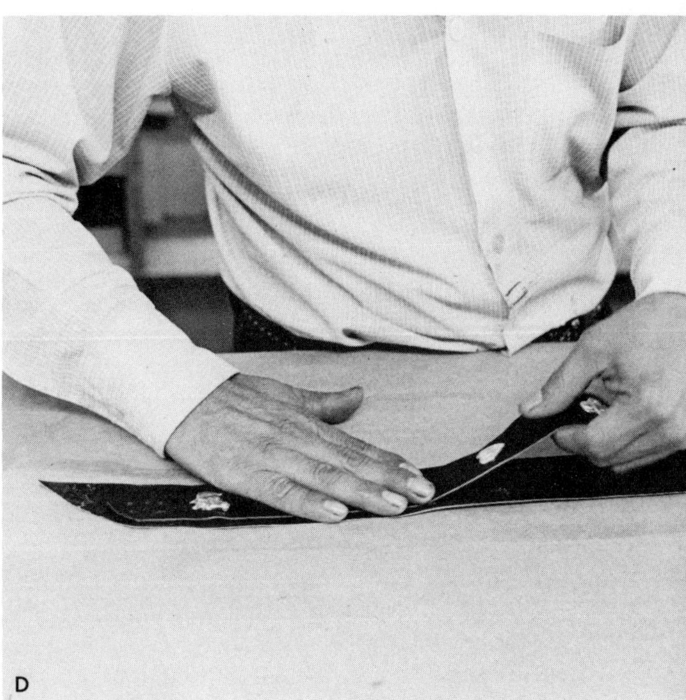

A Abrego cuts a piece of calf strip for a hat band.

B The silver studs are placed atop the leather and marked for the punch holes.

C A revolving punch is used to make holes for the studs.

D After the studs are in place, another piece of calf is cut for the backing and cemented together with Barge Cement.

but the judge will certainly give him some extra attention with all the flash of fine leatherwork." Lucchese's boots have been crafted from all the exotic leathers, including reptile, ostrich, anteater, alligator, shark, and hornback lizard.

A customer might want a matching hat band and belt to complement his outfit. Quite frequently cost is no object. A belt of some rare skin, say shark or anteater, might run as high as $150 and a hat band perhaps half of that. Of course fancy decor on the band, such as silver conchas, turquoise, or gold, might run the cost even higher than the belt.

The belt department of Lucchese is set in one corner of the building and is under the direction of Jorge Abrego. Abrego was a leathercraftsman in his native Monterrey, Mexico, for over twenty years before moving to San Antonio. Like all professional leatherworkers, he is a painstaking craftsman. Abrego suggested we first make a hat band to introduce beginning leatherworkers to one of the craft's easiest projects. Basically a hat band is really a short belt, but making one takes a bit more care than just cutting off a narrow strip of leather and wrapping it around a hat. Since the band shown in the photo was to be decorated with silver studs, it required a backing to cover the stud ends and to protect the felt of a fine Stetson.

A strip of five-ounce calfskin was cut to the proper length to fit around the hat and to a suitable width. The decorative studs were first laid on to make certain they would be of equal distance apart. An awl was used to mark their placement and then a punch was used to make the holes. After the studs were fastened, the back of the strip was coated with Barge Cement and another piece of thin calfskin, cut to the same width and length, was placed over the back and firmly pressed into place. After it was allowed to dry for at least an hour, stitching was run around the edge to finish off the band and hold the pieces firmly together. Such a band may be fastened with a buckle or, in this instance, snaps were used.

Delicate skins such as snakeskin may also be used for hat bands and belts, but they require a backing to give them sturdiness. I have a hat band I picked up in Africa made from python, but it is extremely delicate because the skin was just folded over and glued with a couple of leather thongs for tassels. Lucchese craftsmen exercise more care in their craftwork with fragile skins and use a backing for strength. Rare and exotic skins call for some special care, not only for the final appearance but to enable such skins to be used. Rather than using leather as a backing, gray Fibastay, an almost paperlike material, is used. This may be obtained from Bennett, Goding's and Cooper, 50 Midway Street, Boston, Massachusetts 02210. Since this is a commercial product, it is doubtful if only a few feet would be sold. Normally it comes in 200-yard rolls and most leather-supply houses should have it on hand.

The Fibastay is coated with Barge Cement, as is the skin, and both are pressed together. A half-inch or so of the skin is folded over onto the backing, which is also coated with cement. Both are then allowed to dry. Once this is done, a strip of backing leather, usually a thin strip of calfskin, is cut to the same size and also cemented to the backing. Now we have a piece of thin snakeskin with backing plus a piece of leather to give it strength. Again this may be sewn or edge-laced for contrast, a buckle or snap attached, and the job is done.

Once the two pieces are cemented together, excess is cut away with a sharp knife.

A strong sewing machine is used to run a row of stitches around the edge.

Next the edges are sanded on a machine to smooth them off for the finish. A piece of fine sandpaper can also be used.

The finishing step is to coat the edges with black dye and the hat band is completed.

In making an elegant belt, Abrego shows how to combine two pieces of white ostrich with a fine piece of calfskin. The two pieces of ostrich, previously cut, are coated with leather cement.

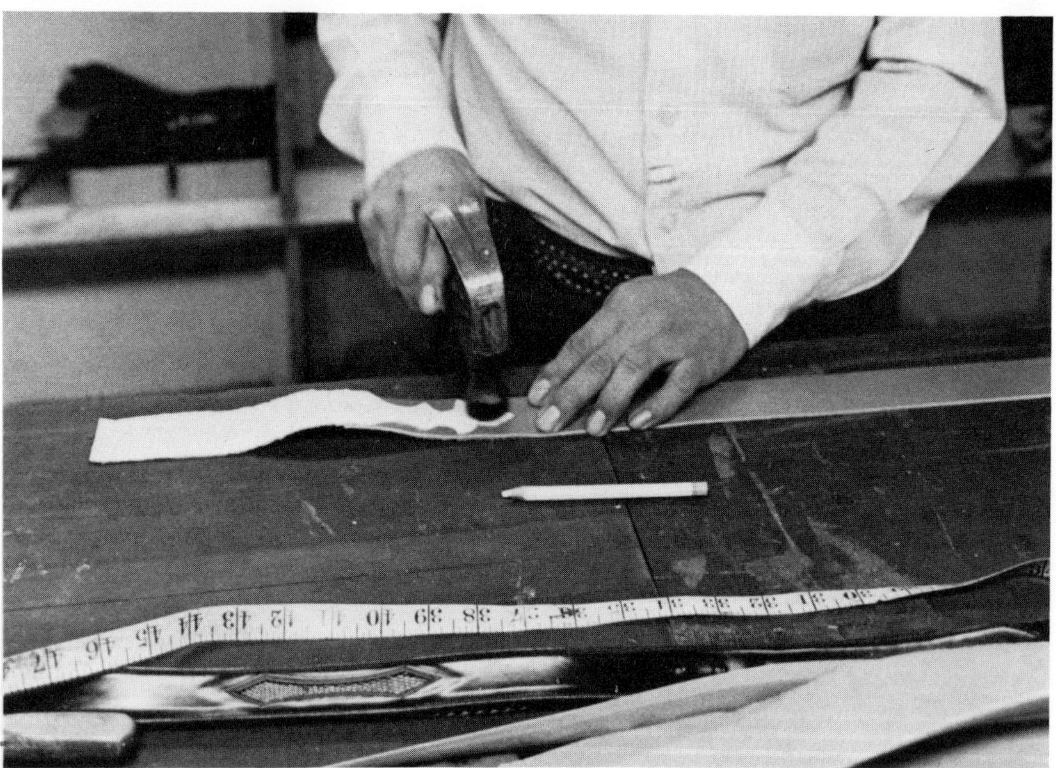

The ostrich is hammered down on the main belt strip.

After the backing is put on, the excess is cut away.

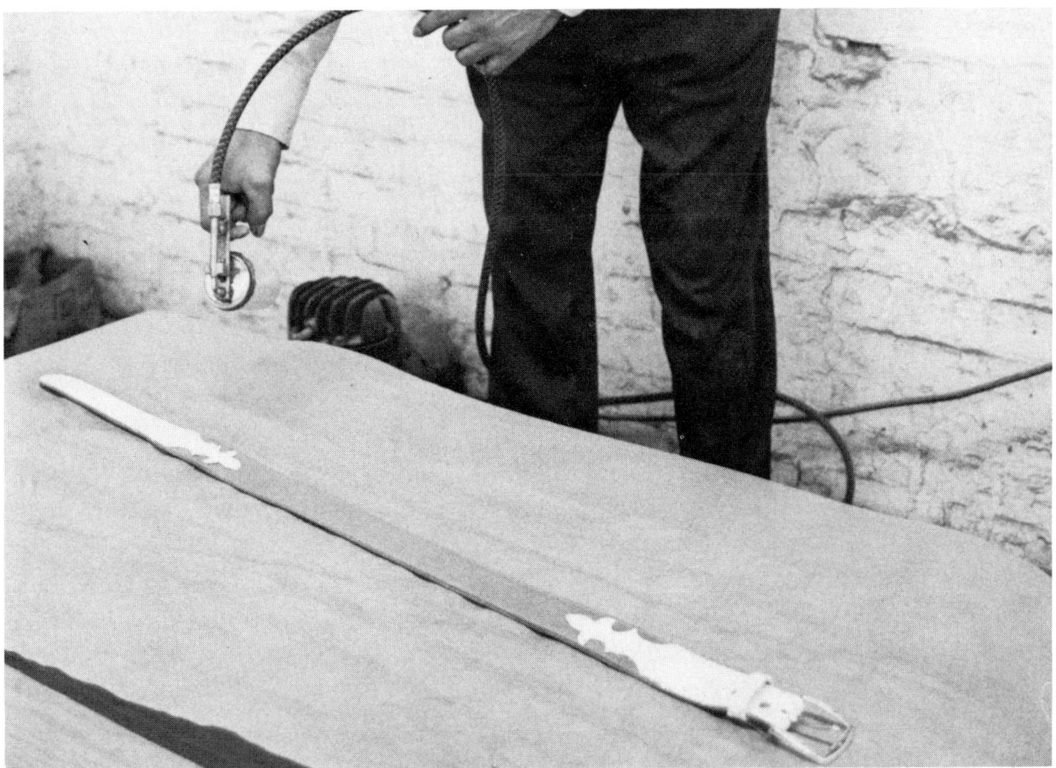

When completed, the leather is sprayed with a glaze finish.

This same technique may be used with sharkskin, lizard, or other skins that are almost paper thin; it will give them strength for the harder use of belts. When making a belt of hornback lizard, the same careful technique of backing the skin is also used because the lizard alone is much too fragile to sustain the constant pull and flexing movement of a belt.

First Jorge Abrego cuts a strip of belt leather to the proper length and width. He then cuts the lizard slightly wider so it may be folded over the strip when glued down. After coating with Barge Cement, a strip of Fibastay is cemented to the back of the skin and then the edges of the skin are folded over. Next the leather strip is cemented down and the ends skived or thinned on a skiving machine (or this may be done by hand with a head knife). The reason for this is that the end will be a bit thinner, allowing it to be folded over for the buckle. Once this step is completed, the entire belt is edge stitched—or it may be hand laced—for a finished appearance. The buckle slots or holes are punched with punches or dies which come in various sizes and shapes. Usually the buckle is attached with snaps so that buckles may be changed. Of course there is no reason a buckle can't be permanently attached and this can be done by stitching, riveting, or lacing. Finally, a revolving thonging punch is used to make belt holes for the buckle. That's all there is to making an excellent belt which, with proper care, should make its owner proud to wear it.

Lucchese also combines various leathers and frequently matches some small pieces of unusual leathers with belting leather for a striking effect. In this instance, white ostrich ends, cut in a design, are used for both ends of the belt and the same technique is followed. The ostrich is stitched onto a piece of calf and Fibastay is cemented to the backing. A stronger piece of leather is used and then stitched together for strength. Remember that most household sewing machines aren't strong enough to sew a couple of thicknesses of leather. While there are some that will take a leather needle, it is best to ask the maker if the motor will take the punishment of sewing leather. Otherwise, a hand awl may be used for sewing. Granted, it's a longer and more tedious job, but the work can be done in this way. Incidentally, the calfskin used in the photographs on pages 42–43 are 3½ to 4-ounce and the backing is 4 to 4½-ounce. The combination of these leathers makes an ideal weight for a belt. The Fibastay probably adds a few grams, but it gives the necessary strength and durability for the hard use a belt receives. When the belt or hat band is completed, the edges are given a touch of dye to match the rest of the leather and to make a finished-looking job.

Such professionals as Jorge Abrego have all the necessary tools and machinery at hand. However this shouldn't give the beginner any cause to be discouraged. Many of the operations can be carried out with the most basic and simple of tools—a good sharp knife, a steel ruler, and a hand awl. Holes can be punched with any hammer and a proper-size nail. Granted, the first efforts may be a bit crude, but care and caution in working will soon result in more professional-looking work.

Sam Lucchese likes to point out that the greater expense of the exotic leathers shouldn't indicate to the wearer they are tougher and more durable than the less expensive type of leathers. He draws the parallel between an inexpensive pair of cowboy Levis and a custom made pair of fine English flannel trousers. The latter are, of course, more costly than a cheap pair of Levis, but certainly won't stand the daily grind

A piece of Fibastay is placed on the lizard skin as a backing to give strength.

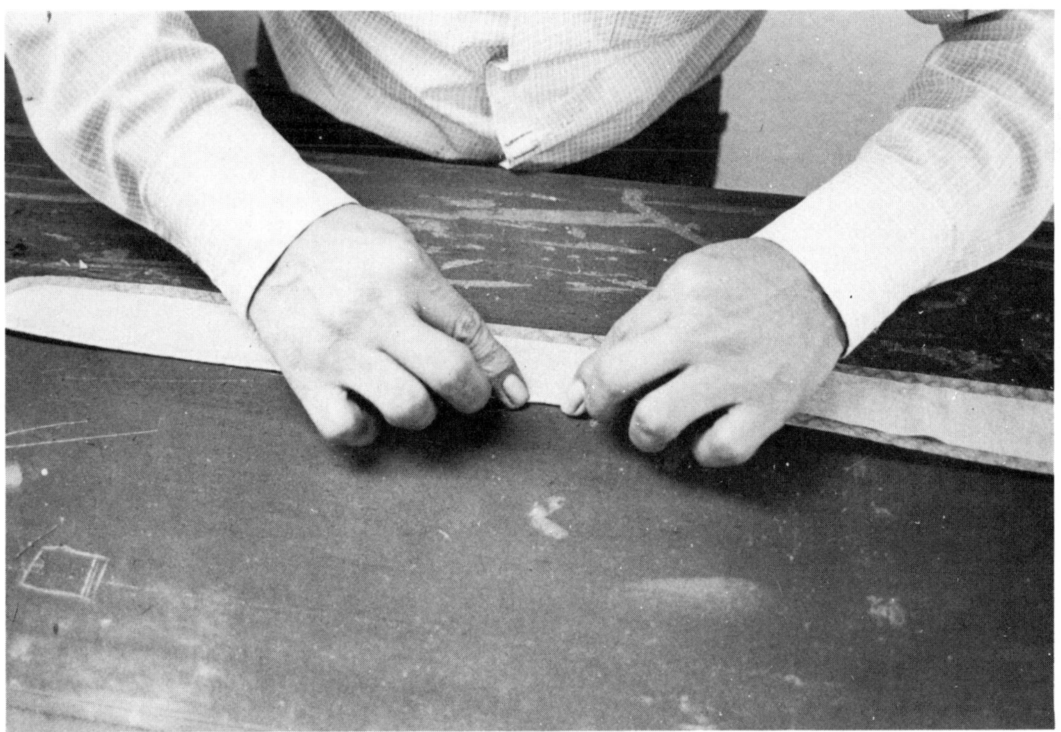

The edges are carefully folded over and cemented to the backing.

of hours on horseback, working around the mud of corrals and horse barns, and occasionally snagging on a piece of barbed wire. Rare leathers are the same. They require more care and attention. While they look well and their owners are proud to wear articles made from them, they are not as sturdy and won't take the hard knocks of a belt crafted out of a piece of vegetable-tanned hide. With the exception of sharkskin, the lizards and snakeskins or even fine ostrich are used for dress belts or, if you will, "show" belts and should be worn to complement a fine pair of boots. Naturally a hat band won't take the stress and strain of a belt, but it's still on top of the head taking the worst the elements can give—rain, dust, hot sun, and, in some parts of the Southwest, driving hail and snow. If these fancy items are given a modicum of care, they will give long life and years of pleasure.

As to cost, Lucchese's belts and hat bands run upward near the price of a modest pair of boots. Anteater belts might cost $150 and a hat band could be as much as $50. While these are not prices attractive to the average pocketbook, for the man who has everything the boots, belts, and hat bands made by Sam Lucchese are considered tops in their field.

For the new leathercraftsman, the purchase of snakeskin, some lengths of leather, and a few basic tools can yield many hours of pleasure. If he takes care in his craftsmanship and pays attention to detail, rare and unusual belts and hat bands can be the result. There is still nothing like making something for yourself, especially when a friend admires it and says, "Boy, I'd like one of those for myself." At this point, the novice has become a professional and he enjoys the satisfaction of knowing that his craftsmanship is accepted, admired and desired.

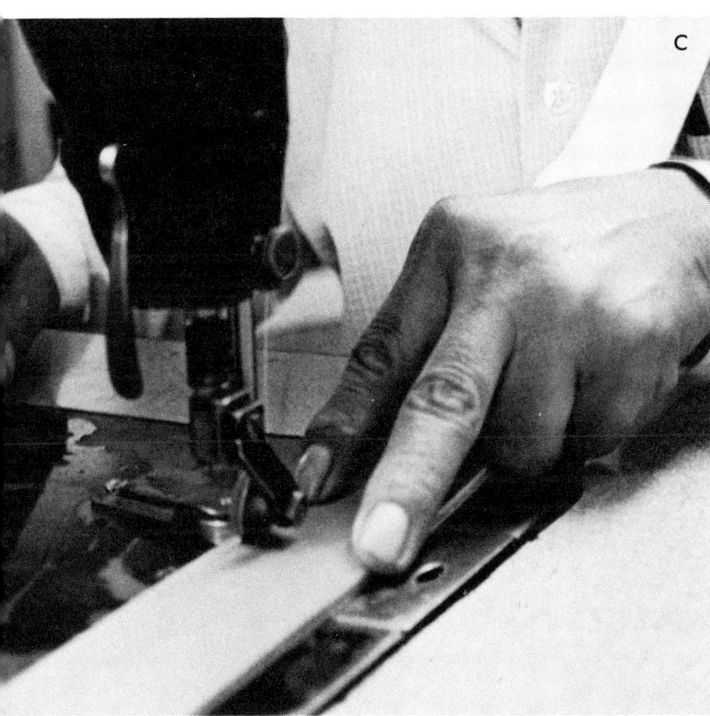

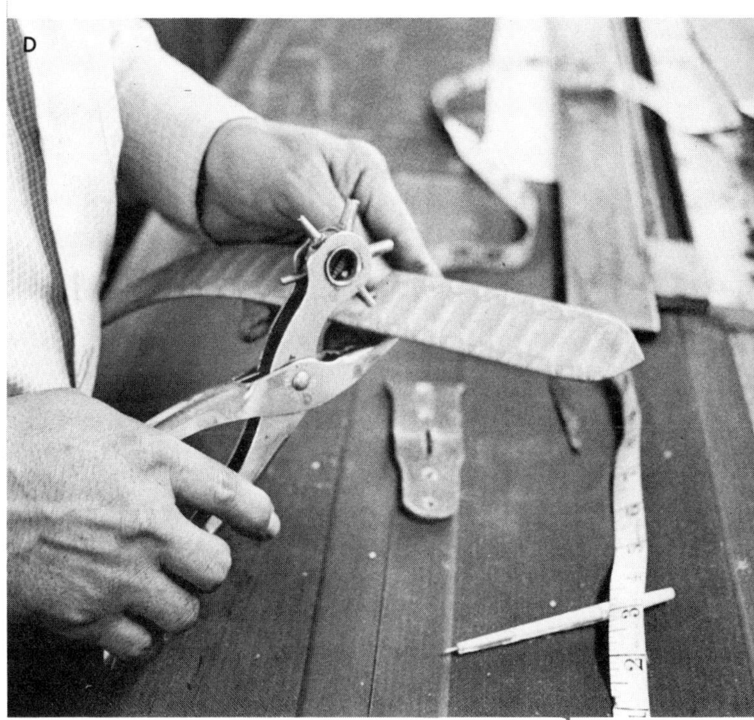

A Typical of all leatherwork, the edges are hammered down for a solid fit.

B The lizard skin, with Fibastay backing, is next cemented to another back of 4/5-ounce leather for strength.

C Although all pieces are cemented, the leather is also sewed for a finished appearance.

D Holes are punched for the buckle.

CHAPTER SIX

Walter Kneubuhler "Mountain Crafts"

Among the fine craftsmen cutting leather today is Walter Kneubuhler of Pioneer, Ohio. WK, as he is often called, is a most unusual craftsman since he has selected for his skills one period of American history that appeals to him—that tough and dangerous time of the fur trade when white men roamed the great mountains and shared the wilderness with the Indians. It was a time when the long barges were poled along the upper Missouri and beaver pelts were piled high on the wharves awaiting the freight canoes downstream to St. Louis. Romantic? Well maybe, but ask Walter if he would have liked to live in those days. An emphatic "Hell no" is his answer. Yet, in some ways, WK is the modern embodiment of those pioneers of old. If he doesn't want to push through waist-high snow drifts or climb high mountains or ford icy streams, he still supplies dreams for many with his expert craftsmanship. And perhaps he even keeps a few dreams alive for his own pleasure.

Take the flintlock rifle, a weapon that was indispensable to the Mountain Men. Kneubuhler, along with many thousands of other Americans, is an avid shooter of the old powderburner. WK also crafts many leather items that went along with it. These include clothing and accoutrements, fringed Indian knife sheaths, highly decorative scabbards of the Mountain Men, and the "possible bag" that carried all those accessories that made it possible to shoot a possible. And WK makes them all as nearly exact as modern materials will allow.

Now seventy, Kneubuhler became fascinated with the fur trade about twenty years ago. He began to research the early 1800s when the French *voyageurs* moved into the shining mountains. Research to a hobbyist is just as important as it is to a scientist and WK, wanting to recreate the knives and sheaths precisely, drove the long distance from

Walter Kneubuhler.

Ohio to the Denver Museum. On other long trips, he has journeyed to New York for visits to the Museum of the American Indian. Observing, sketching, and counting rows of brass tacks in the various designs, Walter strove for accuracy in the smallest detail. Being a skilled knifemaker, he reproduced the blades that were originally made by Sorby or Jukes Coulson & Company of Sheffield. The first blades to hit North America were supplied to the Hudson's Bay Company by the cutlers and eventually traded to the Indians. These knives were particularly favored by the Piegans, Bloods, Assiniboins, and other tribes and they gained their greatest favor during the fur and buffalo trade. The handles were crude; sometimes the owner would simply attach a bear or wolf jaw. Sheaths were highly decorative. Some had beadwork, horsehair, and, if the Indian brave had done well in battle, a couple of scalplocks.

Making a Blackfoot Dag Sheath

In spite of its seemingly complicated appearance, the Blackfoot knife sheath is fairly easy to make. Of course it will take time and patience, but the new leathercraftsman will slowly learn this. While Kneubuhler can make one in a couple of hours (he's crafted hundreds over the years), the novice leatherworker should pace himself, work slowly, and carefully examine each progressive step in the crafting.

The sheath shown in the accompanying illustrations will hold a knife with a seven-inch blade and a five-inch handle, although it can be made any size.

A pouch sheath of this type, because of the buckskin covering, requires a liner to protect the knife and wearer. The first step is to lay the knife on a piece of wrapping paper so that the pattern can be drawn. Allow the handle to stick out the top a couple of inches. Now, after cutting the pattern, lay the knife inside and fold the paper over. Allow sufficient room for rivets, and check the fit. If all is in order at this point, copy the pattern on a piece of 6/7-ounce saddle leather and cut with a sharp knife or leather shears. The rivet holes are punched and the next step is to coat the edge seams with Barge Cement. Kneubuhler allows this to set overnight because the first coating will be absorbed by the leather. Next morning go over the same area with a second coating of cement and allow this coat to dry about twenty minutes. Press the two edges together, lay the liner on the bench, and pound along the edge with a hammer so it will adhere tightly. The rivets may now be set in the pre-punched holes. A pair of scissors or a sharp knife is used next to trim excess leather along the edge. The liner is now complete and should be set aside while the buckskin cover is prepared.

The illustration and pattern on page 52 will show the proper way to cut the cover; however, sufficient material must be allowed for the fringe. As to length, six inches would do for an average size knife with a 3½" blade, while a cover for a larger knife might run to eight inches.

While quality leathers have been stressed, on this sheath a lower-grade buckskin or suede should be used because it will probably be scratched and scruffed up a bit to give a realistic appearance.

The scalplock is important since it will be the most decorative item on the sheath. WK uses cow tails with a bit of hide left on the scalp. When he runs out of material, he crafts his own "scalps" with a tuft of fur cemented in the proper place. It is then circled with beads and a hole is punched with an awl for the horsehair wrapped with thread.

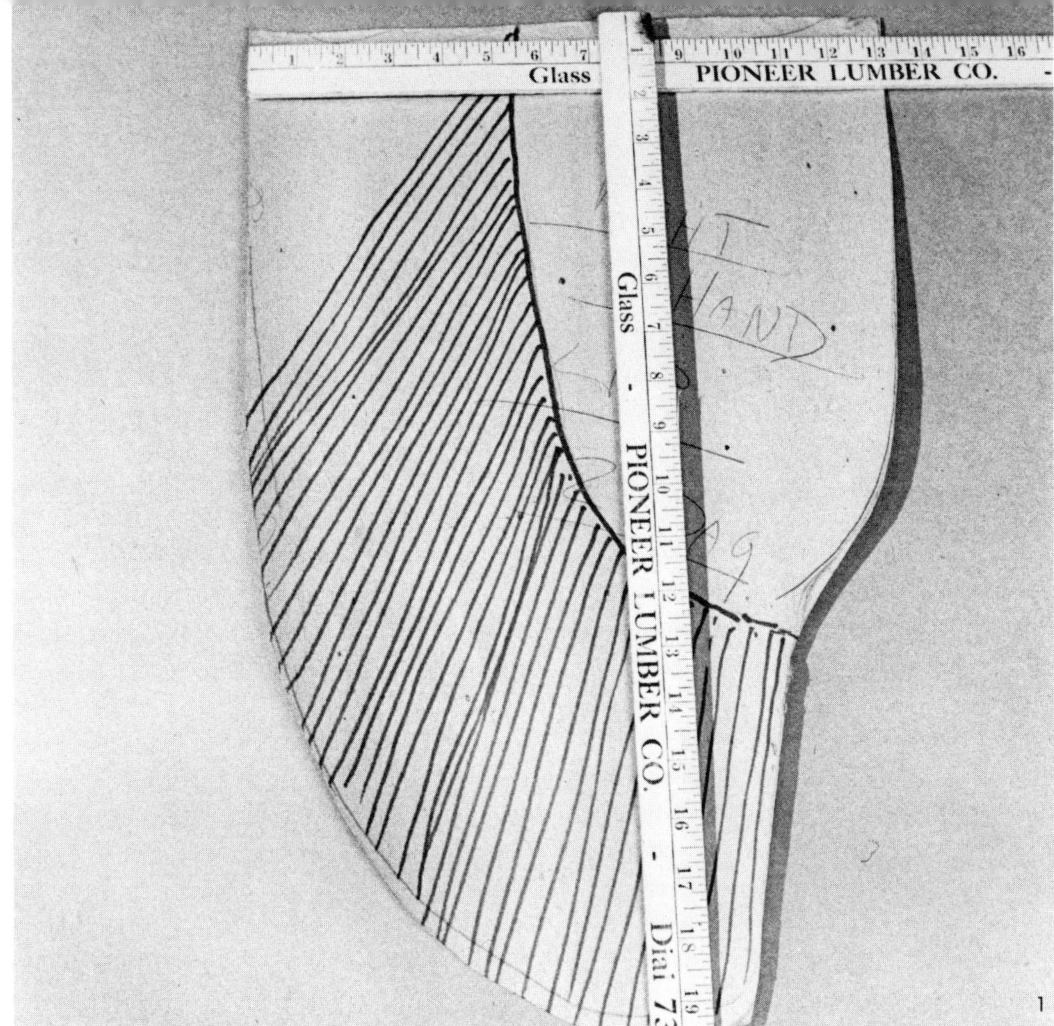

Cardboard pattern used to make the Blackfoot Dag Sheath. Note that the rulers give measurements of the size of skin required to craft the liner cover.

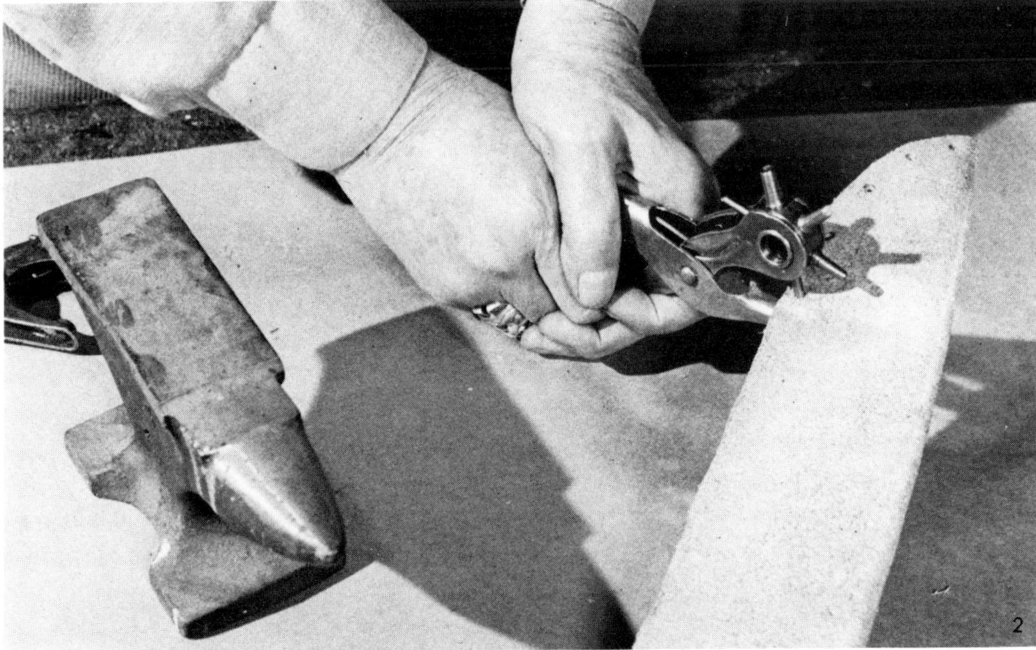

A piece of heavy leather, about 9/10 ounce, is cut to size for the knife sheath and holes punched for rivets. A small hammer and anvil will give a solid support for pounding in rivets. This liner will protect both the knife and wearer.

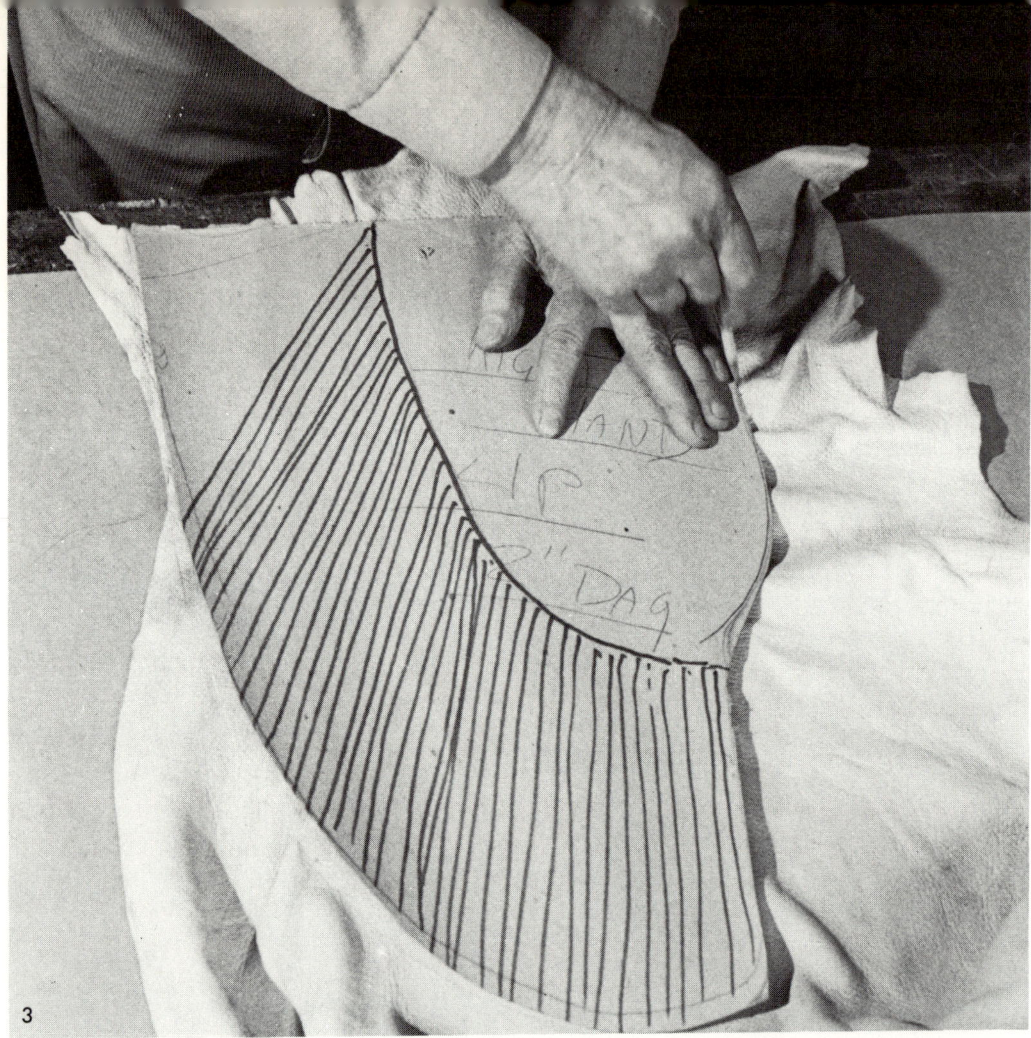

The next step is to cut and prepare the fancy covering. Here the pattern is used; note the amount of buckskin allowed for fringe.

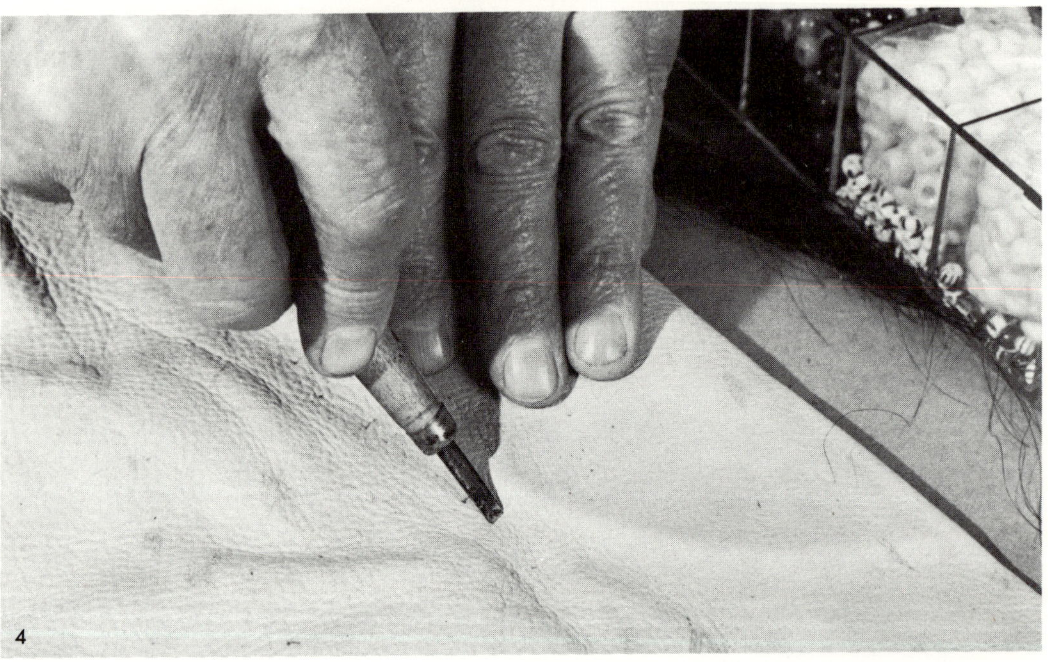

Preparing the scalplock, which is sewn on before covering the liner. After proper placement of the scalplock, and punching a hole for the fastening, both areas are coated with Barge Cement.

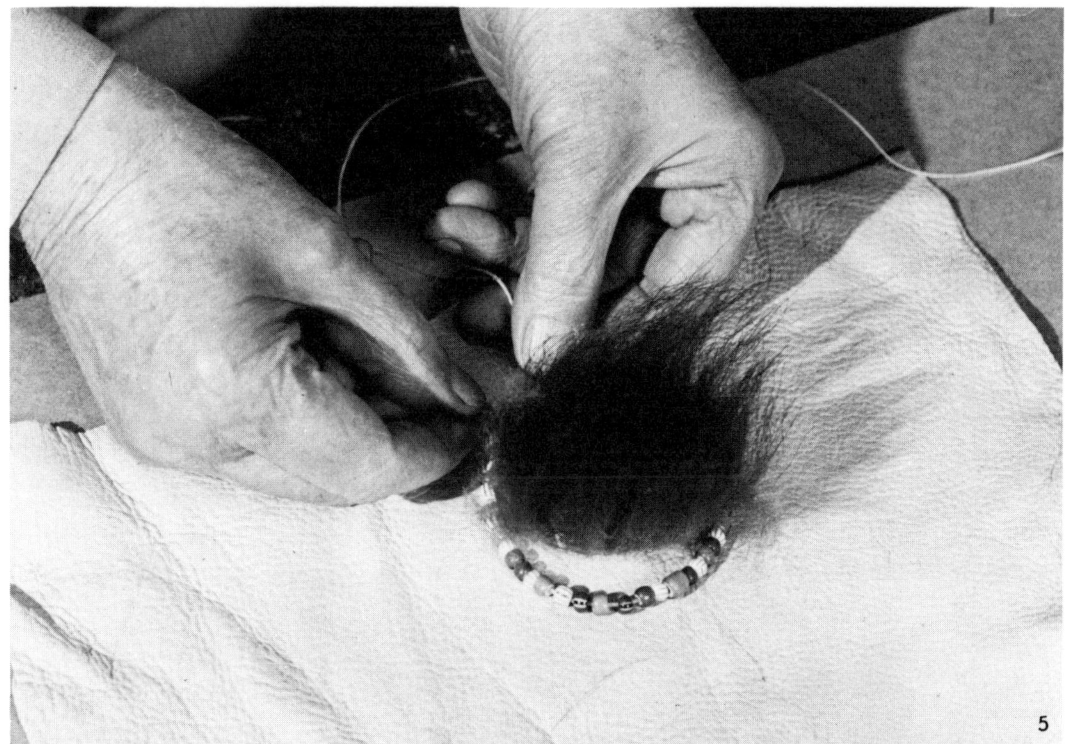

5

After a circle of colored beads is sewn down, a small piece of fur is set into the center. The horsehair thong, simulating a scalp, is drawn into the center and tied in back.

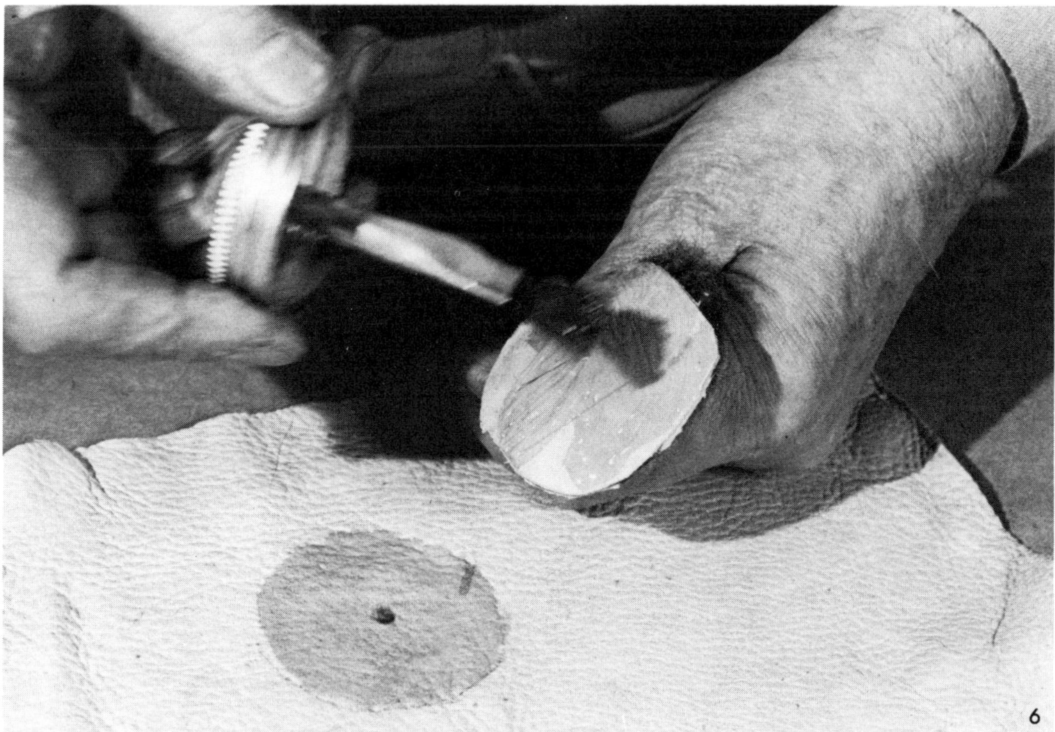

6

Note the placement of the covering on the liner. The darkened portion is covered with Barge Cement to allow a firm fit. The uncoated white area will be cut into fringe.

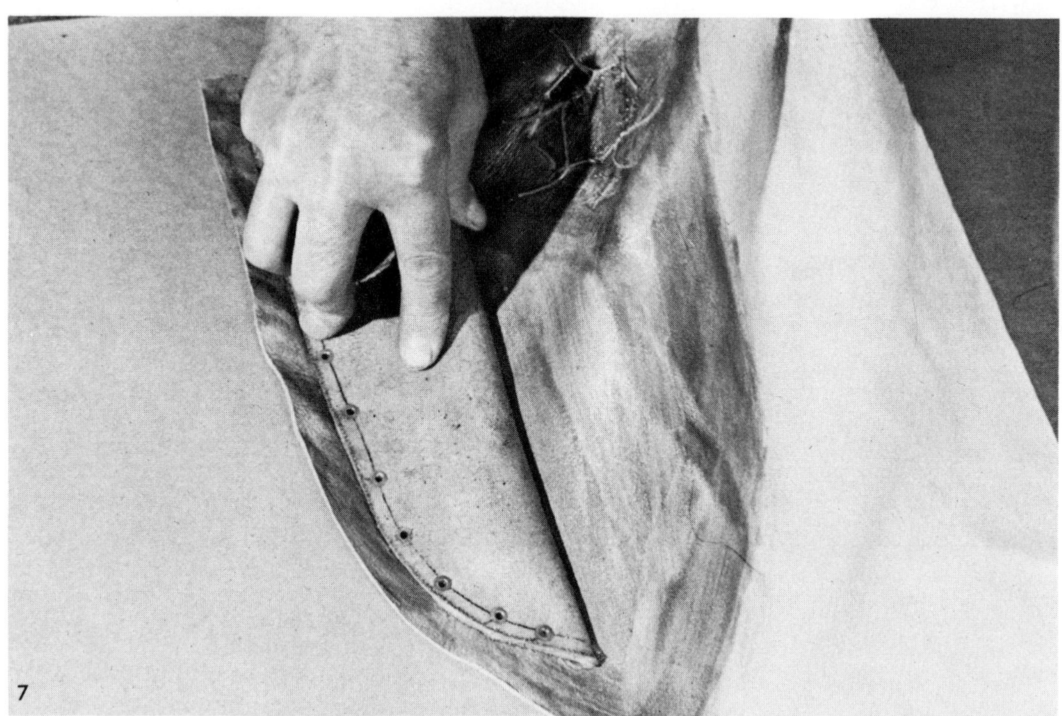

Holes are punched with a small chisel for the lacing. Note the large beads which are placed on each alternate loop of the buck stitch.

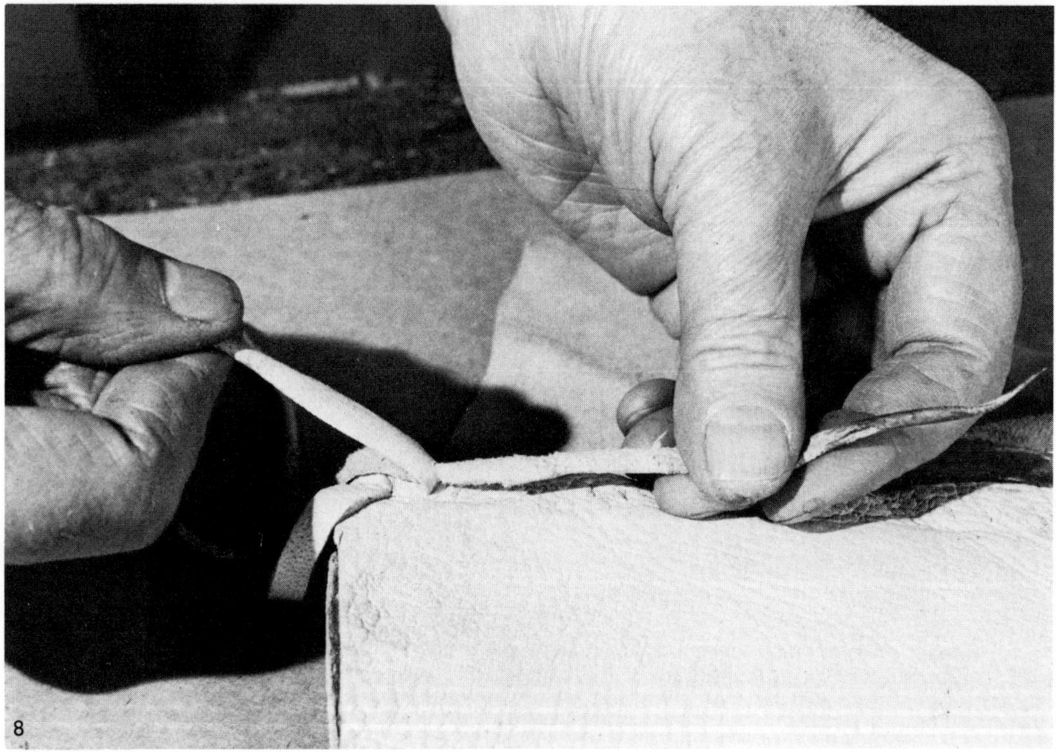

Method of ending the lacing with a slit-end lace to tie the pieces together. This is shown completed in the next picture.

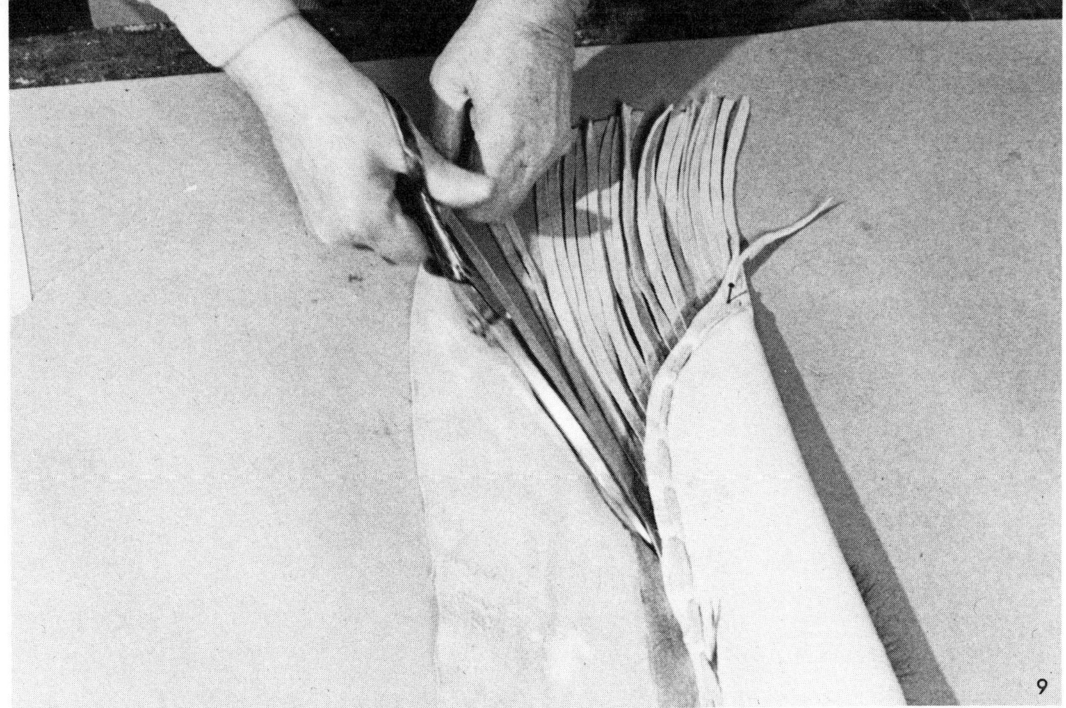
9

Cutting the fringe at an angle will allow it to fall naturally. When arriving at the top, a small triangle will be left and this is simply cut off.

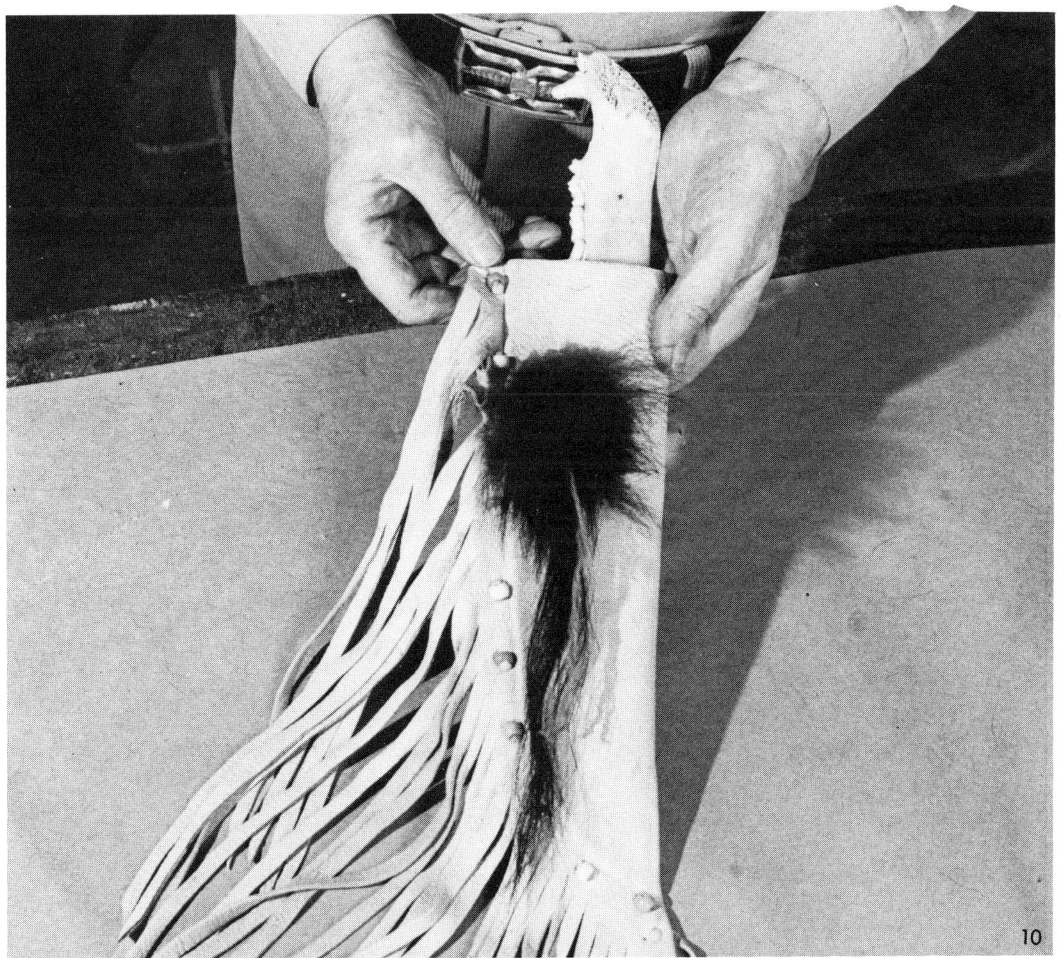
10

The completed sheath. A comb or brush can be used to untangle the hair. The advantage of this sheath is that it can be made for almost any size of knife. However, larger knives will show to more advantage with a greater area of decor and fringe.

When the scalplock is completed, both the liner sheath and the inside of the buckskin cover are coated with cement. Allowing a few moments for it to dry, the cover is then placed over the liner and worked down with the fingers for a smooth fit. Note that only the part of the buckskin that will cover the liner is coated and the fringe area is left alone. Next a long ⅛″-thong is cut for lacing this. Incidentally, it is cut from the same material as the sheath cover.

The larger colored beads are laid out ready to be laced on. There are ten beads used on the large Blackfoot Dag sheath and a smaller sheath would require less. Walter uses an extremely sharp chisel to punch the holes for the lacing. It is exactly ⅛″ wide and works well indeed. But should this type of tool not be available, an awl, razor blade, or sharp, small-bladed pocket knife could also be used. The beads are placed about 1½″ apart, which means there are a pair of ⅛″-holes ¼″ apart every 1½ inches. Picture 10, page 55, shows how the thong is caught in back and from then on it is simply buckstitch lacing. Incidentally, it can often be difficult forcing a thong through leather and Kneubuhler uses needle-nosed pliers to push it through, then turns the sheath over and pulls it from the far side. After the lacing is completed, the excess material is fringed. In order to have the fringe fall gracefully, the cut is made with a pair of scissors starting from the bottom and cutting upward. It will be noted that as the fringe is cut toward the top of the sheath there will be a small triangle of buckskin that can't be fringed. This is simply cut off and discarded. All that is now required is to comb out the scalplock and the job is done. The Blackfoot Dag sheath is authentic, handsome, and will dress up any sportsman or black-powder shooter.

Crafting a Possible Bag

This type of bag is carried by anyone shooting a muzzle-loading rifle and, in fact, a few friends hang them near a brick fireplace to add to the atmosphere. The bag on a scale of difficulty from one to ten might be a number five, certainly a bit more difficult than the sheaths in crafting ability. The leather used should be at least a four-ounce chrome- or buck-tanned leather. It can even run to five- or six-ounce and will perhaps give a bit more body to the completed bag.

The tools used are the same as those used for the sheaths, but with the addition of needles and a spool of eight-cord nylon thread. A study of Picture 1 showing the pattern and measurements will give the basic size and cuts required to begin the bag. Later a piece of leather to go across the back will be needed, as will shoulder straps.

The first step is to place the cardboard pattern on a piece of leather and mark around it for cutting, as in Picture 2. Once the outline is marked, a pair of scissors is used to cut the leather to shape. After all the pieces are cut, each piece is marked with the exact center. This is a seemingly trivial yet very important step. Why? Because the center of all four pieces must match to ensure the bag will be "square" and thus hang properly. A slightly heavier piece of sole leather is cut to shape and this will be glued down inside the bag. This piece gives proper form and shape to the completed bag.

Once the center of the bottom piece is marked, holes are punched through for the dangling laces that will hang from the bottom of the completed bag. These holes are

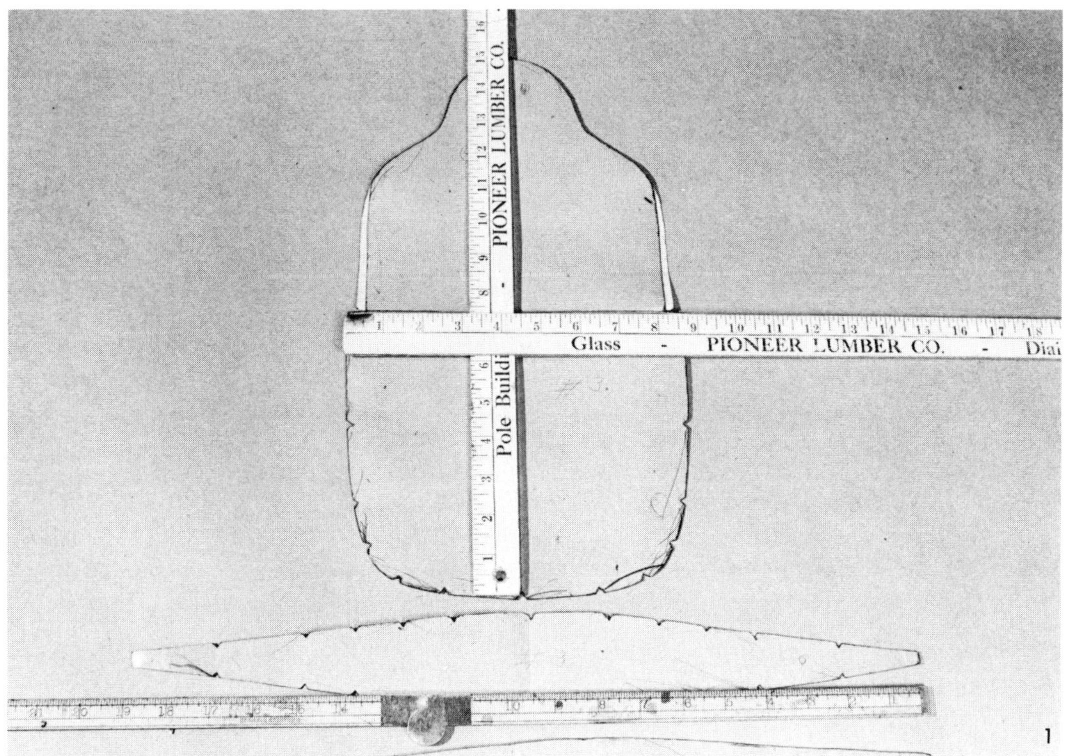

1

As with all his projects Kneubuhler uses a pattern and lays out the various pieces before starting construction. The rulers again show the size pieces to be cut.

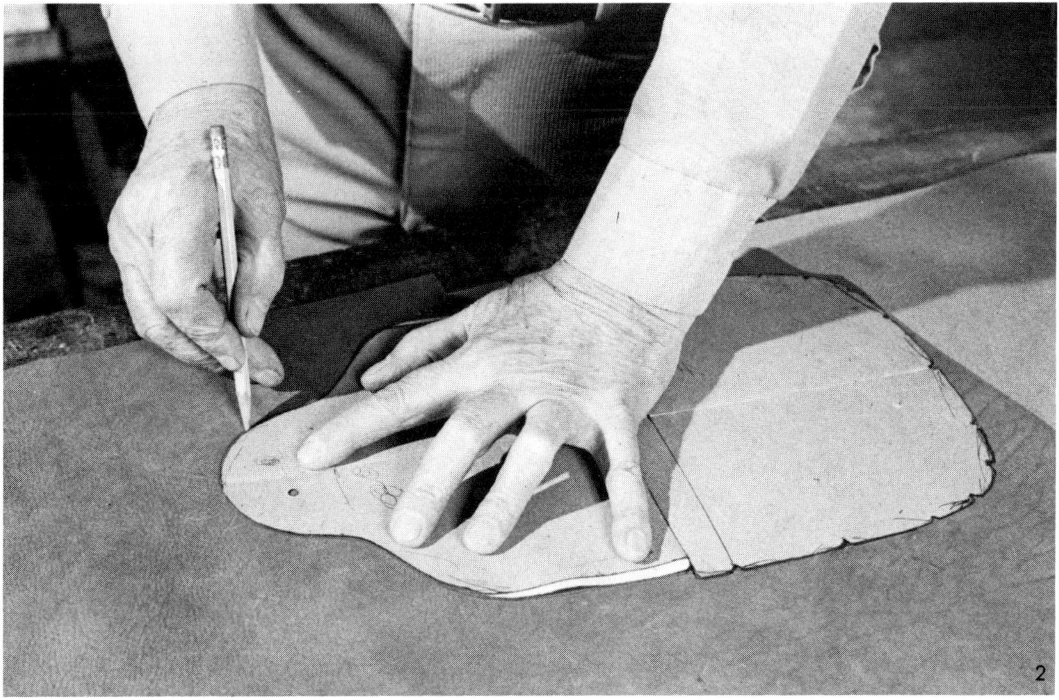

2

The pattern pieces are laid over the leather and outlined with pencil.

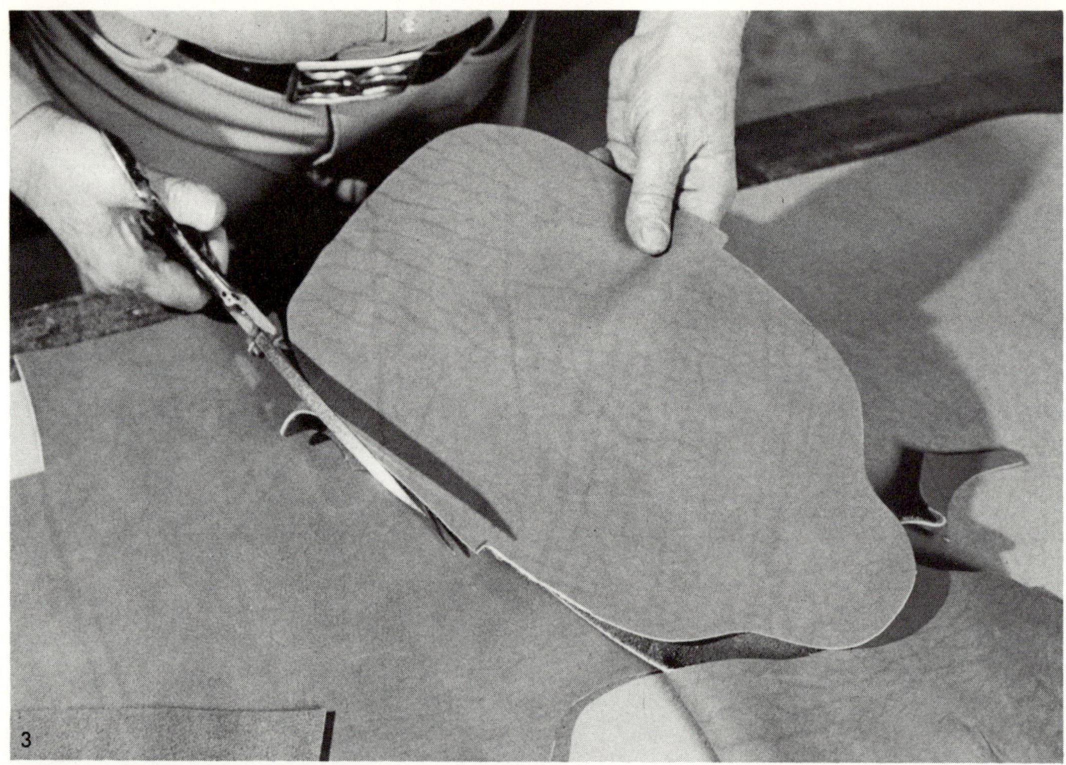

Leather shears are used for cutting the leather to size.

A heavier piece of sole leather is used for the bottom of the bag to keep it open and give support. This is also cut before beginning to make the bag.

5

With the exception of the shoulder straps, all the pieces necessary for the bag are laid out. Up to this point the shears was the only tool used.

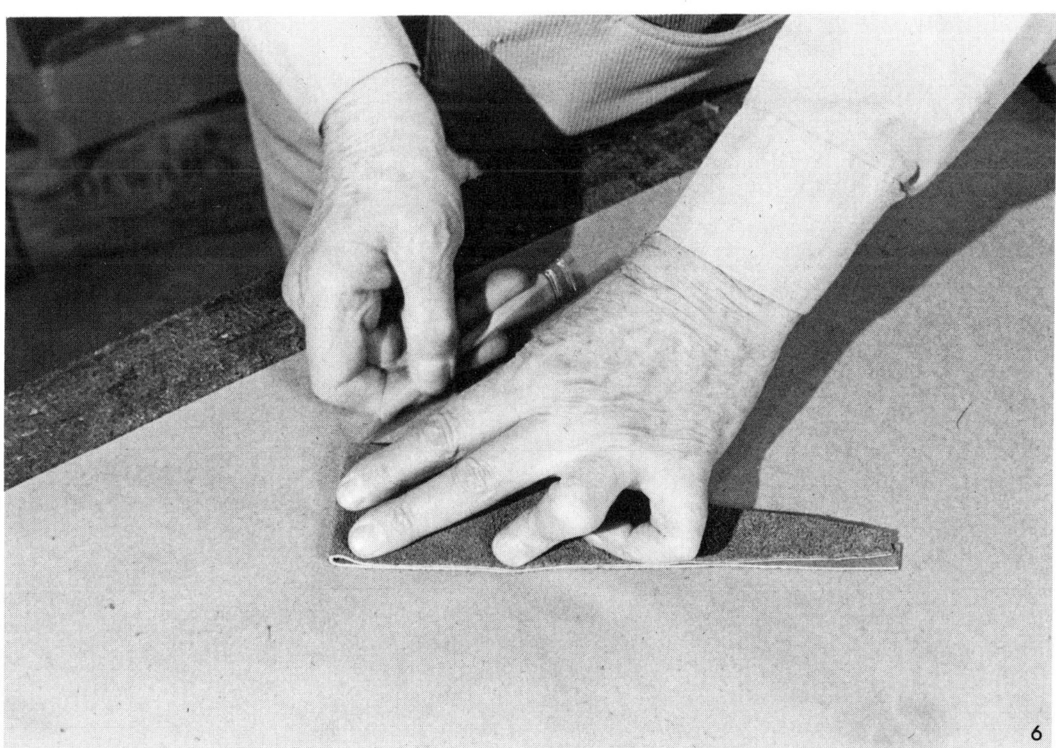

6

In order to have the pieces line up, it's necessary to find the center. This is done by folding the leather and then marking with a pencil.

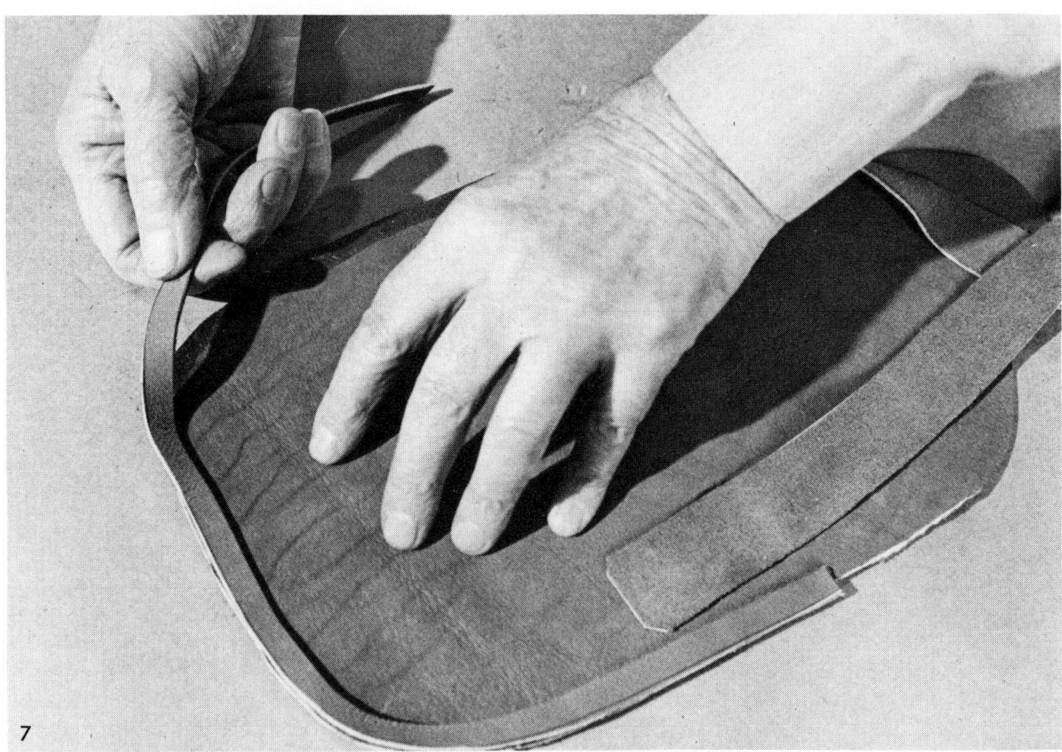

7

A coating of Barge Cement is used for the edge strips and to hold the strap ends for sewing. Here the various pieces are being set in and will then be allowed to dry for an hour. The craftsman will note that pre-gluing will make stitching much easier.

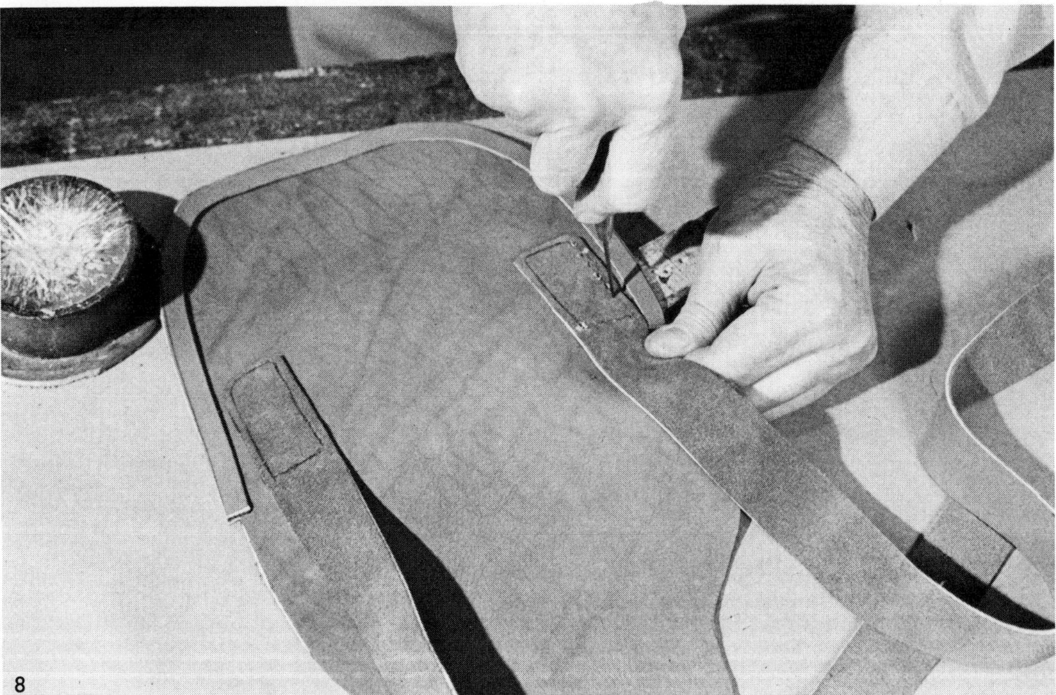

8

An awl is pushed through first to mark the stitching holes. The circle of beeswax on the left will help the needle go through the leather and prevent it from becoming too hot.

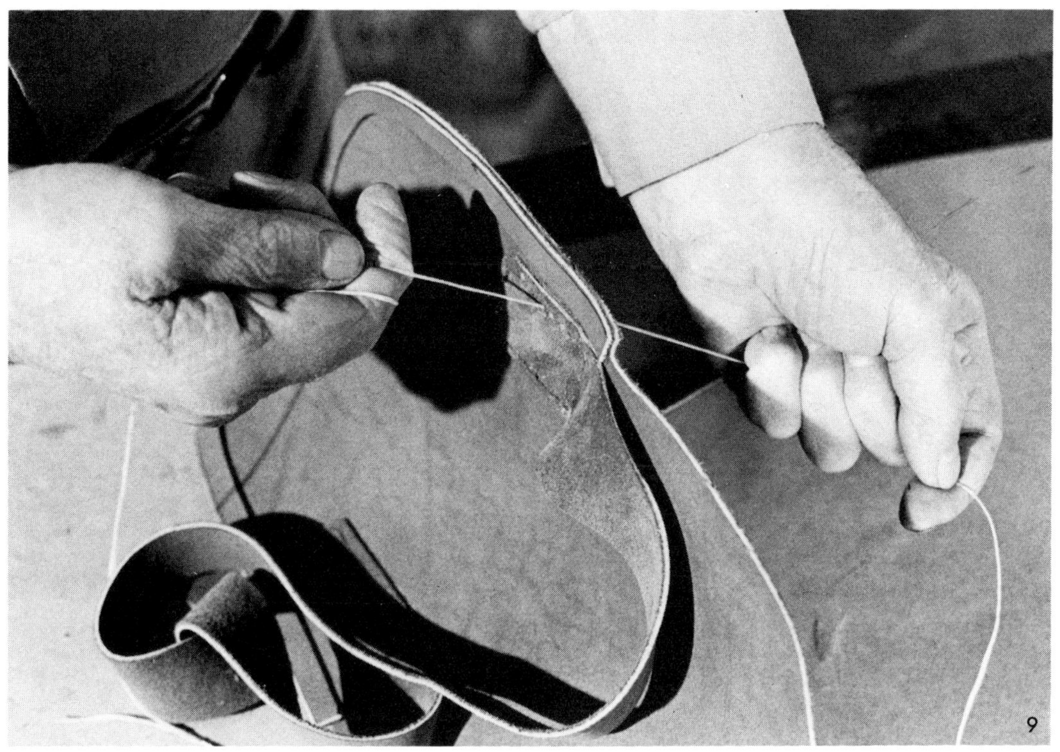

A saddle stitch is used with two needles and pulled tightly.

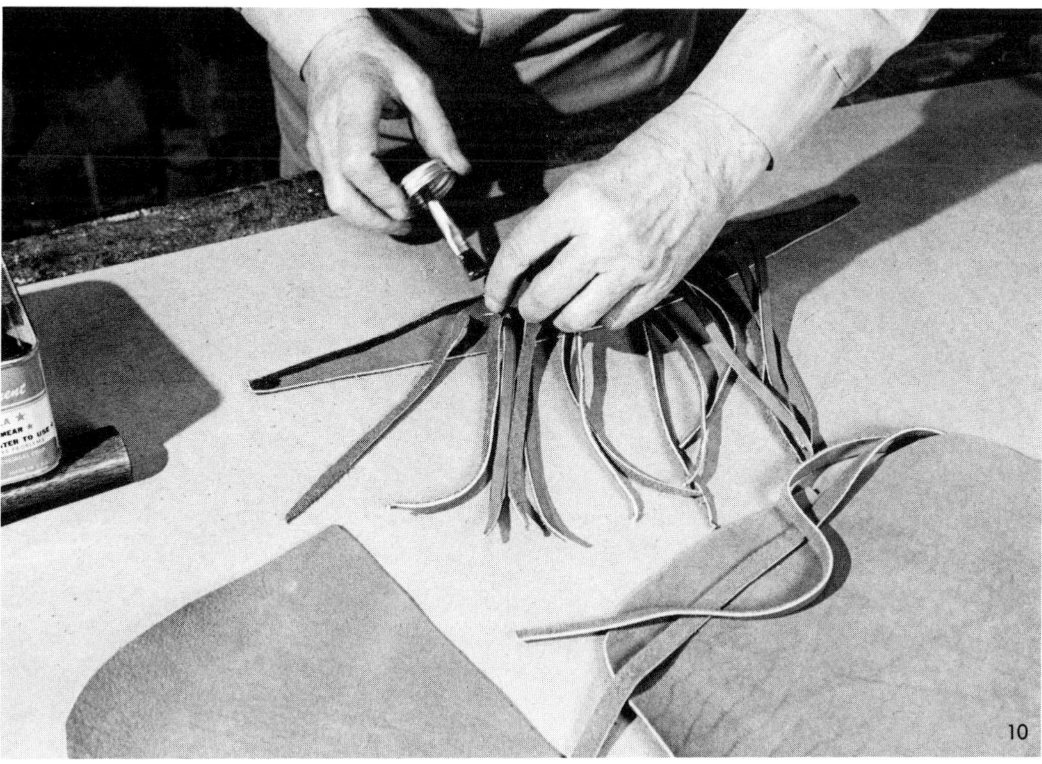

The bottom of the bag is now coated with Barge Cement and set aside to dry while the backing is prepared.

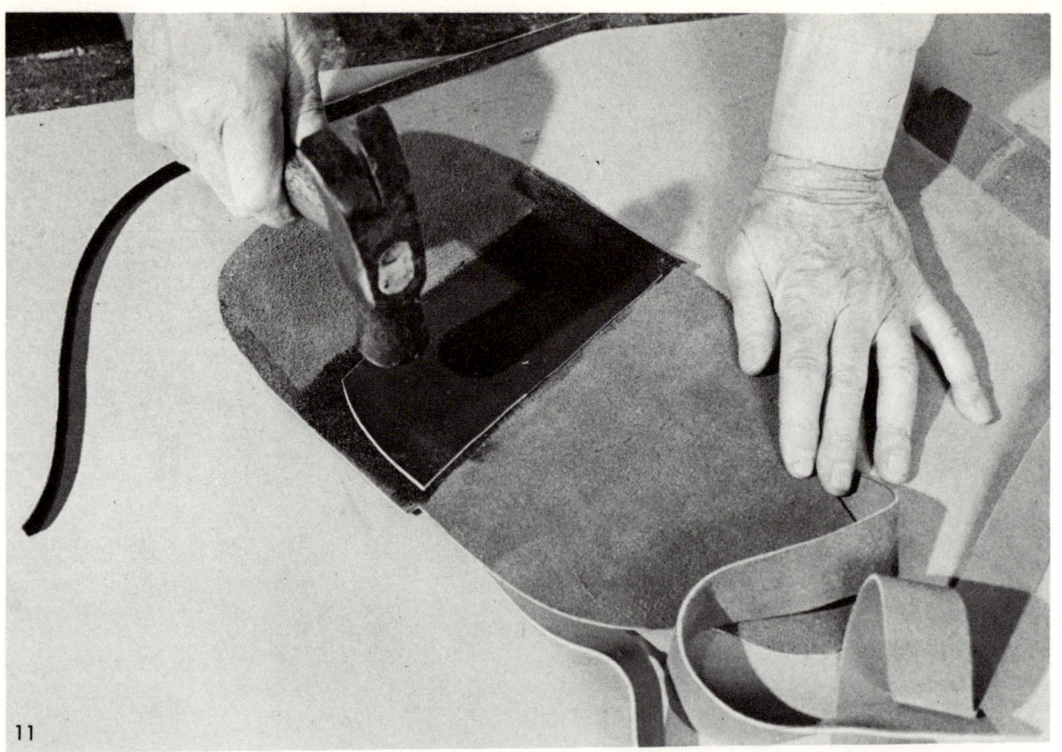

11

A stiffer piece of leather is cemented to the inside back to give support to the completed bag.

12

After the bag is cemented together, the piece of stiffer sole leather is cemented in. At this point, the reader will note the bag is actually made with all the work being done on the inside and, on completion, is turned inside out.

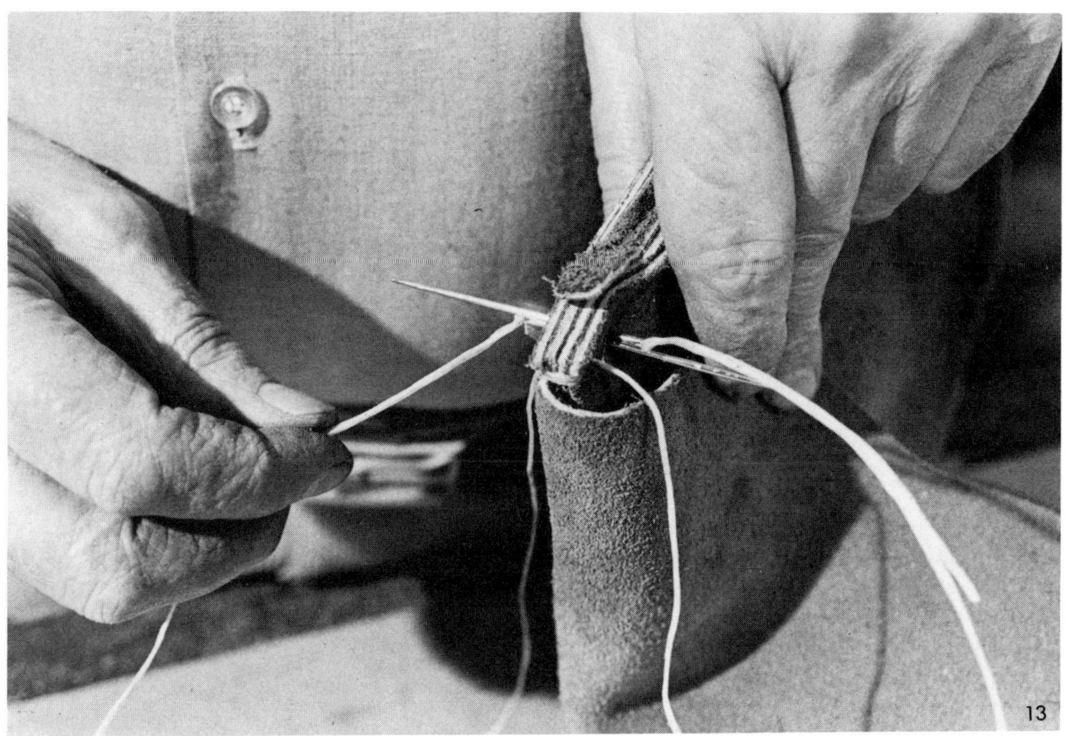

With all the various pieces now cemented together, stitching is done with the sinew-type thread used by Kneubuhler. Depending upon the availability of threads, either linen or nylon may be used.

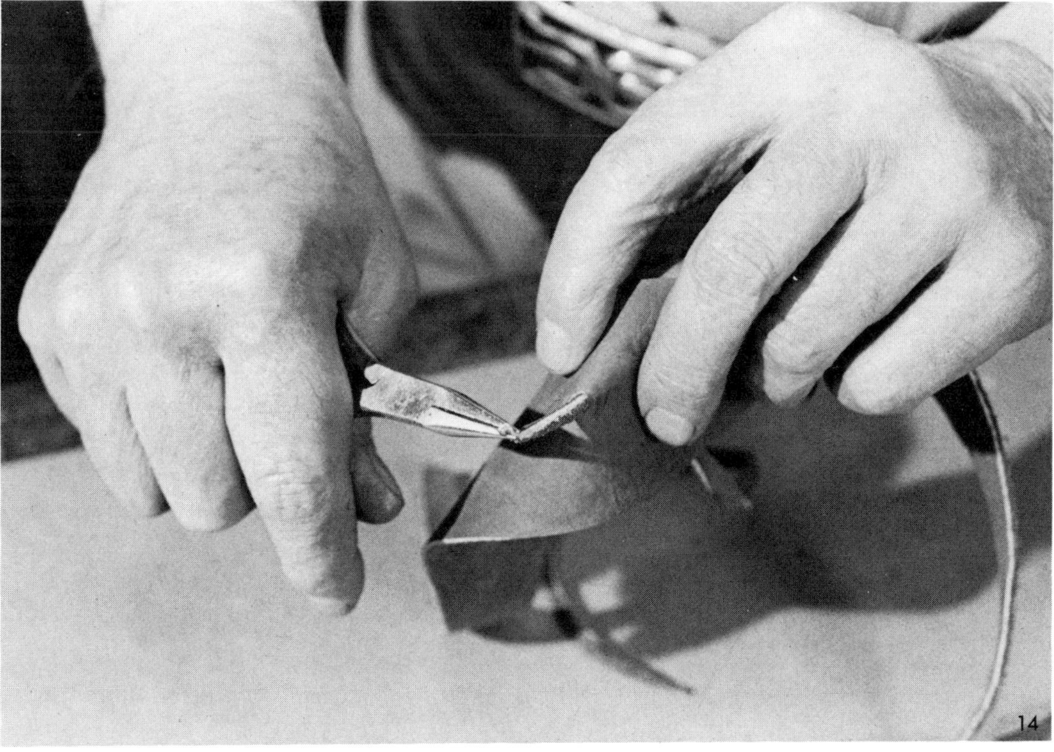

Needle-nosed pliers are excellent for pushing and pulling the various thongs and fringe through the strap.

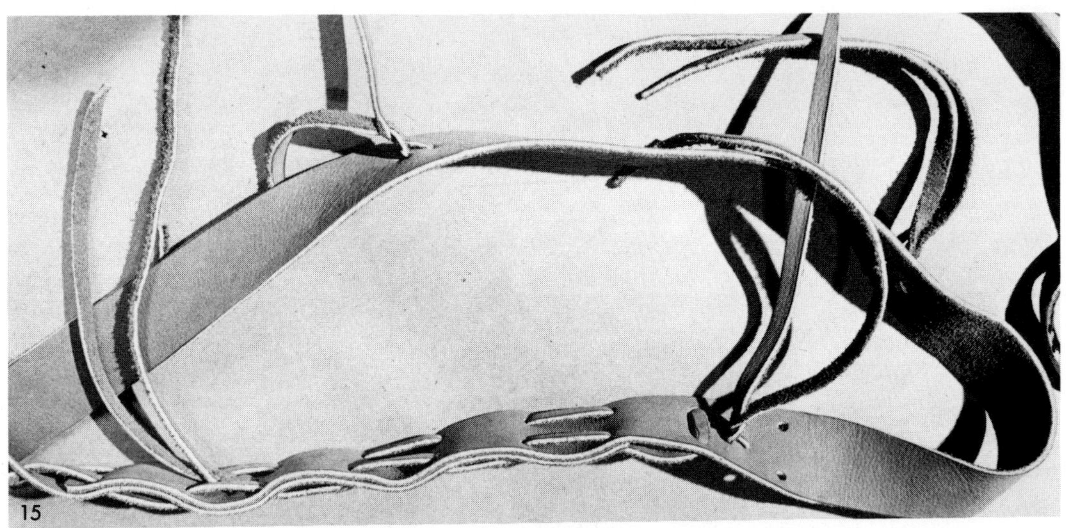

15

The completed strap. Two separate pieces are overlapped and adjusted, as with some rifle slings, by unlacing and moving to the proper holes for correct length.

usually placed about an inch apart, but if more fringe is required they could be placed one-half inch apart. Picture 14 shows the needle-nosed pliers being used to pull the thongs through. After all the pieces are cut, cement is then applied to all parts and set to dry overnight. Barge Cement will hold all the pieces in place for sewing. It is strong and will make this task easier. The next morning a second coat is applied, as with the knife sheaths, and set aside to dry for the required time. A second piece of leather is cut, as shown, to fit the back of the pouch on the inside. This adds body to the bag and gives additional support when the shoulder straps are sewn on. Holes are then punched with an awl for fastening the straps and a block of paraffin and beeswax is used for the needle. This, again, is one of those seemingly unimportant steps that will make life easier for the craftsman. Constant waxing of the needle will allow it to be forced through the leather easier and will, surprisingly, prevent the needle from becoming too hot. After the ends of the straps are sewn, the entire bag is cemented together. When the various pieces are in place, go over them with a hammer to ensure a tight fit.

Sewing with the sinew-type telephone nylon thread requires two needles because the thread will be put through the same hole from the opposite side. The sewing is begun from one end of the open bag and continued to the center of the bottom. Here the threads are tied and cut off and the same procedure is begun from the opposite end. When the sewing is completed the final step, at least for the bag, is to cement in the piece of previously cut sole leather that will give a base to the bag on the bottom and around the sides. This is shown in Picture 12 and, once it is completed, the entire bag is turned inside out. Now we have a finished bag with two long straps dangling in the air.

The strap is adjustable and, for the first time on this project, the punch is brought into play. Aside from the lace to fasten the two pieces together, holes are punched for decorative laces to hang from the straps. A glance at Picture 14 will show how these thongs are placed. Picture 15 shows the method of lacing the two ends together with an additional row of punch holes used to shorten the straps. Normally, when measurements for the proper length of hang are taken, there is no need to constantly take up or lengthen these straps since it does require unlacing a considerable amount of thongs.

To finish the bag, particularly if the user is a black-powder shooter, a patch knife may be hung from one of the thongs, a powder horn may be affixed to the straps, and other accessories such as a touchhole pick or charger may be hung from various convenient places.

With the exception of cement and modern threads, this bag is crafted as it was in the days of the Mountain Men. A diehard purist could probably eliminate the cement—although it does make the bag easier to assemble—and get some genuine sinew to replace the thread and have a bag crafted as did the pioneers.

Whatever its final use—decorative, utilitarian, or a catch-all bag for a frontier-minded lady friend—Walter Kneubuhler's possible bag is an interesting project and a reminder of those days when sturdy men roamed the plains with a Hawken or a Sharps cradled in their arms.

Making a Mountain Man Sheath

The Mountain Man's knife could be anything from a Green River butcher knife to one crafted from an old file. The sheath, however, was developed to fit the needs of the user. Bundled up as pioneers were in thick buffalo robes or heavy buckskins, the knife had to be readily accessible. The pioneer couldn't be bothered with retaining straps or thongs and the sheath was not only required to hold the knife firmly but also to be grasped quickly.

The unusual one-belt slit sheath allowed it to be worn over bulky clothing with the belt passing over the knife and holding it without fear of loss. The highly decorative motif of tacks was originally done by Indians as pure decoration and copied by the Mountain Men as they made their own sheaths.

The most difficult task of crafting this sheath is probably the monotony of pounding in about eighty brass tacks. Otherwise it should be regarded as a fairly simple sheath to make. It requires an awl, needle-nosed pliers, the usual Barge Cement, a short thong for lacing the inner part of the single belt loop, and a longer thong for lacing the edge of the sheath. Probably the best aid in crafting this type of sheath is a small tool Kneubuhler himself made in his shop. It is shown in the photograph on page 24 and is a small block of wood about two inches high with a V cut out with a bandsaw. The leather is placed atop this when an awl is used; it prevents the awl from going through and sticking into the workbench. It is one of those simple yet useful devices that many craftsmen make on the spur of the moment when shops can't supply their needs. Taking a few moments to make one of these for a workbench will be time well spent.

The leather used for this sheath should be, at a minimum, seven- to eight-ounce chrome-tanned hide. While some craftsmen prefer vegetable-tanned hides because of less acid action on the steel blade, Kneubuhler feels chrome-tanned leather will last longer and is probably best in a sheath that will be worn and used.

As can be seen on page 67, a pattern is laid out with rulers to give the reader an idea of dimensions. This can be varied depending upon the size of the knife. It is also simpler and less expensive to experiment with paper than leather. It will be noted the illustration shows measurements of 8¾″ across the top and about 11½″ from top to bottom.

After the leather is cut with the scissors, a divider is used to draw two lines about the edges. One line will show the placement of thong holes for the lacing and the other will be a guide to begin placement of the brass spots or tacks. By the way, the tacks are specially made for leathercraftsmen and come with a split so they may be bent back after hammering through the hole. The next step, shown in Picture 3, is to mark the holes for the awl. The tool may be purchased in any good leather supply house and is not only used to space these holes correctly, but is also used to punch through the leather the second time around.

After the holes are punched, the sheath is laid out and coated with Barge Cement; a knife is placed in the center to ascertain that the fit is correct. Although the cement will dry overnight, the brass spots must now be affixed. The spots are hammered through with another tool of Kneubuhler's making. This is nothing more than a piece of wooden dowel with a slightly dished-out end that will fit over the spots. The tool makes it easy to tap in the spots. After the brass work is completed, the sheath is turned over, placed on another piece of leather to protect the spots, and the split ends are tapped down with a ball peen hammer. This is enough work for one evening and the sheath is now set aside until the next morning.

The next step is to give another coat of cement and allow it to dry for twenty minutes. Then fold the sheath over and hammer down to make certain good adhesion will result. The second step is to measure out the belt slit, as shown in Picture 9. The length will depend, of course, on the width of the belt to be worn. The hold is cut with a wide chisel (Picture 10) and then lace holes are punched with an awl, again using the V-shaped block of wood as in Picture 11. Before beginning the lacing, the thong is run through a can of saddle soap a few times to make it soft enough to allow it to be pulled through the holes made by the awl. Next, the thong is locked in back by putting it under one lace hole. Once the lace is put around the belt slit, dye is used to touch up the edge as shown in Picture 13.

Now comes the tricky part. In order to have a couple of thongs hanging from the bottom of the sheath, a double lace is used. Rather than give measurements it would be safer to cut a thong that is twice as long as the sheath WHEN THE THONG IS DOUBLED OVER since this will allow sufficient length. As the craftsman becomes more experienced in making this type of sheath and estimating the length of thong required, shorter lengths can then be used.

The thong is now pushed and pulled through the top lace hole and evened up to meet at both ends. First one length is laced and pulled tight, then the other end is put through the next hole and pulled tight. This is done until they meet at the bottom of the sheath. As can be seen from a close examination of Picture 14, a small slit is made in each thong. One piece is pulled through one slit and the remaining thong is pulled through the opposite slit. These are then pulled tight and cut off at a length to please the wearer; usually a few inches is sufficient.

These colorful sheaths will dress up anyone wearing buckskins and Walter Kneubuhler shows how well his sheath and possible bag complement each other.

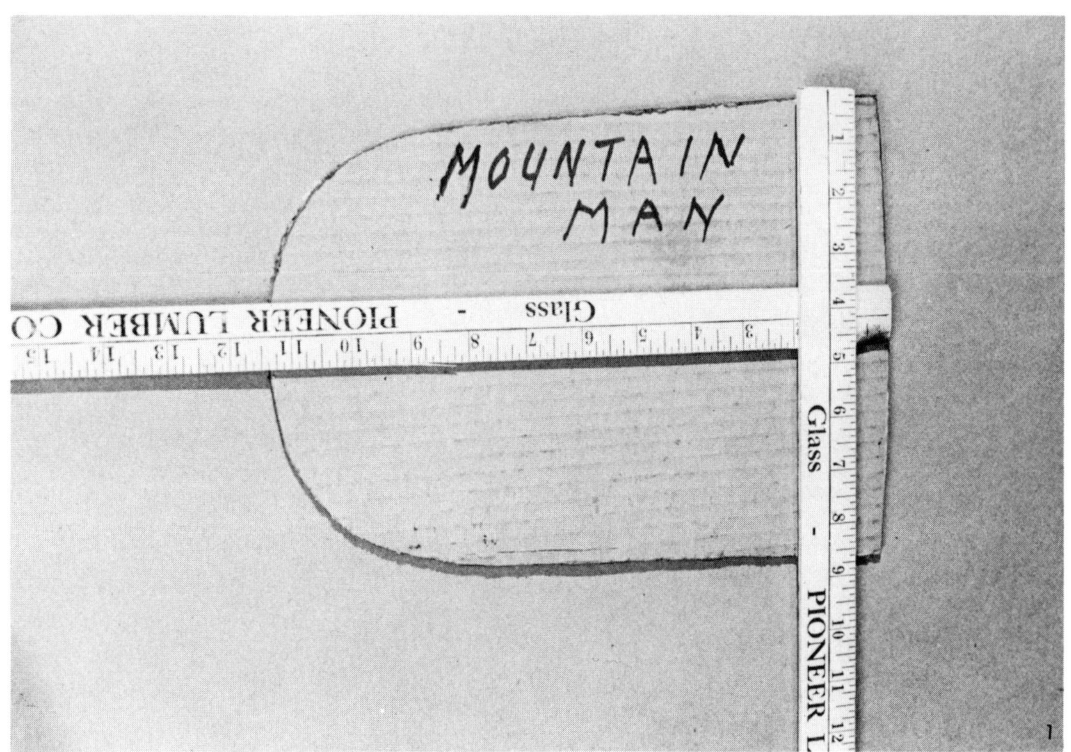

As with the Blackfoot Dag sheath, a pattern is made from cardboard and the rulers give the exact measurements.

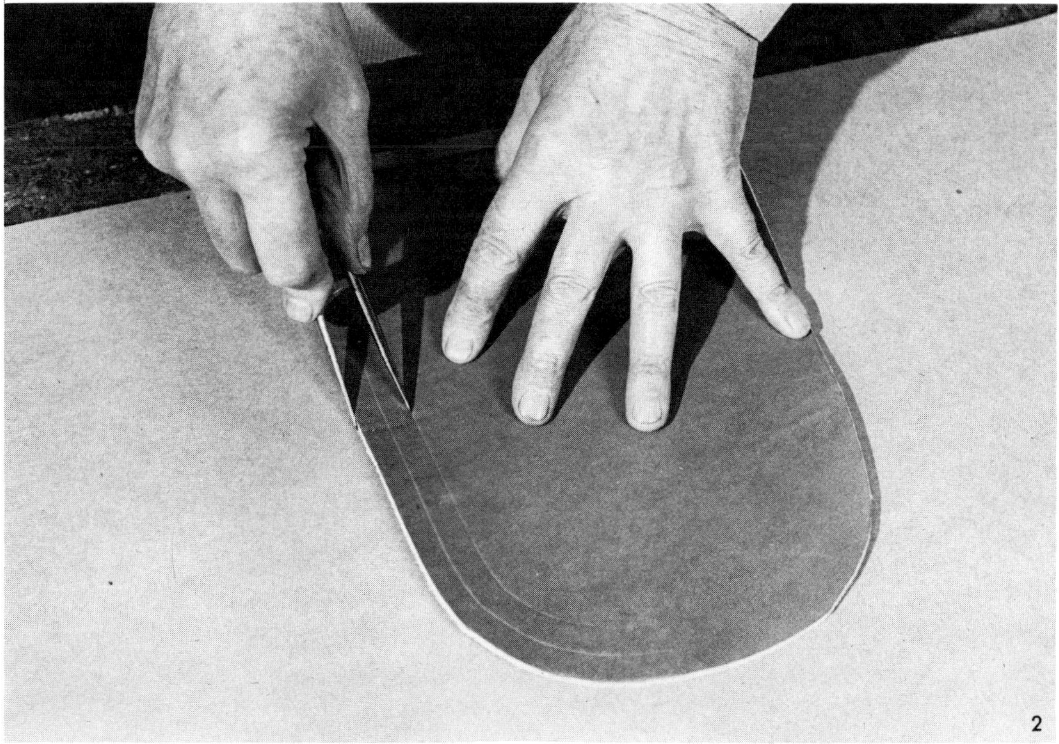

Once the leather is cut, dividers are used to mark lines for proper placement of brass tacks.

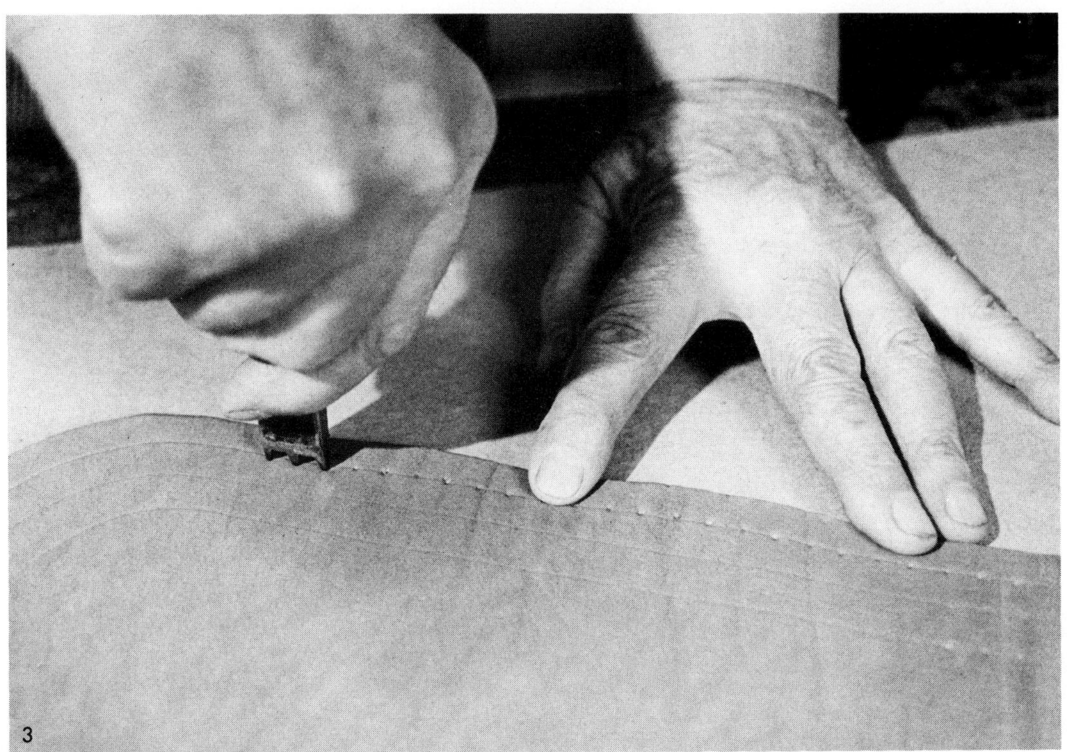

A thonging punch is used to mark holes for punching.

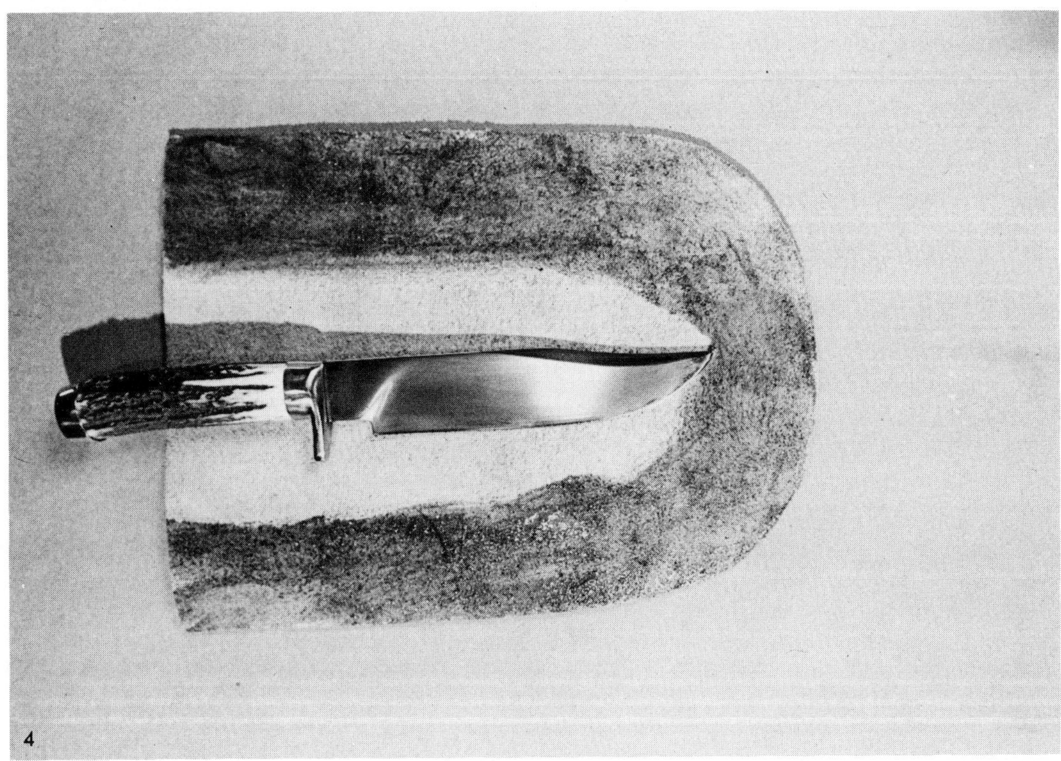

The knife is set onto the sheath for proper fit and coated with Barge Cement that is allowed to dry.

To set the tacks properly, a round rod is used. A short piece of dowel rod is best with the end turned slightly concave to fit over the tack head. A piece of leather is set underneath to allow the studs to come through without sticking to the bench.

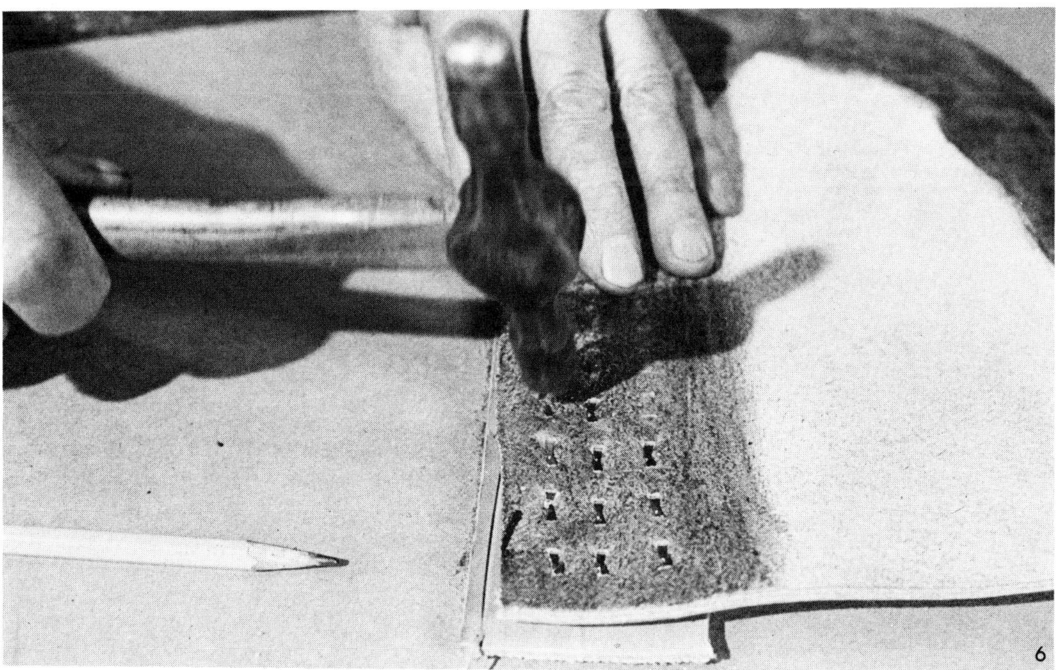

Once a row of studs is set in the sheath, it is turned over, again with a piece of leather underneath to protect the brass tacks. These tacks are special leathercraftsmen's tacks and come with a split stud that must be hammered down.

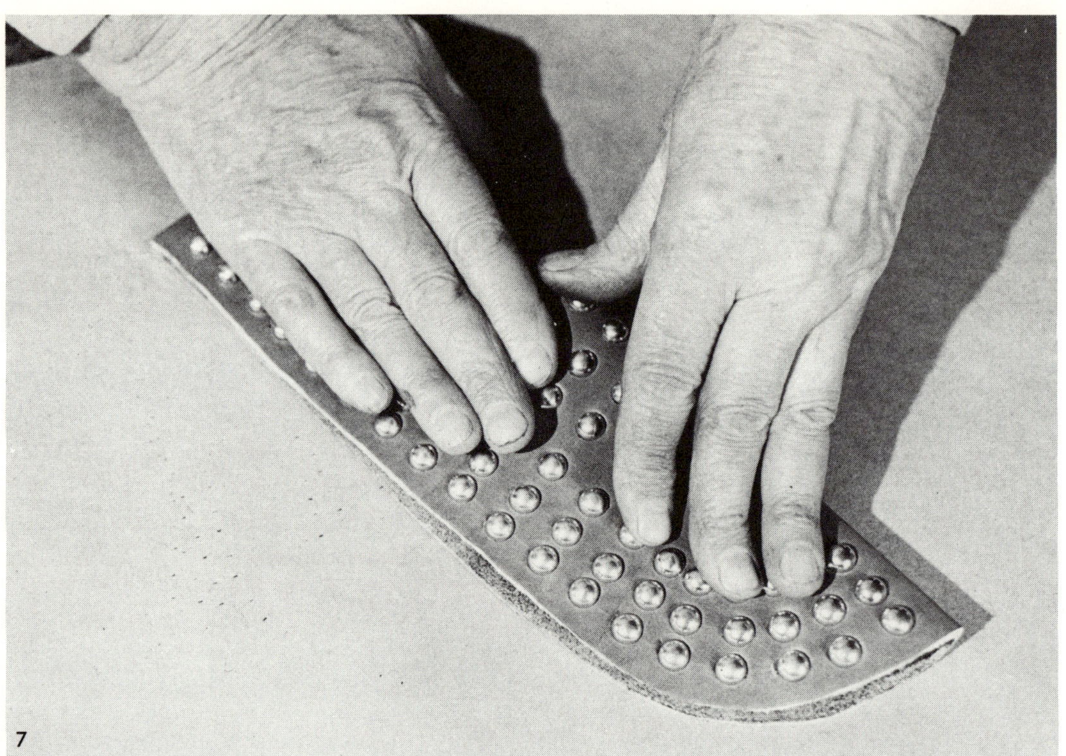

7

A fresh coating of cement is used, then the sheath is folded over and carefully pressed together. The excess leather is trimmed with a sharp knife.

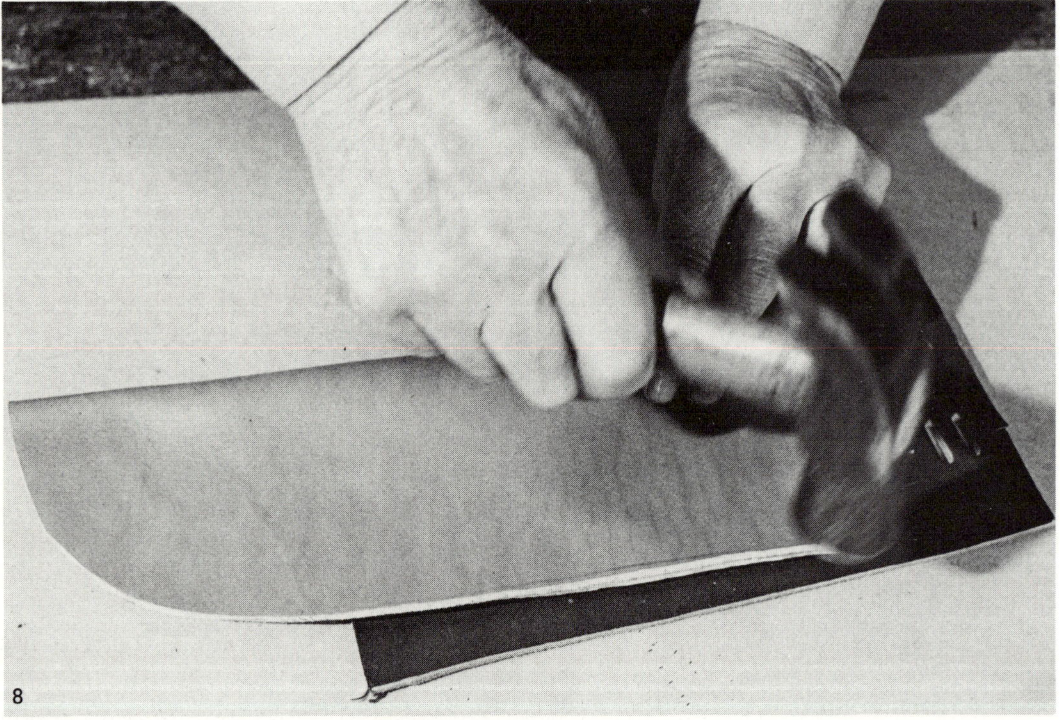

8

Once the sheath has been pressed together it is turned over, again with a piece of leather underneath to protect the studs, and hammered firmly for solid adhesion.

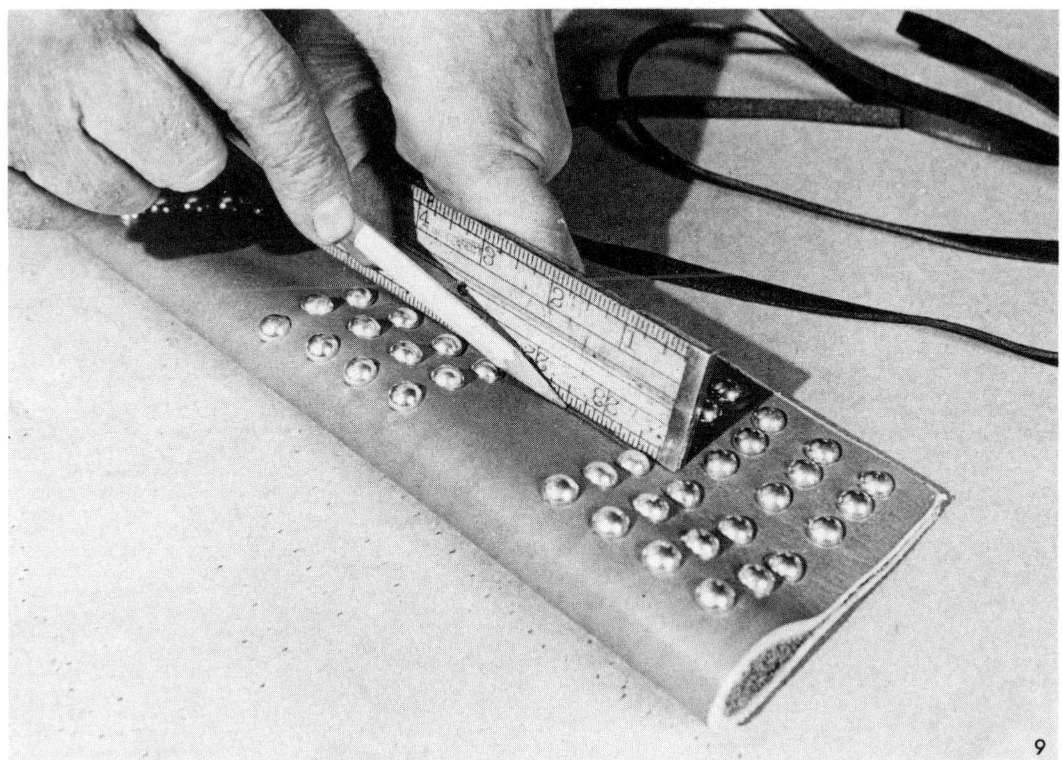

9

A ruler is used for proper placement of belt slit.

A chisel is used by Kneubuhler to cut through the two folds of leather.

10

A small awl is used for the lacing thong above the belt slit. The wedge block of wood is used to allow the awl to go through the leather and not stick in the bench.

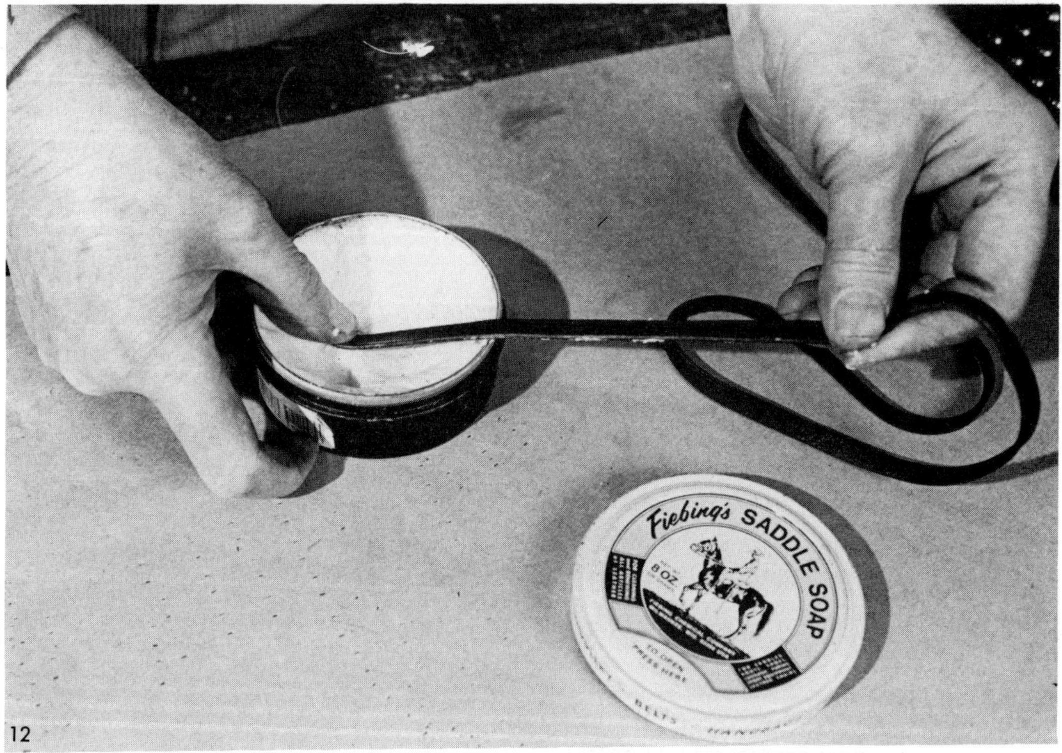

After holes are punched along the edge of the sheath, a thong is cut and pulled through saddle soap to make it easier to work through the holes.

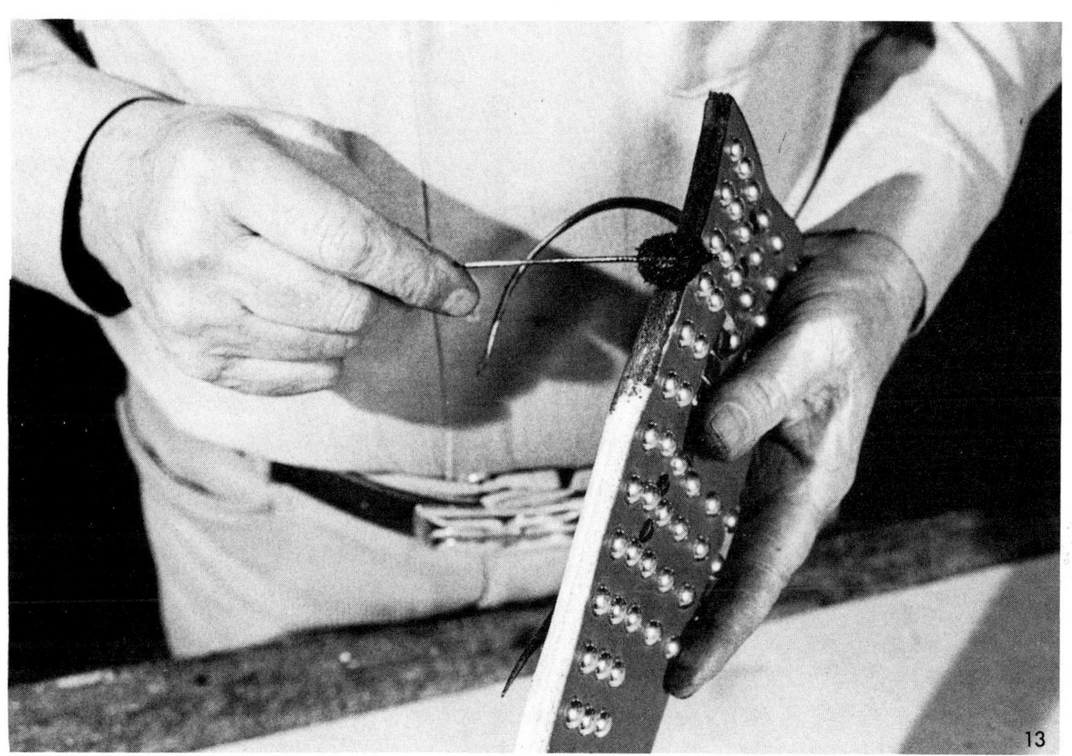

After lacing around the belt hole, dye is applied to darken the edges before lacing is begun.

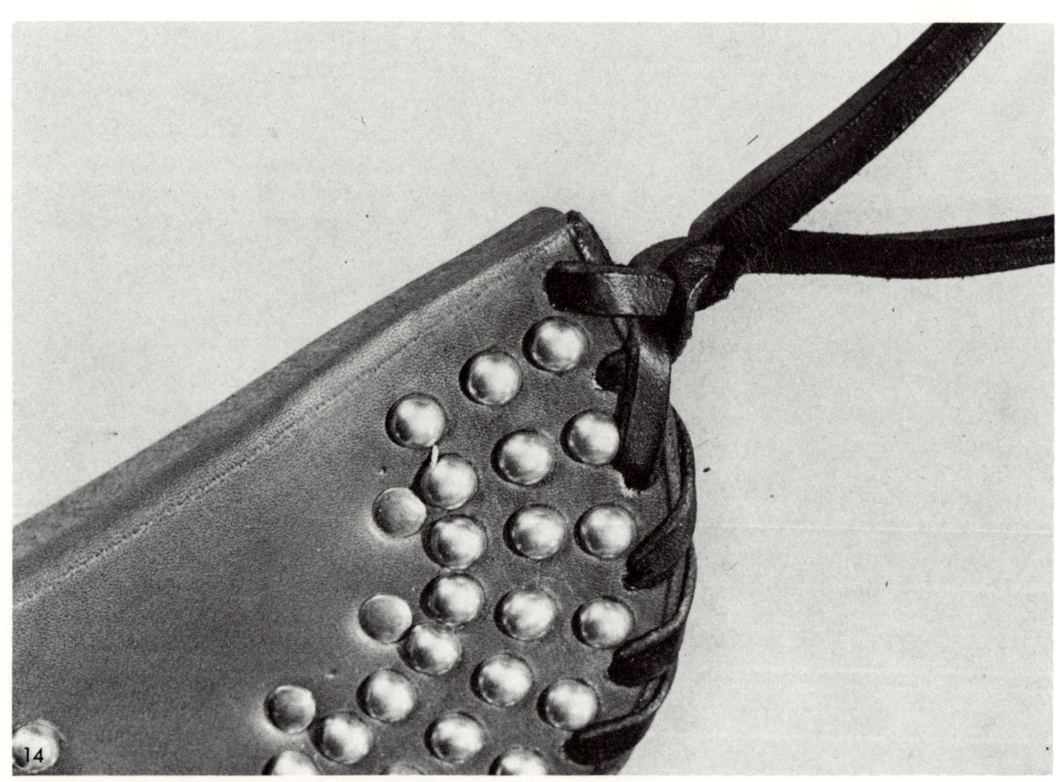

The lace is unusually long and, when doubled, each piece is alternately laced through each hole and pulled. With this type of lacing, both thongs end together and are pulled through as shown.

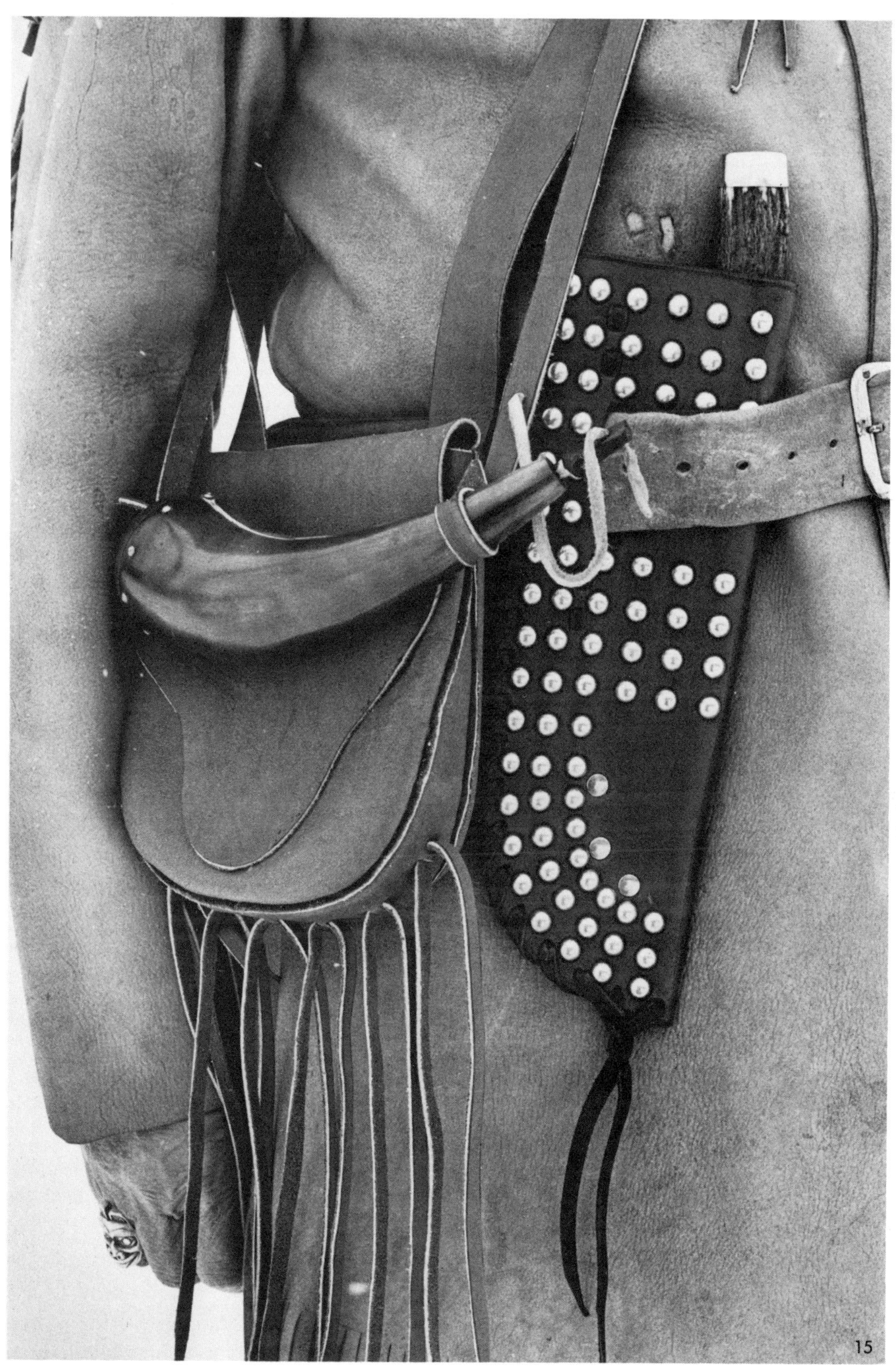

The completed Mountain Man sheath, shown with the possible bag.

CHAPTER SEVEN

The S. D. Myres Saddle Company —"The Art of Tooling"

When "Tio Sam" Myres opened his saddle shop in Sweetwater, Texas, back in 1897, it was a humble beginning for a leather company that would eventually become a leader in fine craftsmanship and quality throughout the West. In those early days, a custom-made saddle could be had for around $40 and gun holsters could be bought for $4 to $6. A finely tooled belt made of the best quality leather straps might cost around $5 and a cowboy or lawman who wanted the best went to Sam Myres.

After World War I, the growing S. D. Myres Company decided to move to El Paso and again it quickly established a reputation as an innovator in leather. During the transition from horse to automobile, "Tio Sam" worked closely with law-enforcement officers—as he always had—and originated and developed the Border Patrol holster. It was a rig that would keep the gun close to the body, yet present the butt to an officer swiftly and efficiently. This fine holster, with minor variations and improvements, is still the accepted standard for Border Patrol officers and has been adopted by many other police organizations around the country.

When the elder Myres passed away, the company was taken over by his son, Bill Myres. Sadly there was never the interest once the old gentleman passed on and the company was eventually sold. Fortunately, the right man came along to buy it. He was an ex-cavalry officer named Colonel Jim Spurrier. Spurrier spent eighteen years in the cavalry at Fort Bliss, Texas. He is a high-goal polo player and was on duty at the Pentagon when the State Department asked him to gather up a team to play Pakistan a few years ago at the Lahore Horse Show. When the horse cavalry became mechanized, he was sent to Nationalist China with the Military Assistance Group to train the Chinese in the intricacies of modern armored warfare. On his retirement, he decided to settle in

Bill Wootres, using a head knife, cuts a long strip to be made into a Western belt.

El Paso. Casting about for something to occupy his time, his fancy was caught by the famous S. D. Myres name and he decided to take over the company.

Jim Spurrier has a solid Western background. Born on a buffalo ranch in Osage County, Oklahoma, Spurrier got his first horse when he was three years old. It would be safe to say he has some modest experience with horses. His skill with leather was gained from experience with the cavalry and leather has been a hobby of his throughout his career. At Fort Riley, Kansas, he spent much time at the saddler's stool of an army saddle and farrier's shop, where much of the tack was maintained.

Spurrier purchased Myres in 1974 and a number of the great Mexican craftsmen came along with the new company. Many of these skilled leatherworkers had been with the original company for over thirty years and brought their high standards of excellence with them. It's interesting to note that, in these modern machine-oriented times, more than 90 percent of the craftwork is still done by hand. There is no compromise on quality since the custom handcrafted process is designed to meet the needs of each individual order. One of the revolutionary processes was the use of a welt in a holster to enable a gun to be drawn properly. For those who want a plug bottom this can be had, and sight-protector welts may also be added. Modern honchos are dedicated to quality and to that end Bill Wootres was brought from the old company to be foreman and manager of the workrooms. "Our craftsmen can't be ramrodded," says Wootres, "and they still do their work in the old way and in their own time."

Myres is among the last of the national organizations that do excellent leather work and pride themselves on fine, fancy carved and tooled holsters and belts. The outfit uses only the best grade leather that is firm plated to ensure a long life for both the leather product and the user; 9/10-ounce leather is used in the belts and holsters. This weight provides the proper stiffness and prevents the edges of a belt or holster from curling. Where holsters must be lined, soft kip leather is used, again of the proper thickness, to provide protection for the weapon. As to sewing—and this is good advice for the beginner—hot-waxed linen thread is used. It has been found by many fine craftsmen that nylon tends to slip and stretch and doesn't provide the strength or protection the thread needs for years of wear. Even Sam Lucchese has commented that nylon will begin to rub the stitch holes of boots and eventually enlarge the holes to the point where they will be worn and allow water to enter the boot. This is something to be particularly concerned about when stitching such large items as gun cases, chaps, or jackets where continual wear could eventually erode the careful stitching.

Among the finest leather products crafted at Myres are the beautifully hand-tooled carved belts and holsters. Foreman Bill Wootres has a lot to do with turning them out. Wootres has been working leathers for almost forty years; he learned his skills from W. H. "Billy" Greene in Las Vegas, New Mexico. In his younger days, when Wootres was following the rodeo circuit, he carried his leatherworking tools around with him. When prize money ran short he managed to work a while in a local saddle shop just to make expense money.

Those with the ability of a Bill Wootres shouldn't be called craftsmen—artists would describe them better, because the skills they exhibit and the ease with which they execute them are indeed awesome. Yet these skills can be acquired by anyone who has the genuine desire to do fine leatherwork.

Before the actual cutting can be done, the outline of the belt is marked on the leather with a ruler.

Crafting a Western Belt

In making the Western belt, Wootres can do the entire job from cutting the strap to the finished carving inside two hours! Admittedly his speed would be beyond the novice. Actually, however, there is no reason for a beginning leatherworker to break any speed records. The work to be done should be relaxing and fun. And the accomplishment of a handsome belt that he can brag about a little should be his goal.

To make a belt, Wootres advises that only a few tools are required. These include a steel ruler, a draw knife for cutting the strip (or a very sharp straight knife), a beveler to round the edges of the strap once it is cut, a couple of background tools with the hammer for tapping impressions into the leather, and, most important, a swivel knife for cutting the design. A bucket or basin of water nearby plus some sponges will help in keeping the leather damp while it is being worked.

The best place to work, of course, is on a solid marble or granite-topped bench. Needless to say, not everyone will have one in his home, but a block or sheet of marble, perhaps a couple of inches thick, will make a fine base and allow the tooling dies to make a firm impression in their contact with leather.

To make your Western belt, simply follow the pictures along in sequence as we explain in the captions what is being done at each stage of the project.

Before beginning any detail work, Wootres outlines the edges.

After the leather is dampened, a transfer is made from a prepared pattern on leather and then stamped into the belt strip.

How the prepared pattern is hammered down. In spite of the light design cut on the pattern, it will transfer properly.

Grooving the edge line to set it deeper. Note how the image is transferred from the pattern and how well it stands out.

The swivel knife is brought into use to deep cut the flower pattern.

After cutting and carving designs, the end strips, unique in this style of belt, are prepared.

The edges are cleaned up by rubbing with a soft cloth.

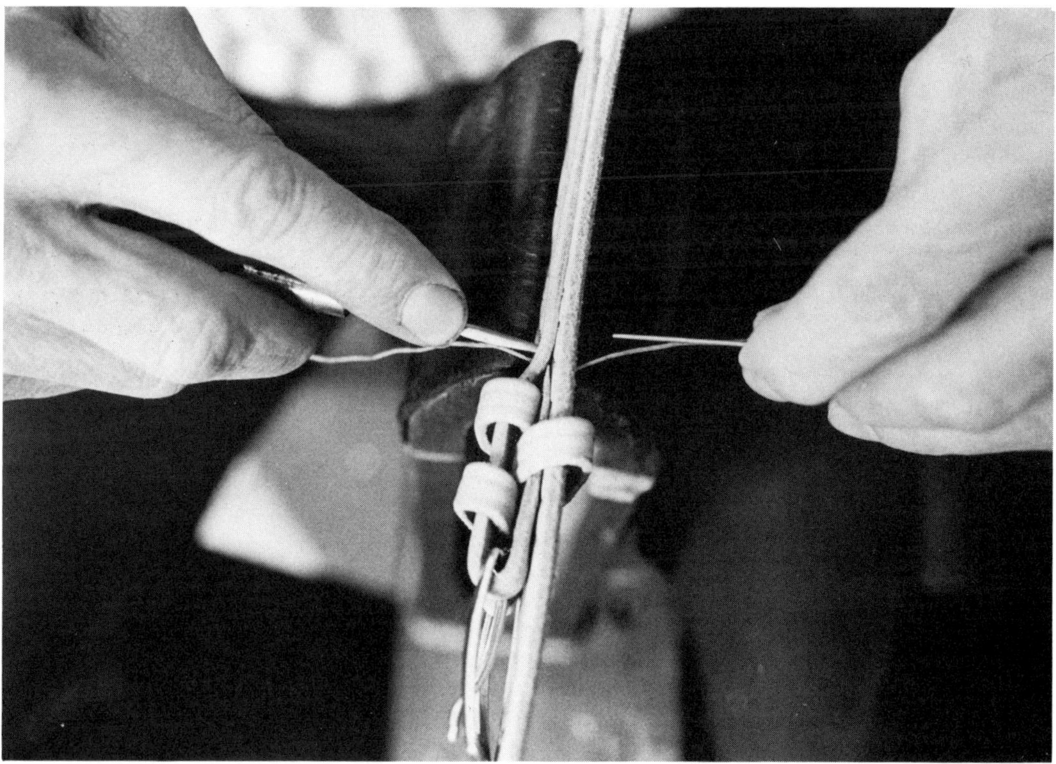

Closeup showing the saddle stitch using two needles. Belt loops and buckle have already been attached.

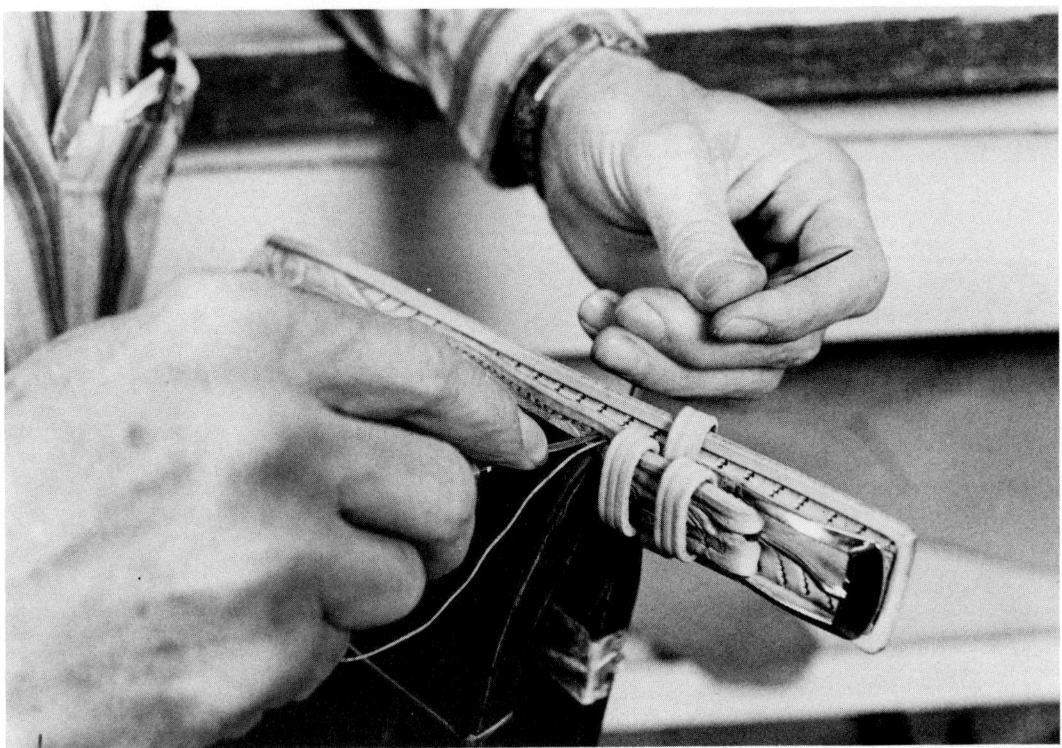

Final stitches are already taken. Note how the belt is held in a lacing pony.

Crafting a Gun Holster

As with a belt, a gun holster is a fairly uncomplicated project. Most important at the beginning is to make a proper pattern for the weapon intended to be carried. The best leather for a holster is 9/10 ounce, as it is for a belt, and the same tools will be used.

To make the pattern, a piece of brown wrapping paper should be used. Set the gun on the paper and run a line down one side with a pencil, as indicated in the accompanying pictures. After the center line is drawn, work along the curved side of the gun. Decide at this time whether or not an open trigger guard is preferred, where the straps, if any, should go, and all the other necessary details.

Once the pattern is complete, cut it out with scissors and then fold it over the handgun for fit. It is important at this juncture to include enough space for the welt so the gun fits properly, rides firmly in the holster, and yet can be drawn with speed if necessary.

The next step is to transfer the pattern to the leather and cut it out. The bevel tool is run around the edges to smooth off the rough cuts and help add to the finished appearance. Now, with a flat piece of leather dampen it and allow it to partially dry. Stamping or tooling comes next and when that's completed the welt is cut. The accompanying pictures are self-explanatory. Before gluing the welt, the belt loop is sewn on. This can be done either by machine—and the local bootmaker can do this—or else it may be hand-sewn using an awl. A lacing pony is also a handy item as shown in the illustration on this page. The angle at which the holster rides on the belt is of particular importance

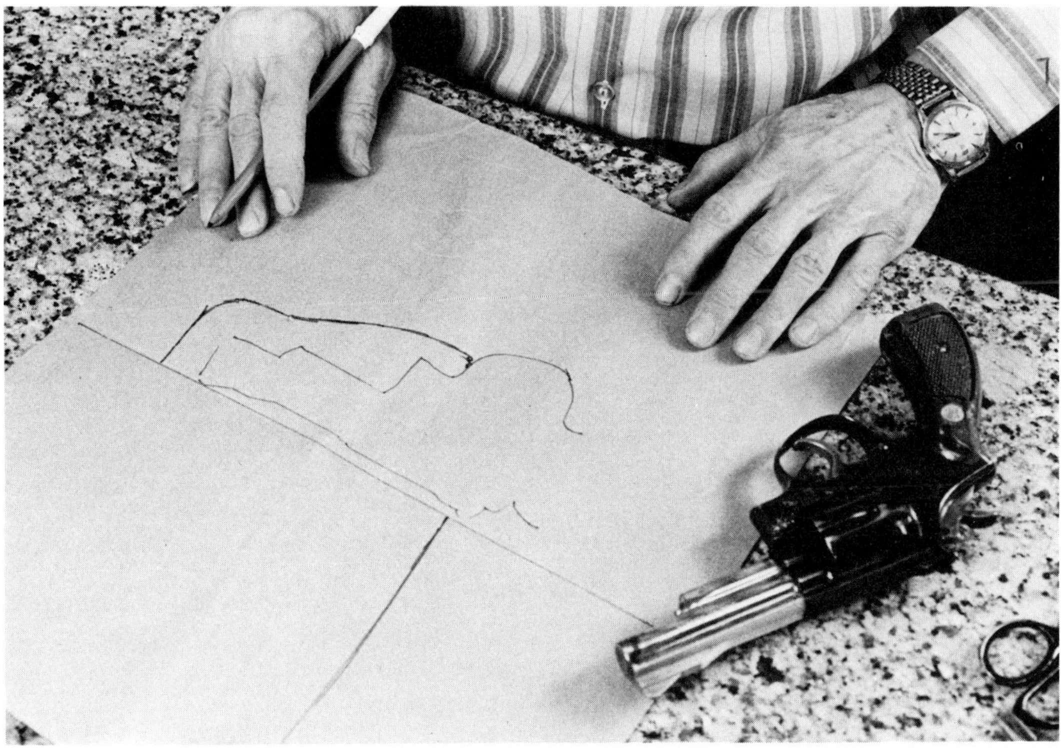

The first step, as with all leather projects, is to draw a pattern onto paper to insure fit. Here the pattern is completed and then cut out.

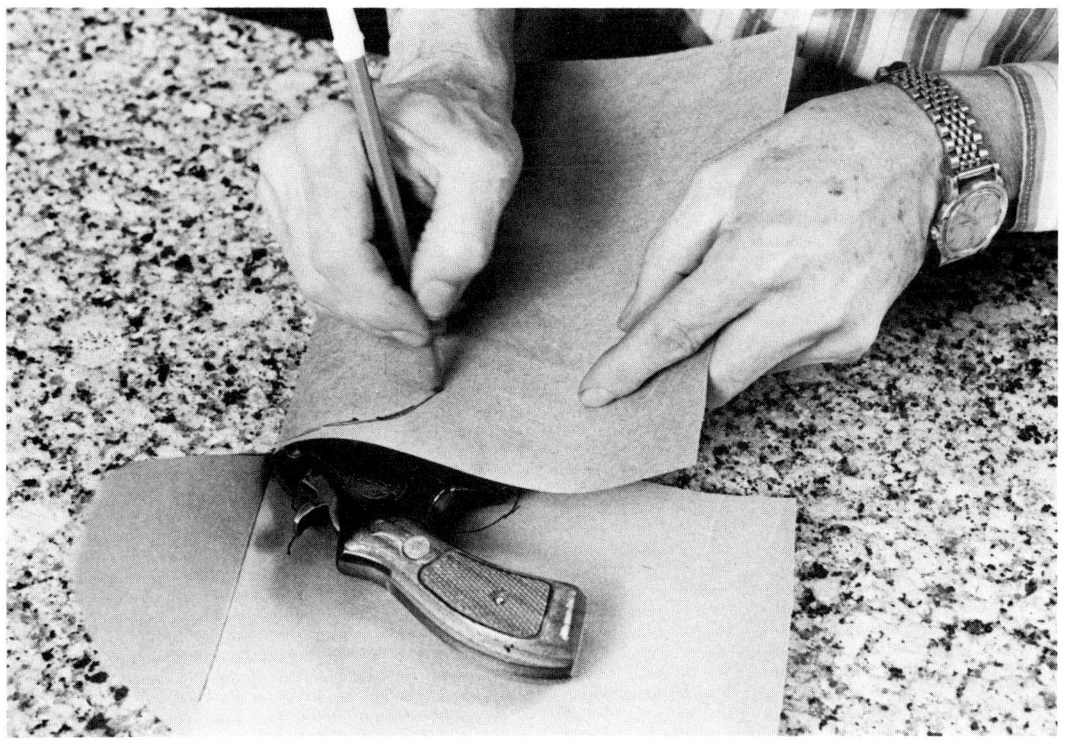

Now fold the pattern over the hand gun, then draw around the cylinder for extra-needed material.

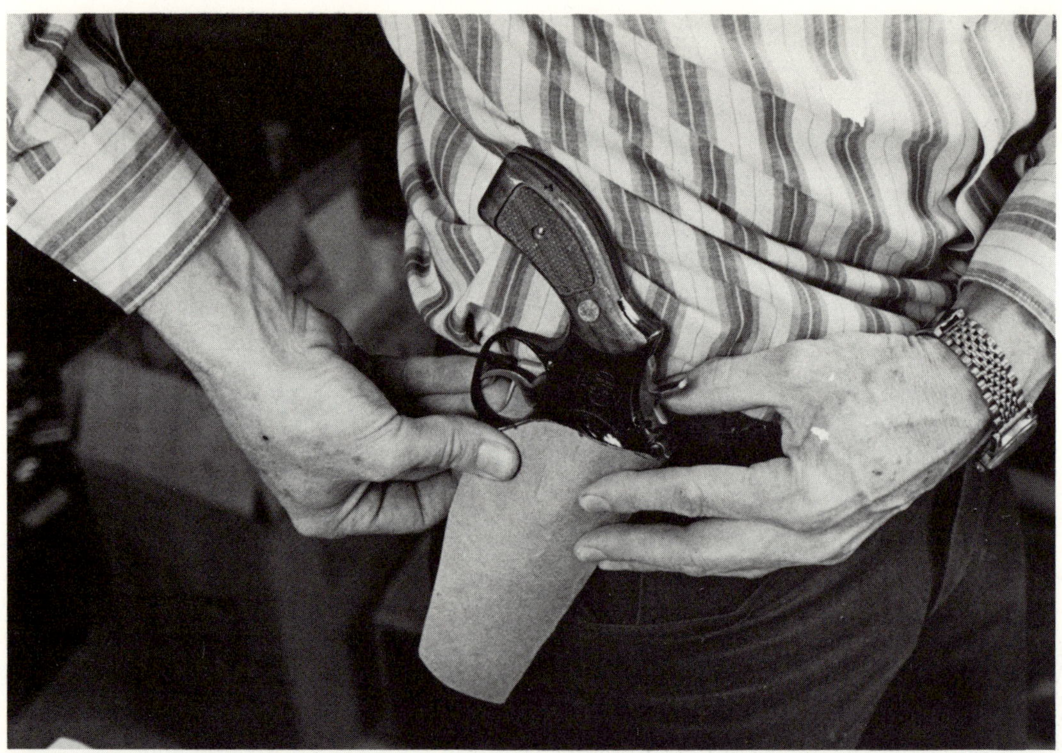

Once the paper pattern is completed, then cut it out, fold around the gun, and set by the waist for the correct slant for belt loop.

The leather is dampened with a sponge and the belt loop folded over and tacked down to hold it in place.

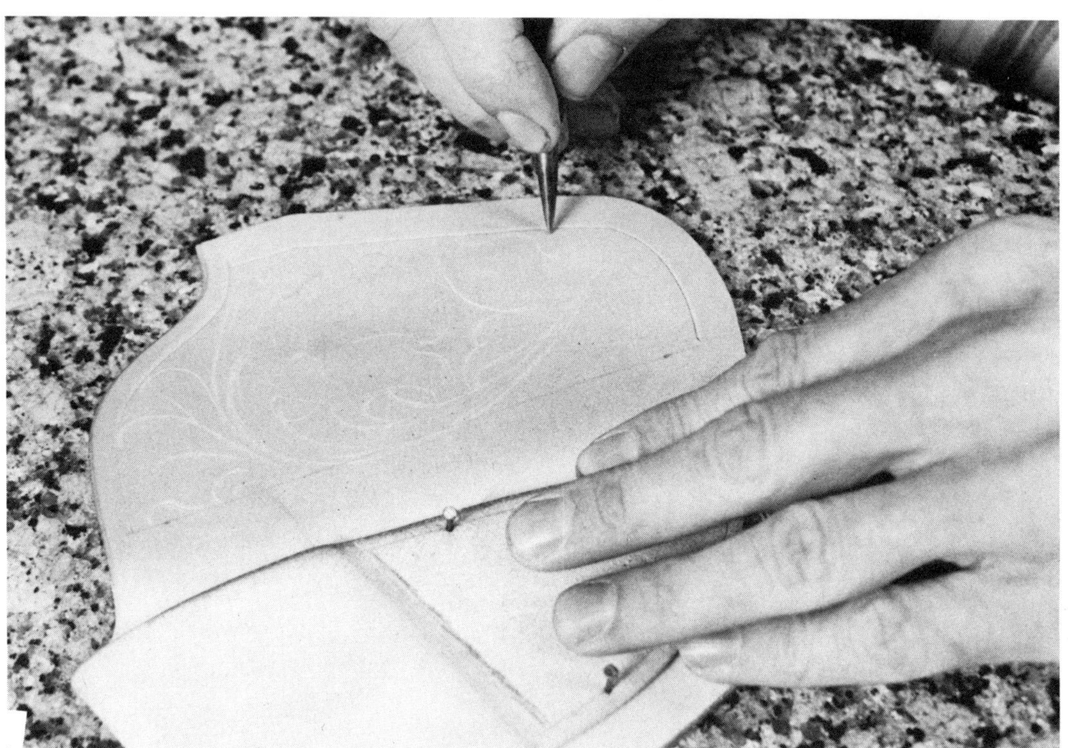

Next the pattern is drawn into the damp leather with a scriber.

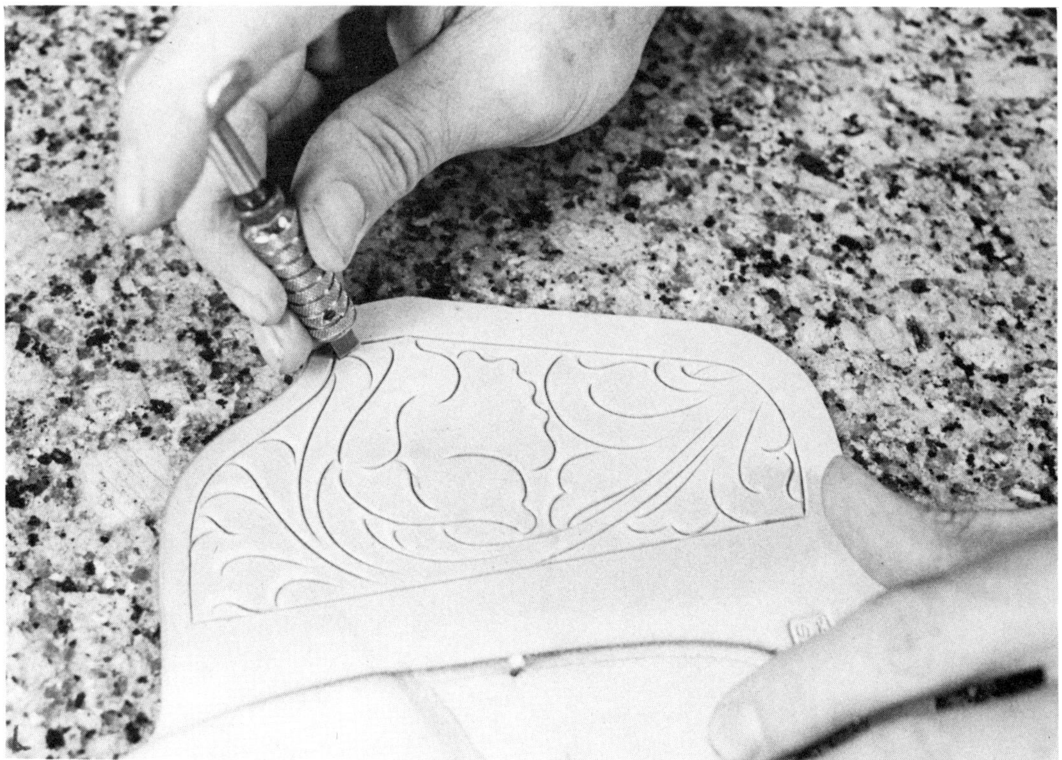

Using the swivel knife Bill Wootres begins carving.

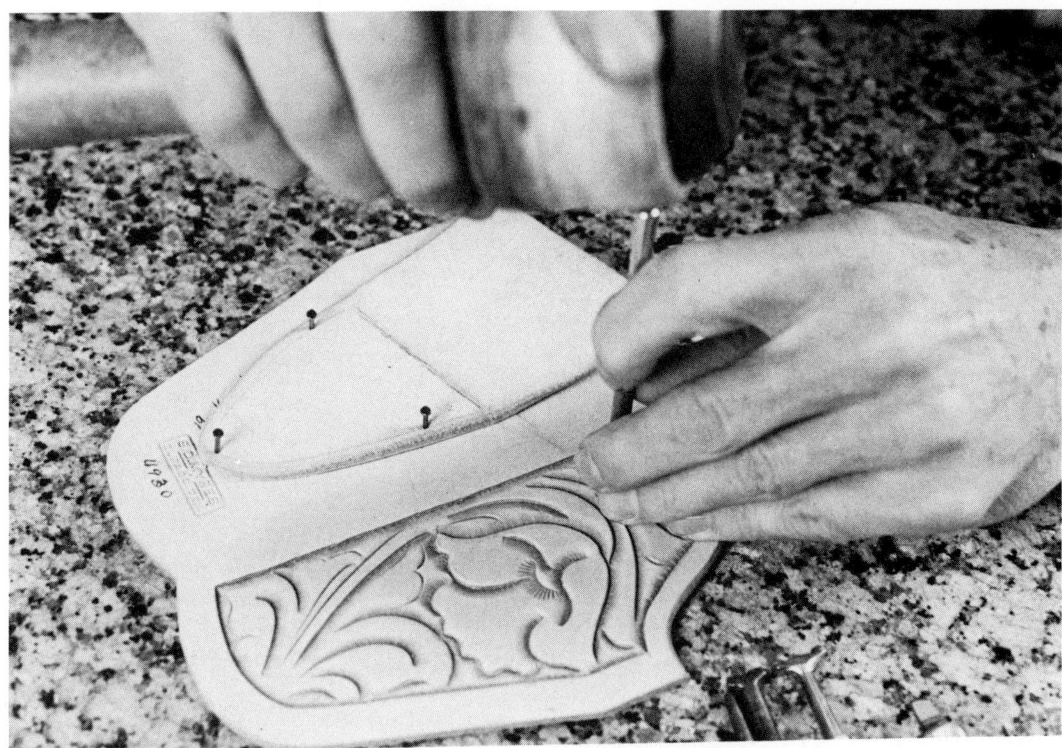

Once the carving is placed on the holster, then the camouflage is stamped on. This rounds the carved areas and finishes the edges of the design area.

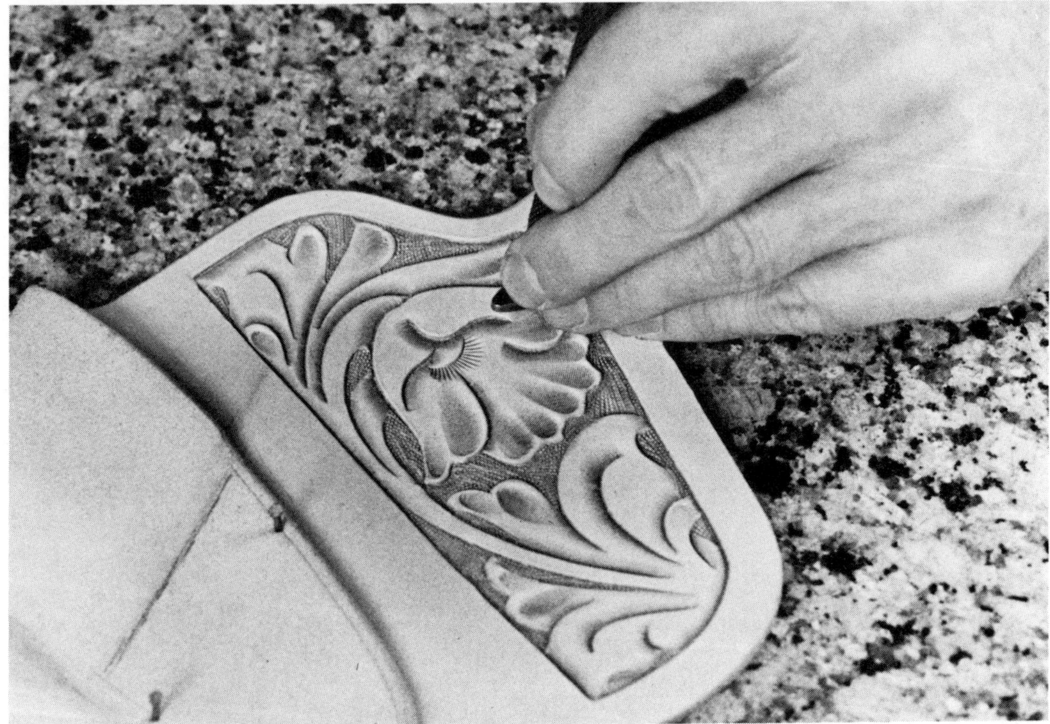

The same camouflage stamp is used to finish the flowers and leaves of the design. Note that it is necessary to redampen the leather as it slowly begins to dry.

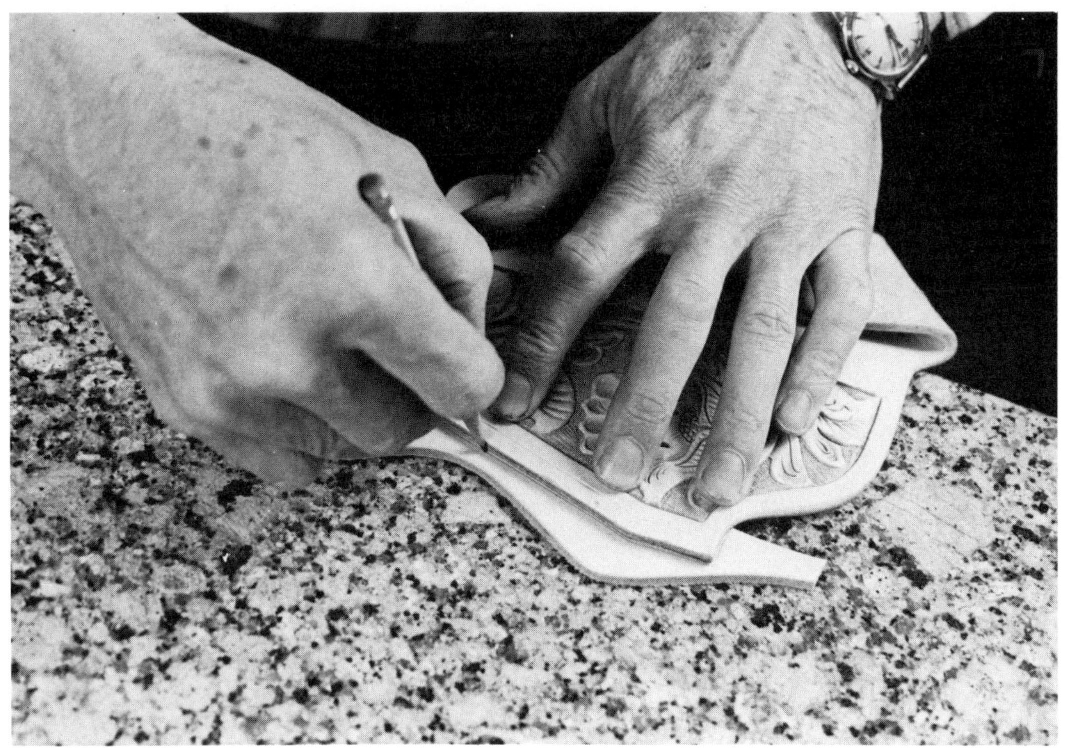

The welt is cut as one of the final steps.

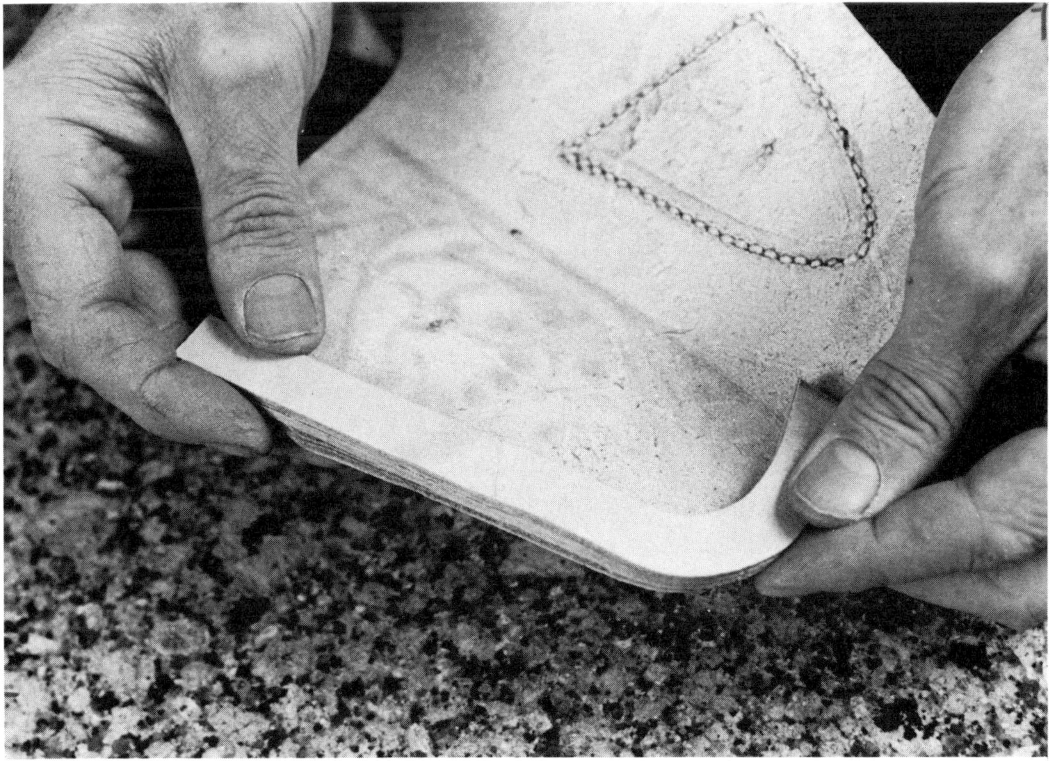

Here the completed welt is set on to insure proper fit.

Coating the welt with Barge Cement. Note the edge of the inside part of the holster is coated with cement as well.

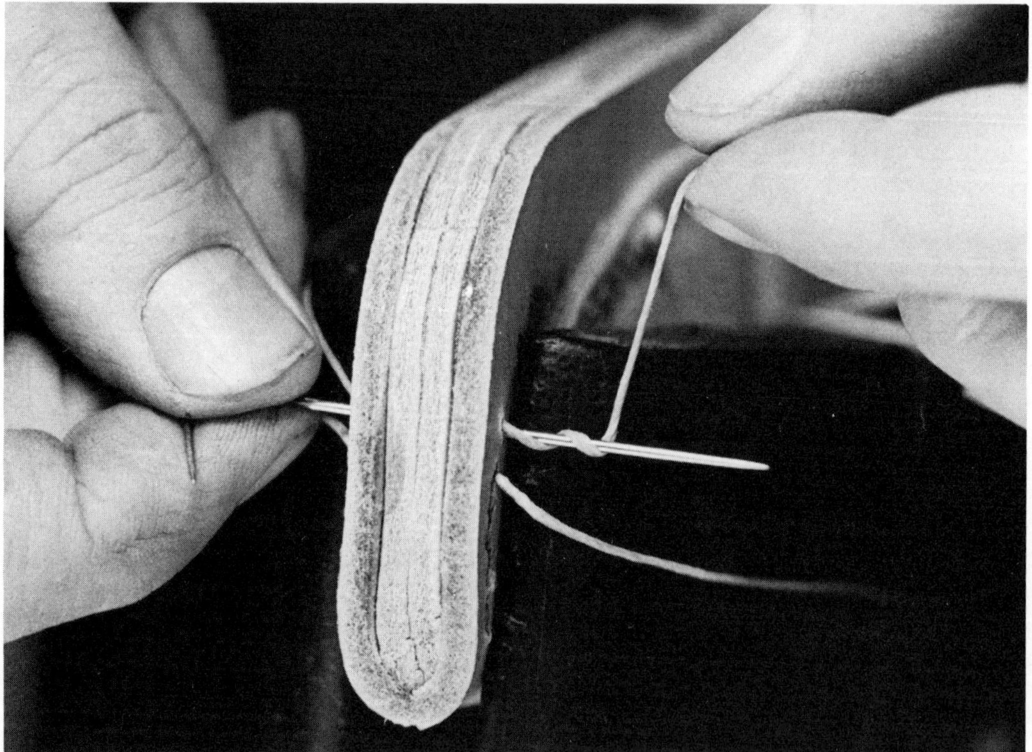

Hand stitching with two needles for a proper saddle stitch.

After the holster is dampened again, the gun is set inside for a good fit and a piece of wood is rubbed against the edge to make certain the fold holds properly.

The completed holster and matching belt. Although this is a left-hand holster, all that is needed is to reverse the pattern for a right-hand model.

to the wearer. This is why care must be taken for the strap to be sewn precisely at the desired angle.

Once the belt loop is sewn, the welt is cemented for sewing. Barge Cement is highly recommended. Both sides of the welt as well as the inner seam of the holster are coated. Set the project aside to dry for about fifteen minutes and then press all pieces firmly together. A hammer is an indispensable tool at this juncture and the entire seam is hammered, along both edges, to ensure a tight fit of holster and welt. Once this dries, it can either be hand-sewn or taken to a cobbler's shop.

Wet-fitting is a trick that ensures that the leather is molded to a correct fit for the gun. It may be done in a number of ways. One technique is to wet the leather thoroughly, first covering the gun well with oil, then forcing the gun into the holster a number of times until it feels secure. Then it is set aside to dry. Another method that works almost as well is to dampen the outside of the leather, place the gun in the holster, and work it a while with the fingers. Both methods will ensure an excellent fit and once the holster is molded properly it will remain that way.

There are a number of finishes that Bill Wootres uses and they are a matter of personal preference. Here are some of them:

Natural. As the name implies, the leather is left in a natural finish—a golden tawny color that will darken with age.

Natural with oil. Oil is applied. Either a good neatsfoot or Lexol is used to darken the leather to a tan brown. This finish will also darken with wear.

Antique. This is a two-tone effect that darkens the depressions in the basketweave or carved design.

Cordovan. This is a deep red wine color that provides a dark finish.

Black. Most black leather is for military or police use and it can be given a brilliant shine.

Making Spur Straps

Before we get into complicated leatherwork like chaps, let's try to craft a pair of spur straps. These may be as attractive and fancy as desired, or they can be a plain, unadorned strap just to hold the spurs. The pattern selected is a popular Western model and is easy to make. Again, the first step is to cut a pattern. It will be seen that there are two pieces to the strap; one piece of leather with the buckle attached and the other that fits over the spur knob. Now transfer the pattern to the leather and cut it out. A head knife will be handy since it allows ease of curving cuts. The edge-beveler is run around the edges to clear up the cuts and the leather is then dampened preparatory to tooling or stamping. It will be noticed in the pattern of these spur straps that only three different stamps or dies are used. First, the basketweave; second, camouflage along the edges of the basketweave; and third, the circular pattern on the ends or circles. It took Bill Wootres about twenty minutes to make one strap and even the most inexperienced hand should be able to craft a pair in an hour. Once the tooling is completed, holes are punched toward the end of the strap about one-half inch apart. The buckle is then fastened on with a rivet and the job is done. Just one more point: Don't forget to make a slit in each end of the straps so they will fit over the spur knobs.

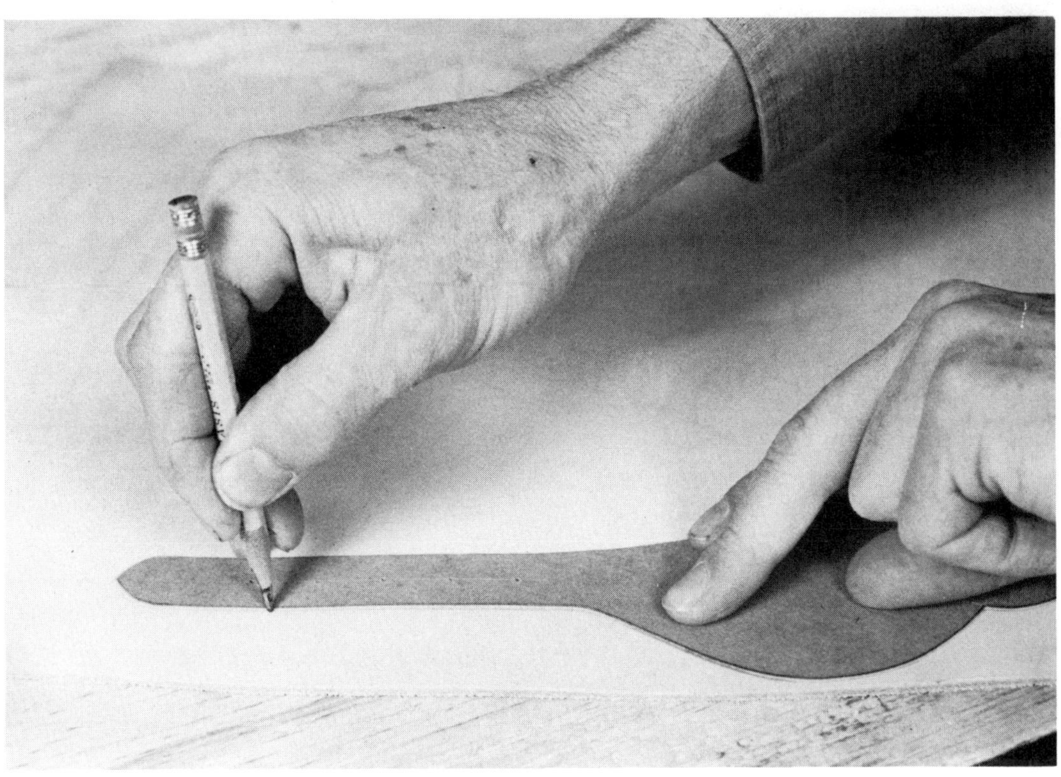

Bill Wootres draws the outline for a spur strap from a cardboard pattern onto the leather.

After cutting the pattern, the edge is beveled and stamping begins.

After basket-stamping the large piece, the smaller section is completed as shown.

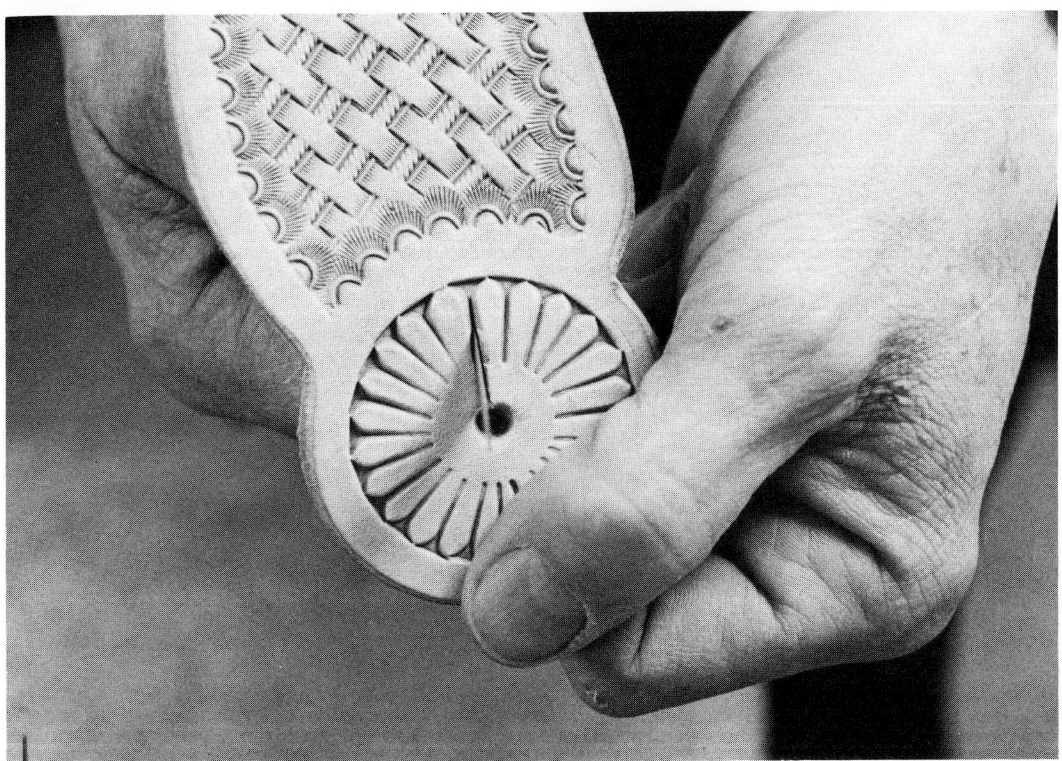

A slit is cut for the spur knobs.

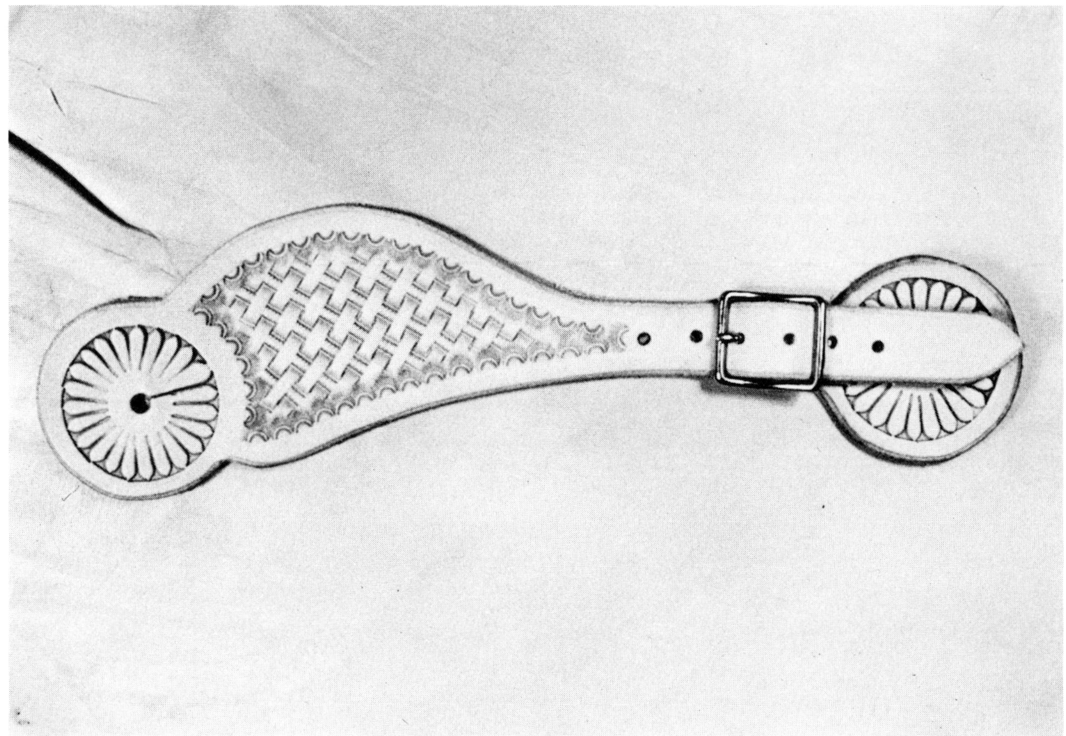

One of a pair of spur straps.

Crafting a Pair of Chaps

Now to a project that may frighten beginning leatherworkers—a pair of chaps. Actually, however, these are not unreasonably hard to craft. If the measurements are carefully taken, there should be no problems or surprises along the way.

First, note the illustration at the top of the next page, indicating the measurements to be taken—the waist, inner seam, outer seam, the largest part of the thigh, the knee, and the calf. The chaps shown are shotgun chaps and were introduced to the Southwest by Mexican *vaqueros*. In some quarters, they are known as polo chaps and are also quite popular among bird shooters in the thickly briared quail country of the South.

Shotgun chaps should fit fairly close to the leg in order to give a slim, trim line. But they should not fit so closely as to bind while riding or walking and become uncomfortable. Chap hide should measure about twenty-one or twenty-two square feet for the type illustrated and be three- to four-ounce chrome-tanned cowhide. The color of the chaps is a matter of taste and a decision should be made whether to make them rough-side-out or smooth-side-out. The roughened side will give a Western or frontier effect which can be quite attractive; however, it will wear out much faster and also absorb more moisture. The smooth side will offer far greater protection against briars and branches and it will wear longer.

The few tools required include any sharp knife, a steel rule, an awl, a small buckle for the belt, and a Number 5 or 6 industrial zipper. There is a considerable amount of

Bill Wootres makes his measurements with a long piece of wrapping paper.

Transferring the pattern to leather.

Cutting leather for chaps. The paper pattern is reversed for the opposite leg.

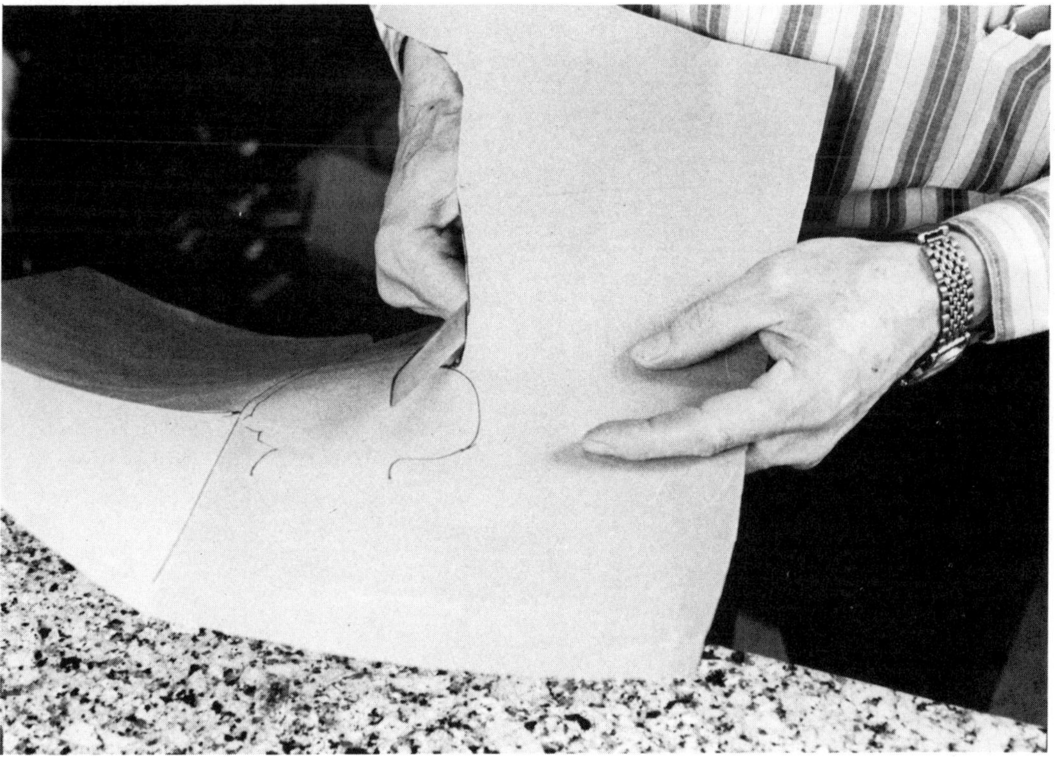

The top section of the chaps being cut out. This will be stitched on and will then take the various straps and keepers.

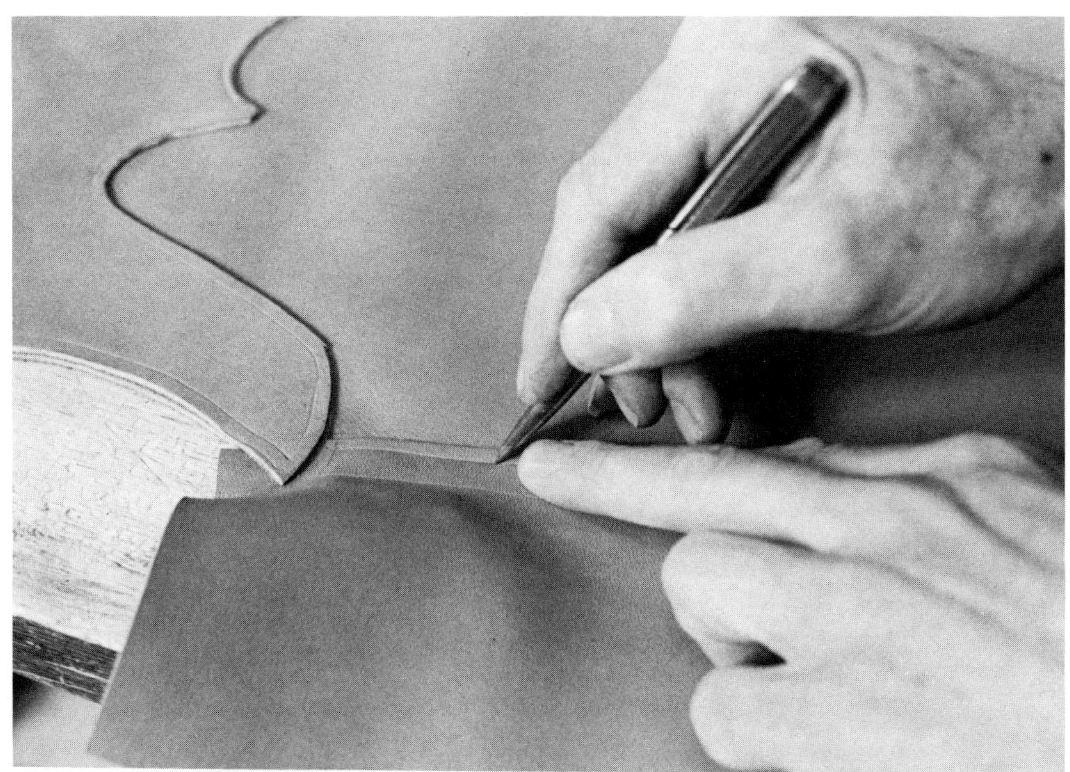

Dividers are used for centering the top for the belt and sewing the extra piece that will hold the belts.

After cutting the belt, pieces are covered with Barge Cement and then stitched.

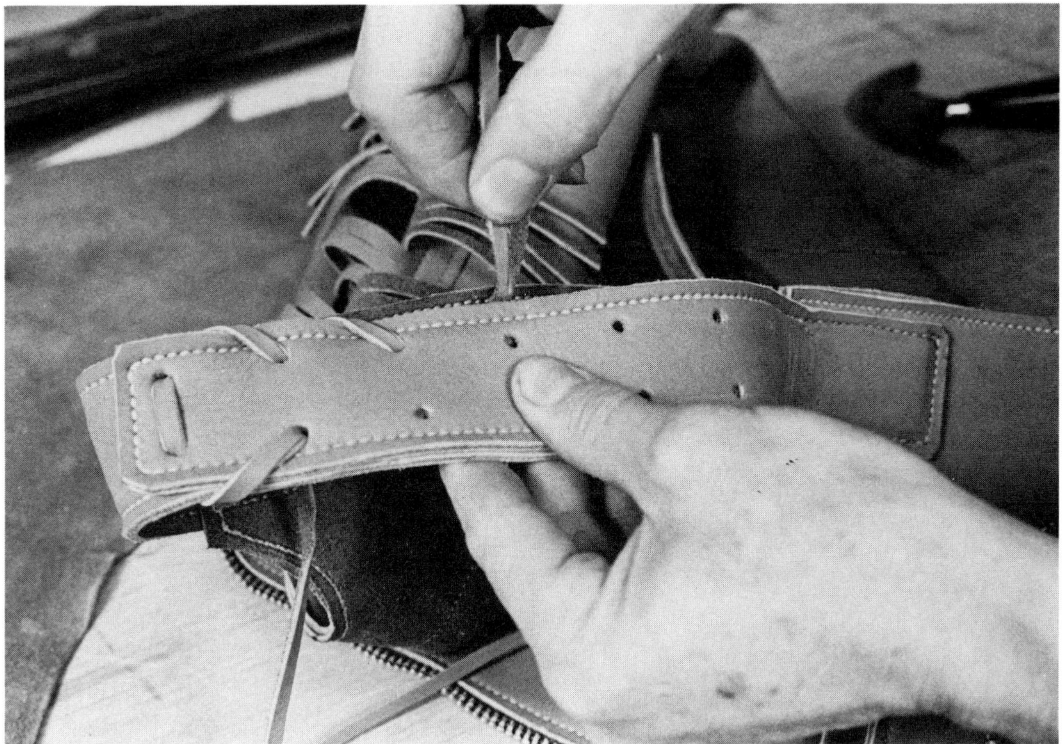

The back piece is punched and laced. Usually, when worn by one person, the lacing will not have to be readjusted.

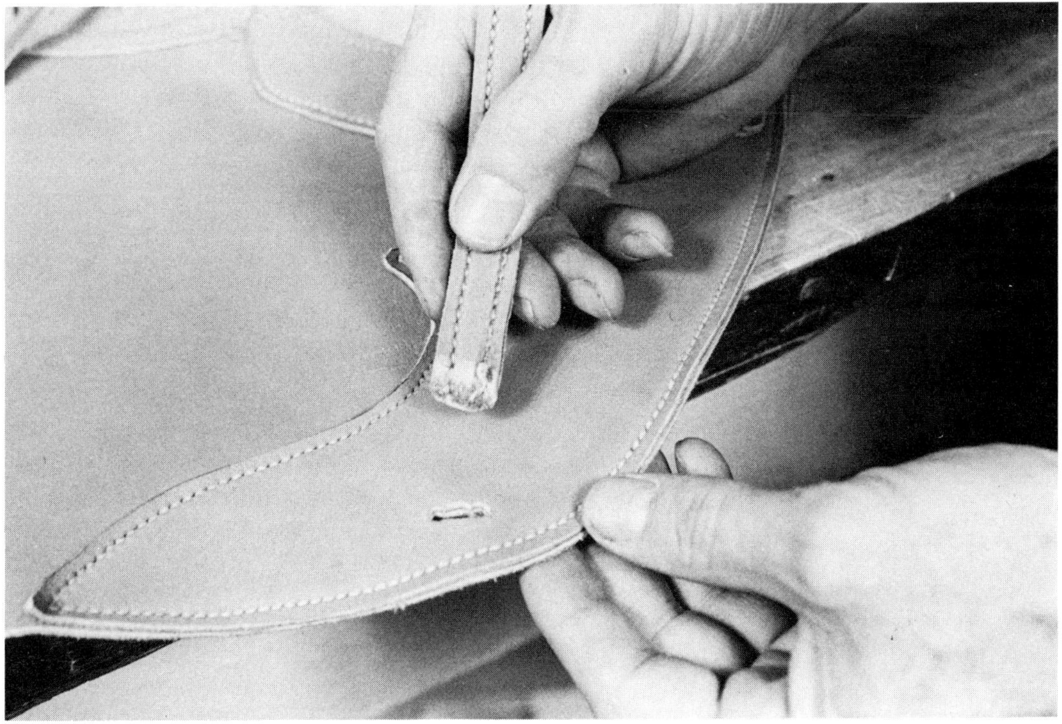

The front belt, with buckle, is set through a slit and fastened with a rivet.

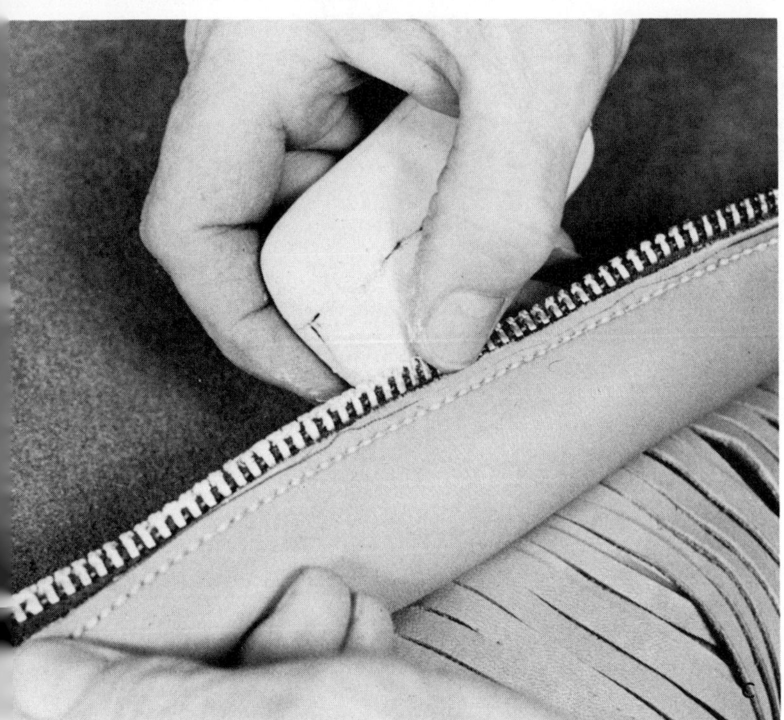

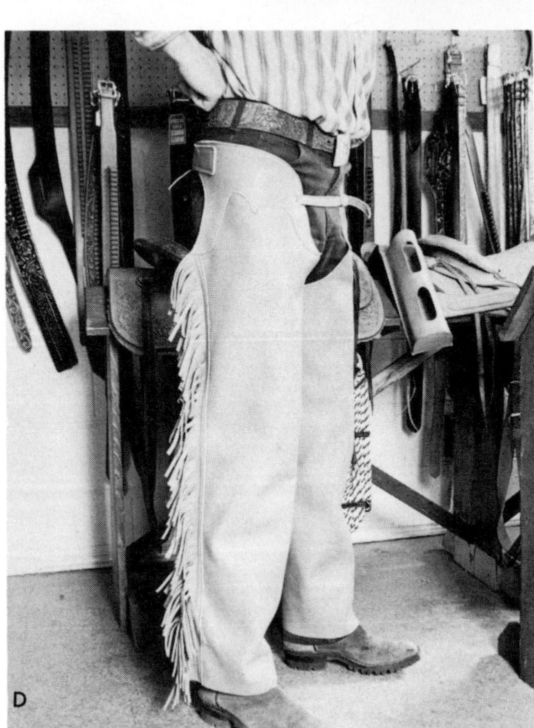

A Once the industrial zipper is placed in position, the additional leather for fringe is set over before cutting. Be careful not to set the zipper too close to the edge; otherwise it will bind on the leather.

B Once the zipper and fringe piece are sewn, the fringe is cut. Note the use of a head knife and the fringe being cut at an angle. This will allow it to hang better and add perhaps 1/4" to the length.

C Once the fringe is cut, run soap along the zipper to insure easy running.

D The completed chaps. These normally set low on the waist.

sewing; however, holes can be punched with an awl and chaps can be buck-stitched with an awl or sewn with needle and thread. An experienced leatherworker should be able to make a pair of chaps in four or five hours. Someone less skilled might double that time without too much effort.

To begin with, the most important factor is to examine the hide with great care for flaws and lay out correct measurements on a paper pattern. Once this is done the pattern is placed over the skin to make certain all areas fit, including sufficient added material for the belting. Basically, chaps are really two separate leggings joined together with a belt; if this is kept in mind it will make the project easier. Once one leg is cut, allowing sufficient extra leather for the fringe, the same pattern is reversed and the other leg is cut out. A few words about the fringe: with some skins it may not be possible to allow enough material for one piece WITH fringe; in that case, an extra piece may be found elsewhere on the skin of sufficient length and this can be sewn on with the same stitches that will be used for the zipper.

The belting can be as simple or fancy as desired. Usually the back straps are punched and laced after being sewn on. Small slits are made in front to accommodate the strap. The strap may be fastened after being passed through the slit, either with a rivet or laced. Once the zipper is sewn on—a local shoe shop will have the equipment for this—the fringe is cut. There is one excellent trick to cutting fringe so it will hang down and that is to cut it at an angle. The illustrations plainly show how. A knife or pair of scissors is excellent for this. When cut at an angle there will also be a gain in length from 1/4 to 1/2 an inch. In spite of its beauty, fringe should seldom be longer than four or five inches on chaps. If it is longer it will get in the way and possibly tangle with briars; it also adds weight.

Once the chaps are finished, they must be "set" to the wearer. Old time cowboys usually dumped them in the horse trough, then put them on wet and wore them all day while going about their duties on horseback. The sportsman can do the same thing before setting out for a couple of hours of quail hunting. Just give them a quick dip in the bathtub—three or four minutes will suffice—then put them on and wear them as long as possible. In this way the chaps form to the body. Once they are dry, a light coating of neatsfoot oil or Lexol (not on the suede side) will give enough treatment to preserve the natural oils.

Chaps can be decorated with conchas if desired. These may be purchased at any leather-supply house and are simply put on by punching two holes and fastening with a piece of thong. Most conchas today are stamped, although real Indian-made conchas may still be found in some of our Western states. Be warned, however, that the genuine silver concha can be expensive. Since at least six will be required for each leg, be prepared to pay something like $20 or more for each concha.

The cowboy, of course, had no aversion to spending a couple of months' salary on his fancy accoutrements. Silver hat bands, inlaid pistol grips, finely carved belts, silk scarves—all helped to brighten his day when he rode to town. With the resurgence of nostalgia in our country, finely crafted items are becoming more popular and the art of the West is again taking its rightful place among more modern crafts.

CHAPTER EIGHT

Knife Sheaths

With the growing boom in knifemaking, craftsmen are so busy filling cutlery orders that few have the time, patience, or desire to make a really good sheath. Truthfully, most knifemakers abhor leatherwork and would prefer to spend their time grinding steel rather than working with leather. While most custom cutlers supply a commendable sheath, few of those made can really complement a $200 blade.

Corbet Sigman, one of the leading exponents of the bench-made knife, has said he can't stand leatherwork, and considers it a waste of time since it takes him away from the grinding wheel. Even so, he considers it a necessary evil since something must be provided to carry a sharpened blade. Actually, Sigman can and does make an excellent sheath which is a tribute to his fine reputation as a knifemaker.

For those many sportsmen who might seek something a little better or are on the lookout for a handsome sheath for a new knife, we've visited with two excellent leather-workers and asked their advice and instruction. One is a leathercraftsman and the other a new but superb knifemaker who firmly believes that a quality sheath not only complements a fine knife, but also provides a safe way to carry a blade.

Doug Hutchins heads up the leather shop of Gerber Legendary Blades in Portland, Oregon. Gerber is one of the few cutlery firms which has its own leather department; it supplies a quality sheath for every straight-bladed knife, as well as pouch sheaths for many of its excellent folders.

There are diverse opinions as to what makes the best knife sheath. As with telescopic sights, rifle calibers, or make of handgun, everyone has his own strong views and what may please one man may definitely not please another. Keeper straps, snaps, toggle thongs, and various clamps annoy some hunters, while others feel these are the only

DOUG HUTCHINS

way to ensure the safety of a knife under adverse conditions.

One style of sheath that has gained in popularity is the pouch sheath and it has much to recommend it. It protects the man using the knife better than any other style of sheath. We also decided to show the crafting of this type of sheath because it's probably one of the easiest to make. So attractive did Gerber find this type of sheath that it decided to use the same style on all its straight-bladed knives. Al Mar, Gerber's design director, is a hunter who has tramped about most of his home state of Oregon. He has also ventured into the Southwest and Mexico with his knifemaking buddy Clyde Fischer and roamed much of the vast wilderness area of Utah and Wyoming for deer, elk, and bear. An experienced sportsman, Mar believes in functional items. The pouch sheath will hold the knife firmly, particularly when it is wet formed, keep the blade in place when running through the underbrush or riding horses, and present it to the user with the advantage of a quick-draw holster.

Making a Pouch Sheath

The plans shown here will make a sheath for any size knife and Doug Hutchins will lead us through the few simple steps of crafting an excellent pouch sheath. The accompanying illustrations show how the pattern is made, cut, and fitted around the knife. How much leather should you buy? Make the pattern first and then purchase slightly more than required.

Keep one thing in mind: extra leather can always be trimmed away, but it can't be added to or glued on particularly when crafting a knife sheath, pistol holster, or belt. The weight of the leather should be about 7/8-ounce. Gerber uses this weight and it will make a strong, firm scabbard. When the pattern is drawn, sufficient extra material should be allowed for the welt to be sewn for a proper fit. Quite simply, the pouch sheath is a fold of leather cut to fit the knife. Making the pattern isn't tricky and requires little drawing ability, but a fair amount of common sense will be a help. As the knife is set on the center line, draw around the left side for the piece that will fold over and allow sufficient leather for the top piece to fold down for the belt loop. When the paper pattern is cut out, now is the time to check carefully for fit.

When the pattern is satisfactory, transfer it to the leather by laying the pattern on the leather and outlining it with a ballpoint pen. Before picking up the knife to cut the leather, make one last check to make certain all points fit properly. Also be sure that the belt loop is correctly placed and that it will fit the belt. A good sharp knife will do much to aid in making clean cuts. An expert can do a beautiful job of cutting leather with a head knife; others will work as well with an X-Acto knife that has a well-sharpened blade. One word of caution: before beginning to cut on a good table, a piece of white pine should be laid down. It makes a fine cutting base and will prevent the table top from being ruined. Another tip is to practice cutting a few pieces of scrap leather before starting. The center line, where the leather folds, should be grooved. The leather must be dampened with a wet sponge and allowed to dry for a few moments before a grooving tool is run down the center line for the fold. The grooves will allow the center line to fold neatly.

Some sheath makers use two grooves about 1/8″ to each side of the center line; however, one will suffice. Once the leather is cut to size, the next step is to fold and fit

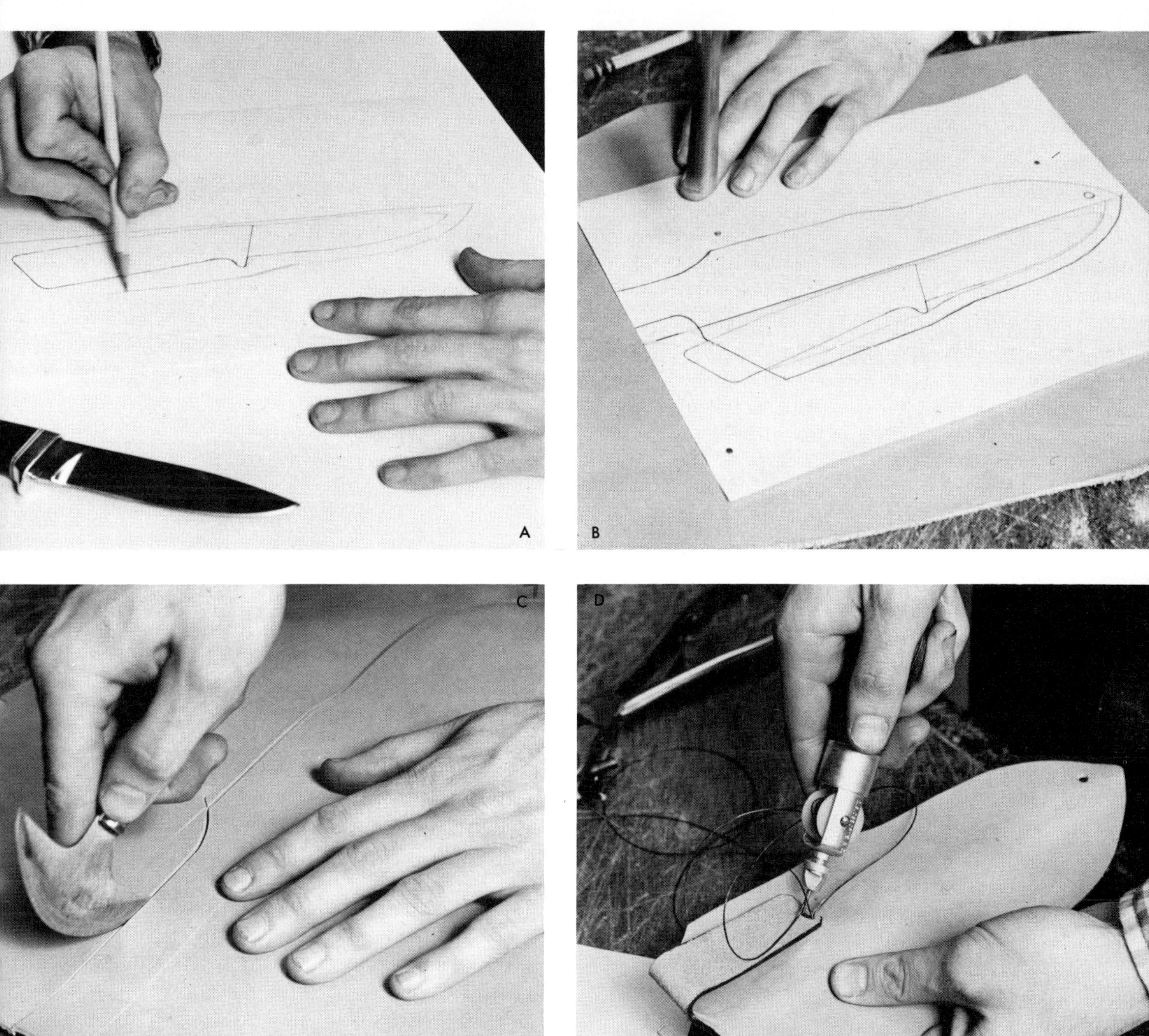

A Hutchins shows how to craft a simple pouch sheath for a straight-bladed sheath knife. First he draws a pattern on paper before transferring it to leather.

B Once the pattern is completed, it is tacked to a piece of damp leather and scribed with a sharp pencil. This will transfer the pattern to the leather.

C Hutchins prefers a head knife for his cuts, although any sharp knife may be used.

D A stitching awl is used to sew the belt loop.

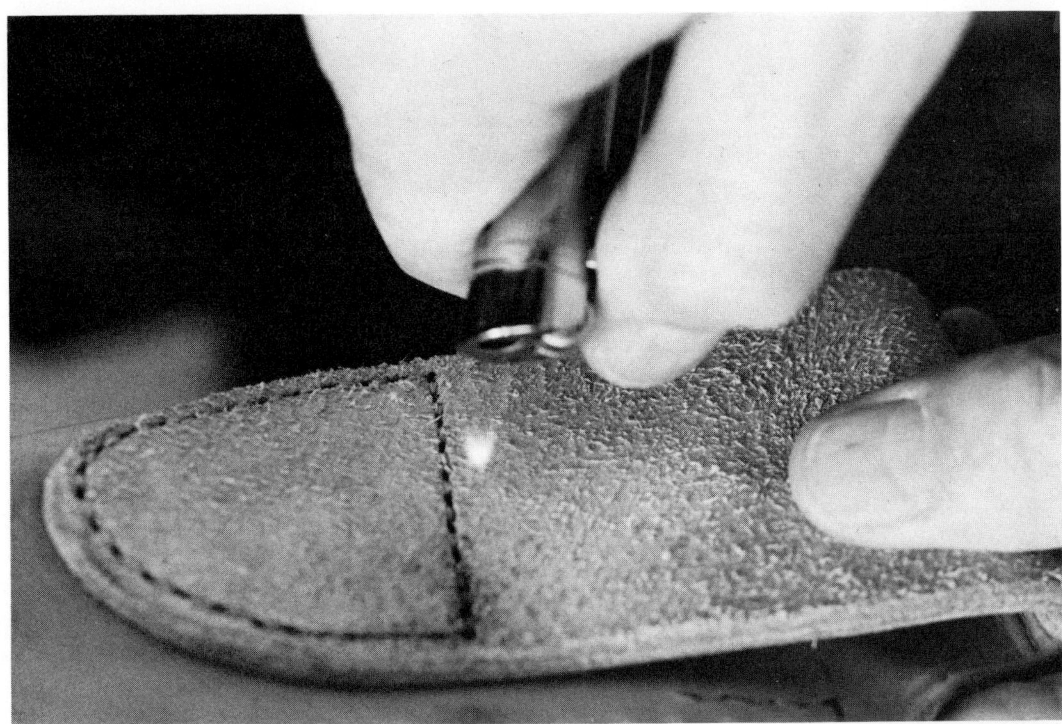

Since nylon thread is used, a couple of back stitches are taken and then burned off with a lighter to fasten securely in the stitch hole.

After cutting the welt, it is tacked onto the sheath and the knife set in to ensure proper fit.

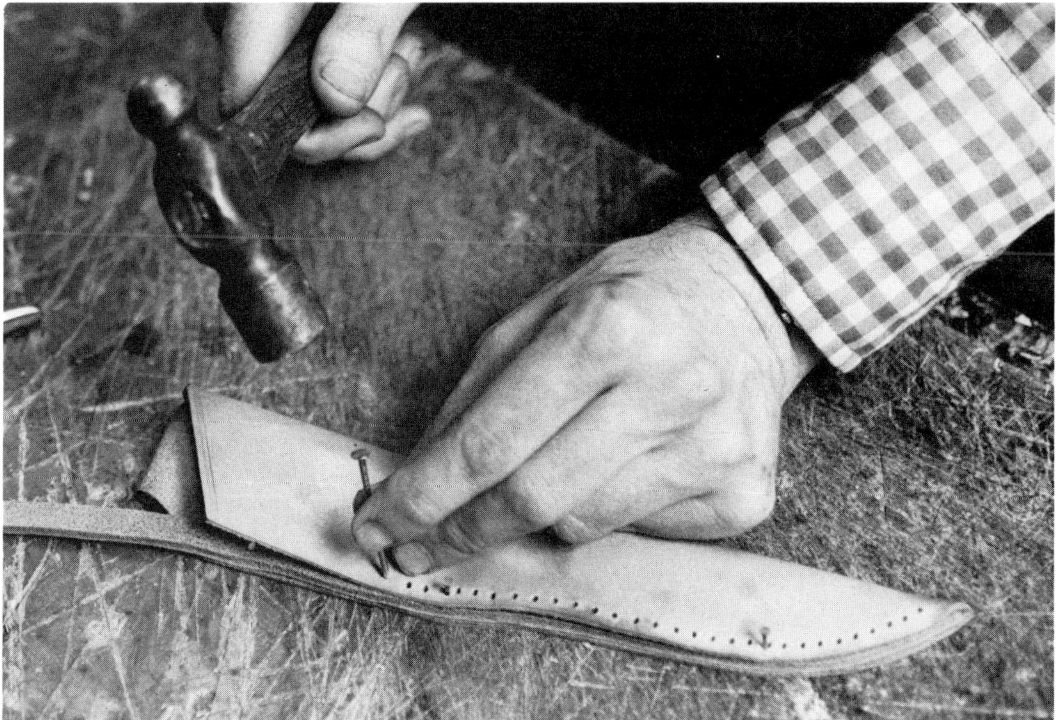

On a hand-crafted sheath, Hutchins uses a nail to hammer the stitching holes in order to go through the top layer and indent the welt.

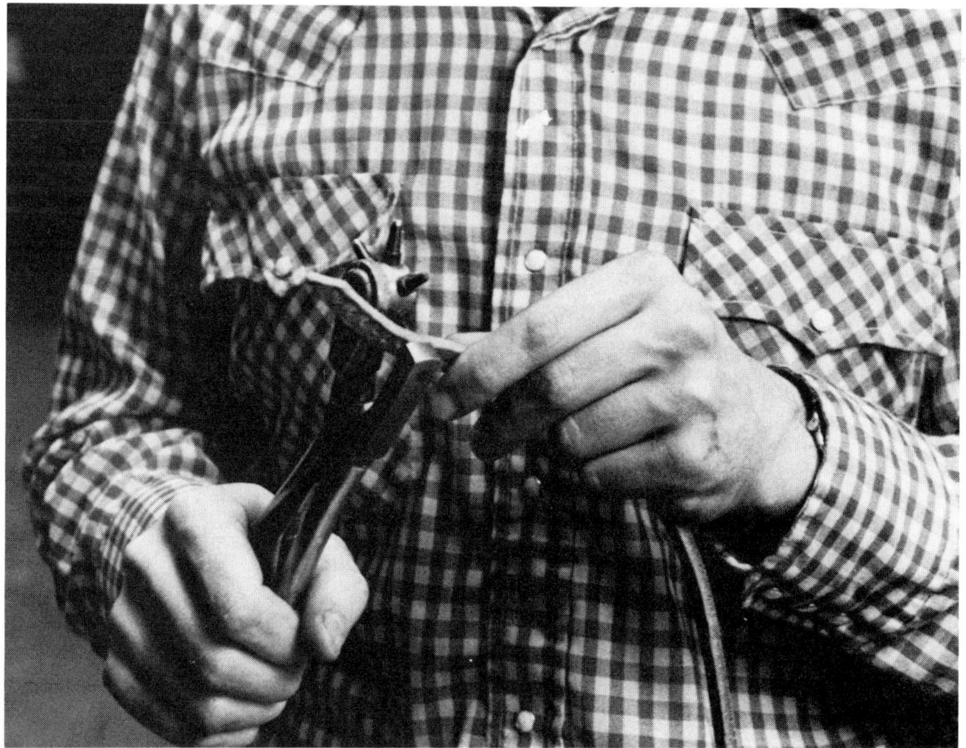

Hutchins uses a punch to clear the sewing hole on the welt.

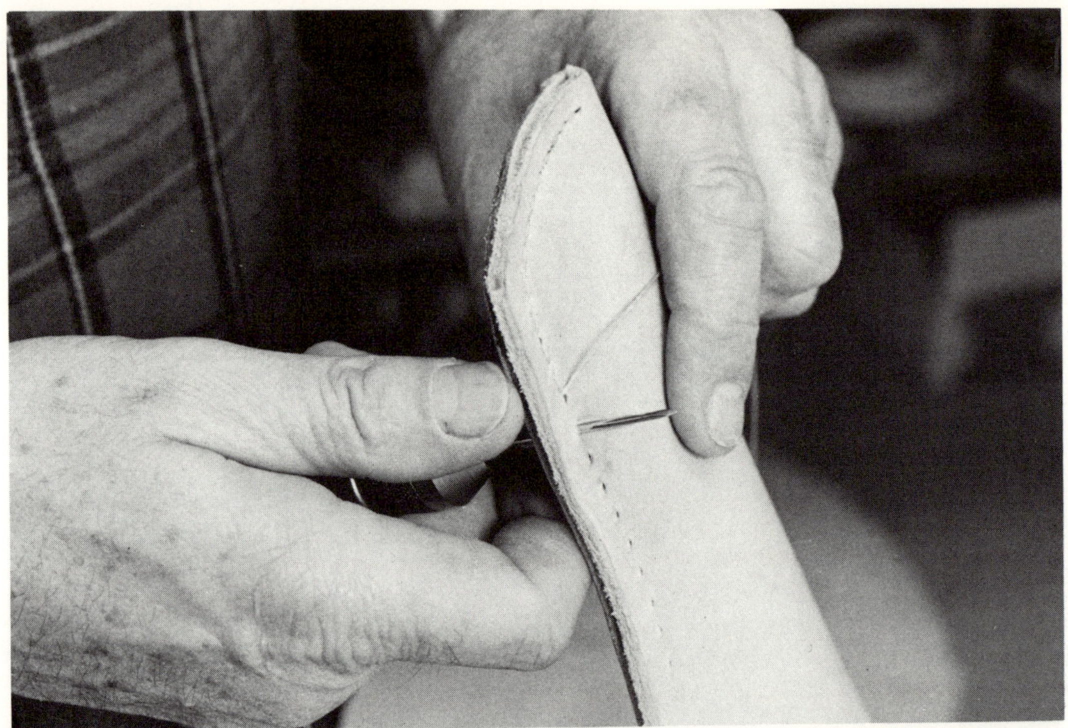

After cementing the pieces with Barge Cement, Doug Hutchins uses a stitching awl to hand sew the edge of the sheath.

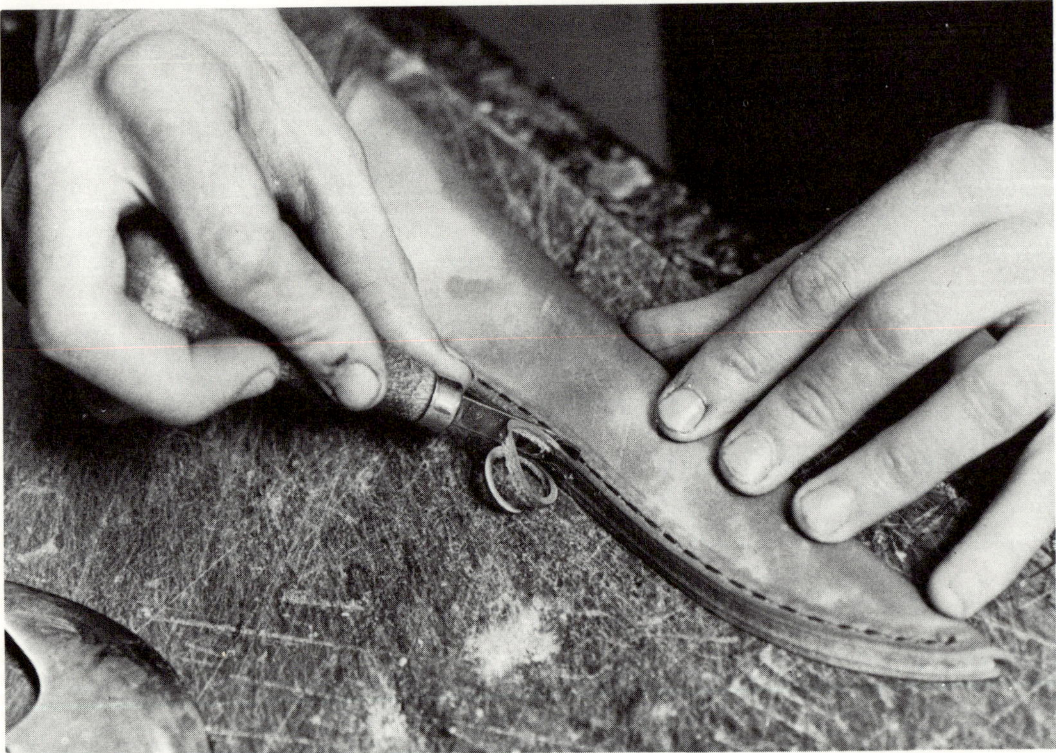

An edge-beveler is used to trim around the edges and give a finished strip to the raw leather.

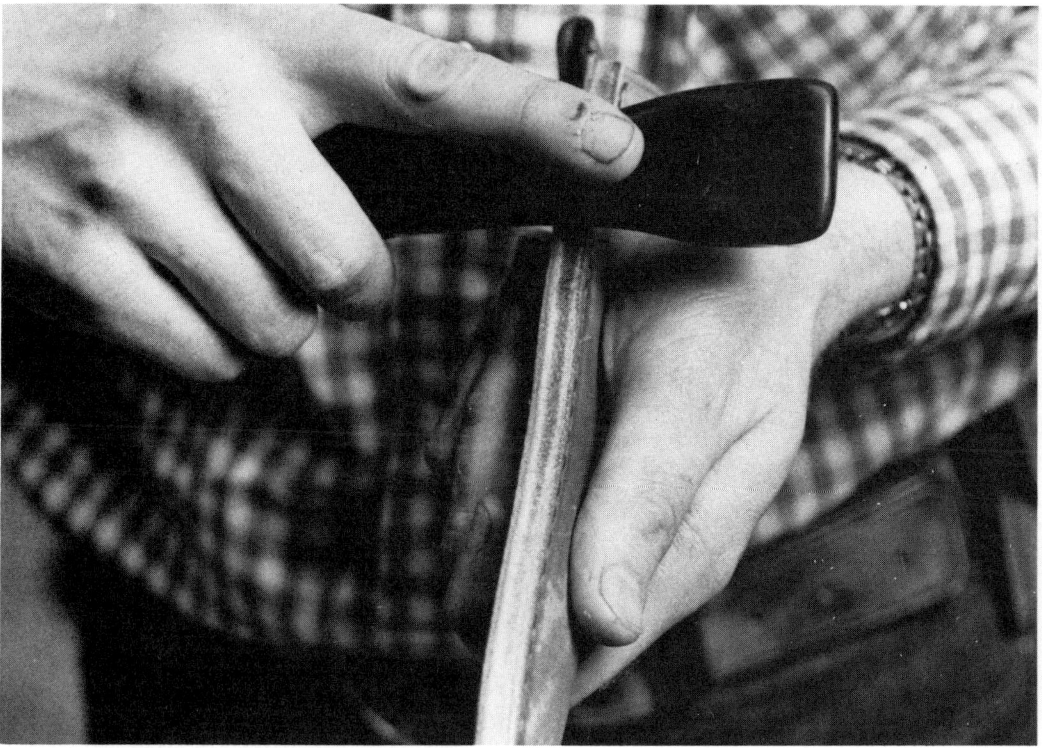

An ebony stick is used to rub the edges and smooth them out.

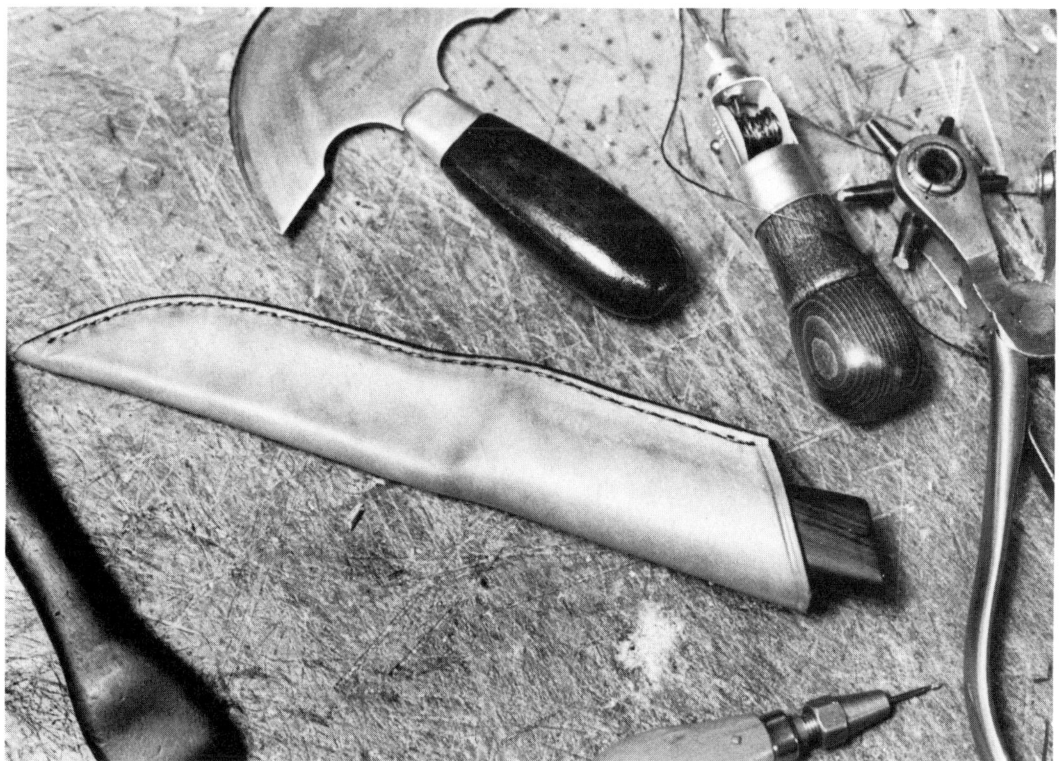

The finished pouch sheath and the tools used.

the belt loop. Here the loop is folded over and the correct placement marked with a scriber, ballpoint pen, or pencil. Now, before the loop is sewn down and it becomes difficult to trim the edges, a beveler is run around the top of the sheath and around the belt loop for a finished appearance. Barge Cement is used to lightly cover both the inside of the loop and the marked-out spot on the back of the sheath. Coat both sides lightly and allow to dry a few moments. In this project, it is important to refer to the pictures frequently so that the wrong side or piece of leather isn't glued or sewn up before it's too late to undo errors. Once the cement has become almost dry to the touch, the pieces are firmly pressed together; in fact, they should be hammered down to ensure a tight smooth fit. Before any other work is done, the loop is now sewn. A sturdy sewing machine that will take a leather needle will do the job. Otherwise one of the lockstitch sewing awls on the market can also be used.

Next comes the welt—that piece of thick, stiff leather that lies between the two sides or edges of the sheath to protect the sharpened edge of the knife and give stiffness to the sheath. A piece of stiff sole leather is best, however a length of 7/8-ounce leather, the same as used for the sheath, will work nicely. Note that the welt is cut on a curve, so some care must be used to obtain a proper fit. Once the welt is cut, set it on the sheath and place the knife in position to ensure a good fit. If all matches up well, coat both sides of the welt with Barge Cement to hold it in place and also glue the inside matching faces. Now, with both sides covered with glue which is almost dry, press both pieces together gently and work the knife in and out a couple of times to ensure a good, firm fit. If all has gone well up to this point—there is no reason it shouldn't have—take a hammer and pound along the welt line and then let it set a while. Since we now have three thicknesses of leather, it may be difficult to force a hand awl through all this leather, so a trip to the cobbler's shop might be in order. Any shoemaker will have the equipment to stitch the sheath and he'll know exactly what's required.

At this point the sheath is almost completed. Run the finished sheath under the faucet to dampen it slightly and force the knife into the scabbard. Work the fingers around the knife to wet-form the sheath. Then, before setting it aside to dry, run a beveler along the sewn edge to give a finished appearance. Incidentally, once the knife is removed, dry it thoroughly. Even such rust resistant steels as 440C or 154CM can be damaged by wet leather and a slight coating of oil on the blades will help to preserve their beauty. Once the sheath is dry, a clear finishing wax can be buffed on to help prevent staining and provide some amount of waterproofing.

This, then, is how a pouch sheath is made. A good sturdy sheath will give years of service, protect the knife, and give the wearer satisfaction in knowing he has crafted something of practical use.

Barnett Knife Sheaths

For those who may want to attempt something a bit more intricate two other styles of sheaths are shown by knifemaker Jack Barnett of Littleton, Colorado. Barnett is one of those unusual craftsmen who is both a superb maker of impeccable knives and a top leatherworker.

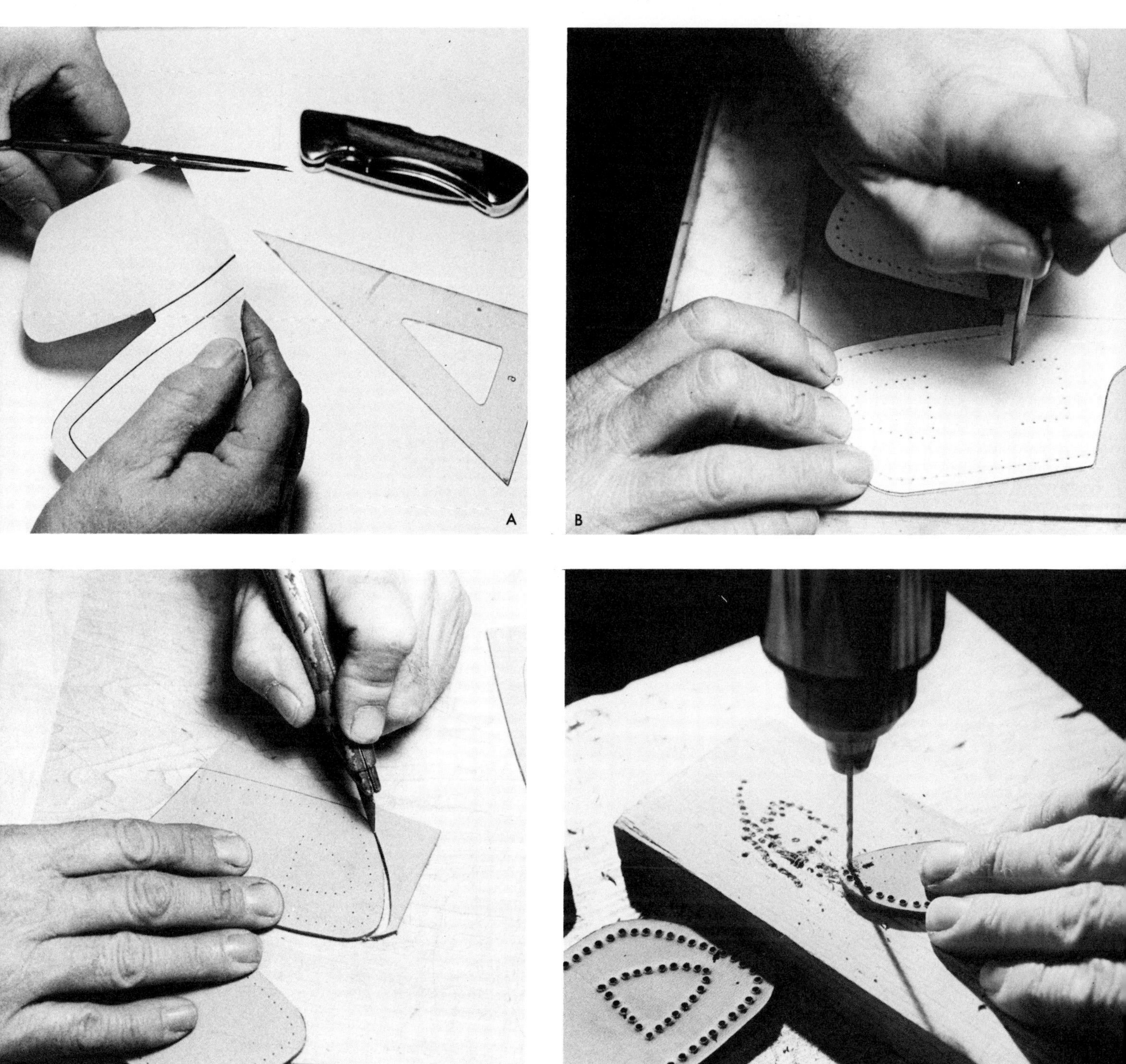

A As with all leather projects, a paper pattern is made and cut out.

B Dividers are used to place the stitching holes, pressing through to the leather underneath.

C The leather is cut to size with a sharp knife. Note the belt loop on the right.

D A drill press is used to drill the stitching holes.

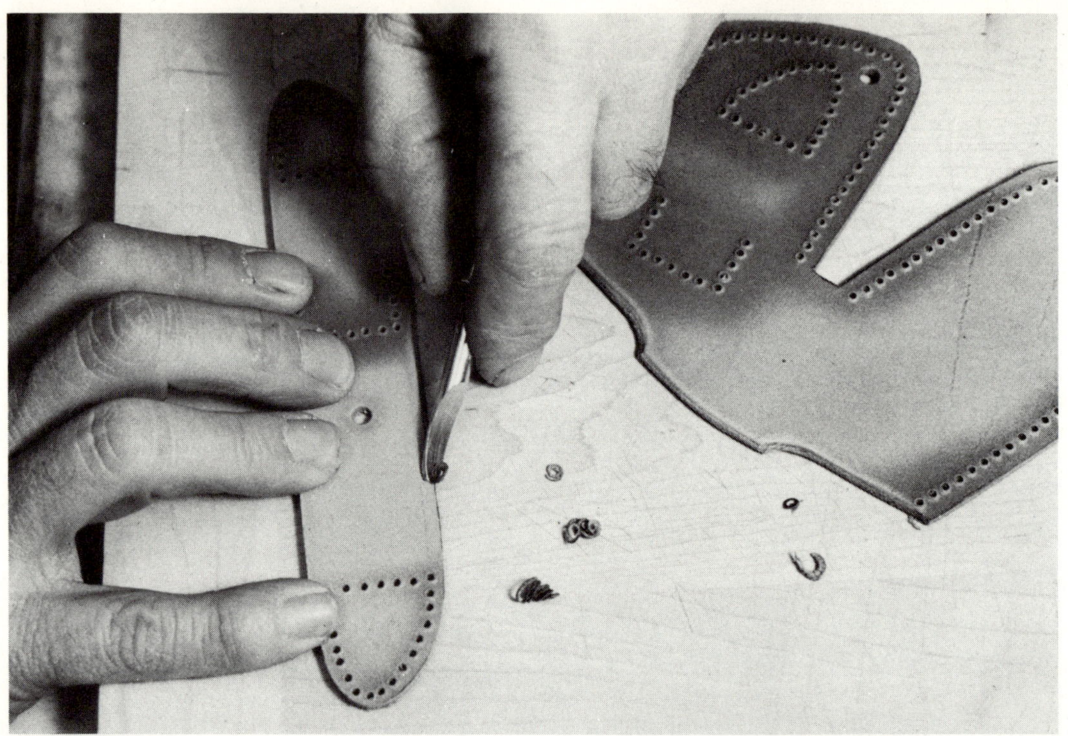

After the holes are drilled, an edge-beveler is used to trim the edges since it would be difficult to do this once the scabbard is sewn.

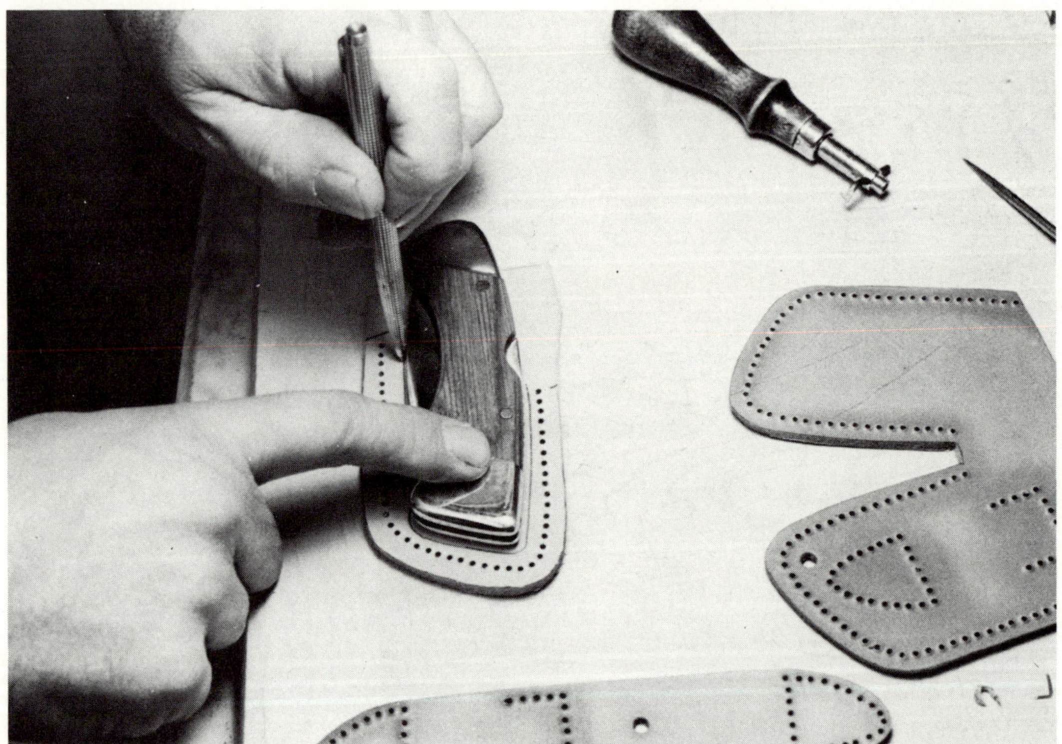

After the stitch holes are drilled and the edges beveled, the welt is carefully drawn out with the knife placed in exact position.

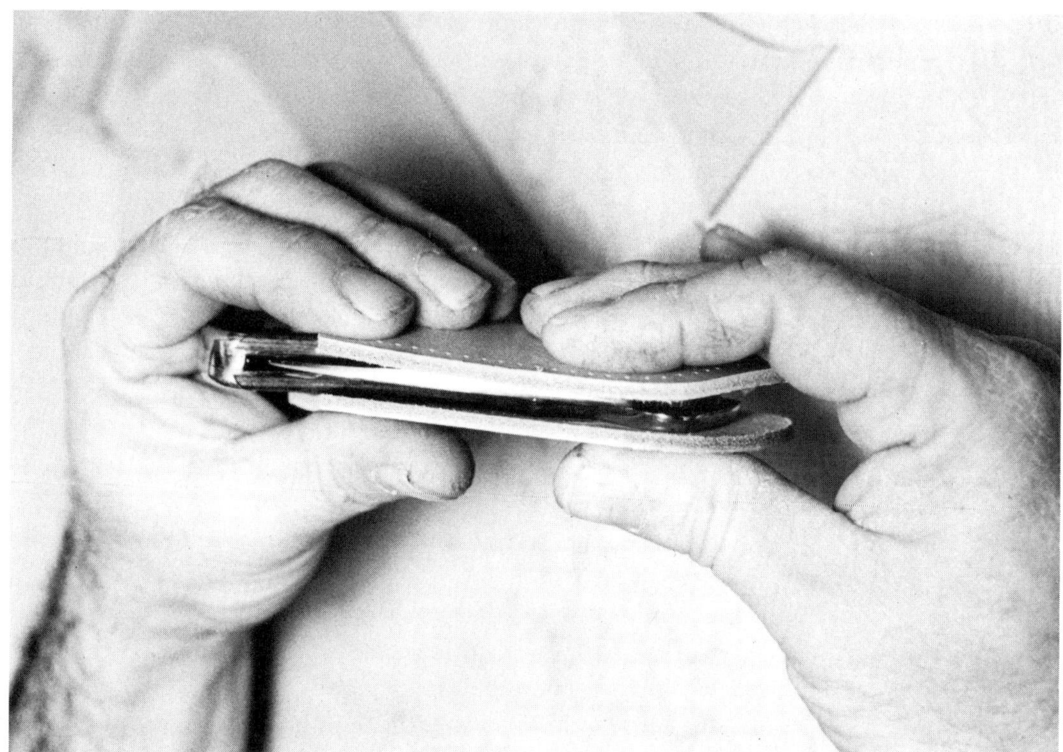

The leather is folded over to ensure tight fit of the knife.

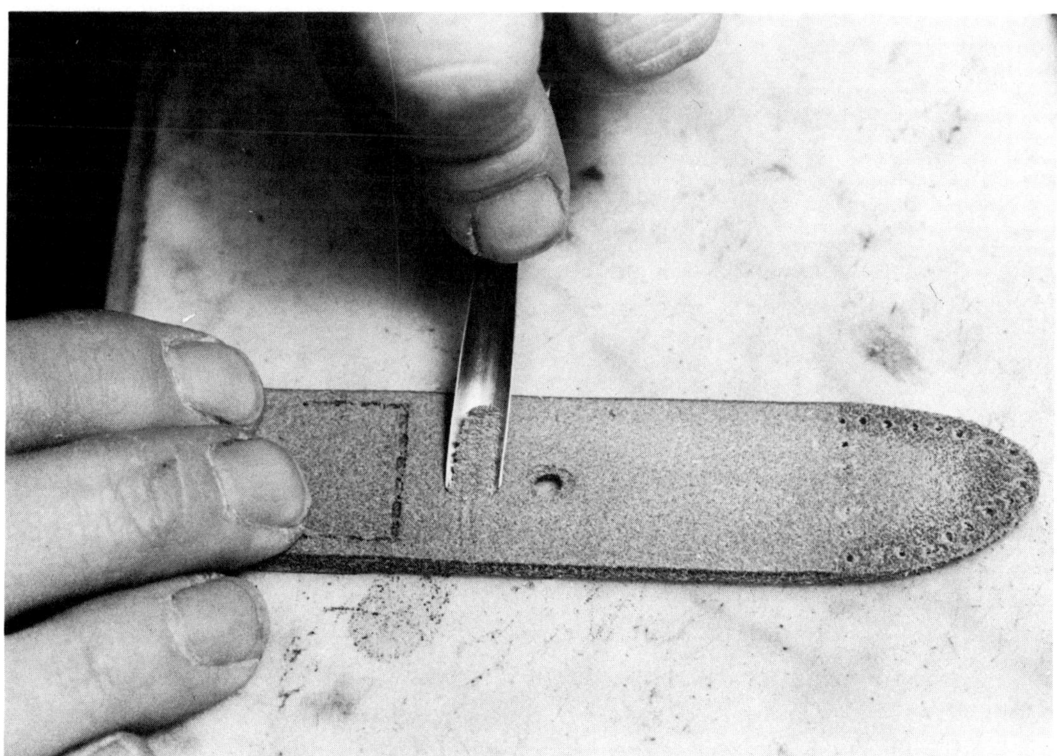

A gouger is used to thin the leather at the fold line to ensure a proper fold. The hole is for hanging in the gun cabinet and will be lined with brass.

For a knifemaker, Barnett has one of the most unusual backgrounds to be found. He was an identification expert with the Federal Bureau of Investigation for a number of years. Returning to his home state of Iowa, he went with the Iowa Bureau of Criminal Investigation for ten years and then moved to Alaska where he joined the State Police. As an investigator he worked over most of Alaska for seven years and eventually returned to the "lower forty-eight" due to a family illness.

Jack's attitude toward knife sheaths is completely different from most knifemakers. "I love to take a piece of leather and do something completely different with it," Jack told me. "In fact, I don't go to my work bench and completely finish a sheath at one sitting. There are too many steps to my sheaths, including tooling and a different style of finish. And there are too many stages where the sheath must dry or set before other work can be done." The perfection of Jack's work could be called the Rolls-Royce of knife sheaths with their precise construction, artful tooling, and careful hot-waxing along with wet-form fitting. Indeed, a number of knife aficionados have ordered Jack's beautiful sheaths just to hang in their collections, knowing full well they complement the handsome knives they encase.

The hallmark of a Barnett sheath is the excellent tooling done on it. One of the most outstanding designs is a simple pine bough with a few pine cones and needles in subtle colors. It is almost Japanese in its effect and the simplicity adds to the beauty. Jack did his first tooling while in the U.S. Navy in the South Pacific and he made many of his first leatherworking tools from old toothbrush handles. As a youngster, he gathered scraps of leather from harness makers and started making sheaths for more simple knives. As his work improved, he began crafting sheaths for friends and soon the hobby developed into a business. He once told me: "I'm utterly fascinated with making knives and I love to do leatherwork, too. I'd hate to have to put one above the other. Personally, I consider a fine handmade knife is deserving of a fine individual type of sheath to go with it."

Surprisingly, Barnett has never taken a lesson in these crafts. It has been entirely trial and error for him, with lots of reading of leather books in between. He is particularly fond of a pouch-type sheath for both folder- and straight-bladed knives. A word of advice: for the straight-bladed knife, the drop point is best for this type of sheath. Blades with an upswept curve won't work and it's best to go to another type of sheath.

As was done for the Gerber sheath, a pattern is made on a piece of paper and slightly enlarged for the welt and stitching; 7/8-ounce vegetable-tanned leather is ideal. Avoid chrome-tanned or latigo leather. Not only do vegetable-tanned leathers form to the contours of the knife, but a proper fit is also ensured and it is excellent for tooling. Jack cautions, however, that once leather is wet, any mark will show and remain forever. So be careful with wet tools and where the damp leather is set down. Even handling leather with wet fingers will show, and once the marks are on it, they can't be removed.

The craftsman must be extremely meticulous about the pattern because it is of the utmost importance to get the proper fit. It is impossible to say that such-and-such a fraction of an inch must be used, but allow for the weight of the leather and realize that the welt will take up a certain amount of space. The welt that Barnett uses runs 9/10-ounce leather. Make the pattern for the outline of the sheath first, then make the pattern for the belt loop that goes on the back of the sheath.

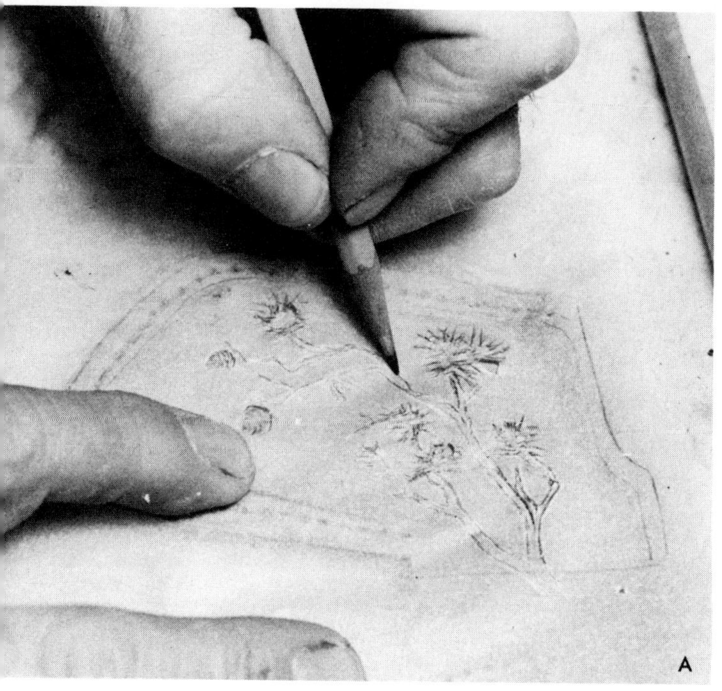

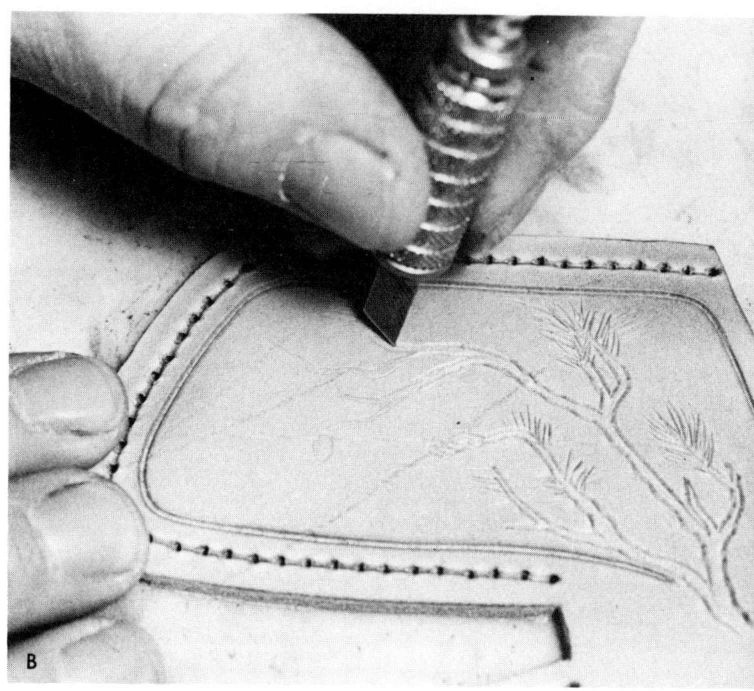

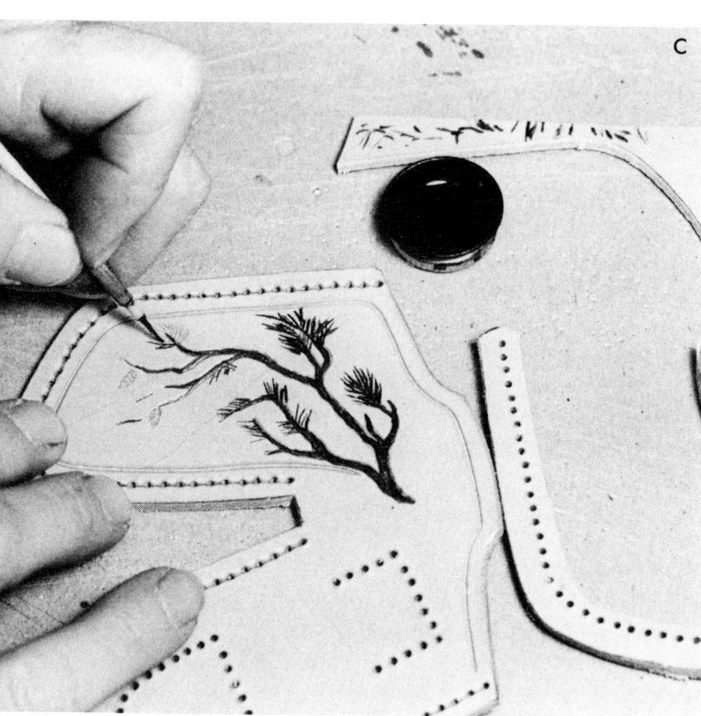

A Before any sewing or assembly is attempted, the design is drawn onto the dampened leather. Here Barnett draws free-hand, but various patterns may be used. A sharp pencil will easily transfer the design.

B Once the pattern is drawn on, a swivel knife is used to cut the design into the leather.

C The next step is to use small brushes and cover the design with dye. Care must be taken here not to spill drops of dye on the clear leather.

D Once the design is dyed and allowed to dry, leather toner is used to cover the entire sheath. Note all pieces are ready for assembly.

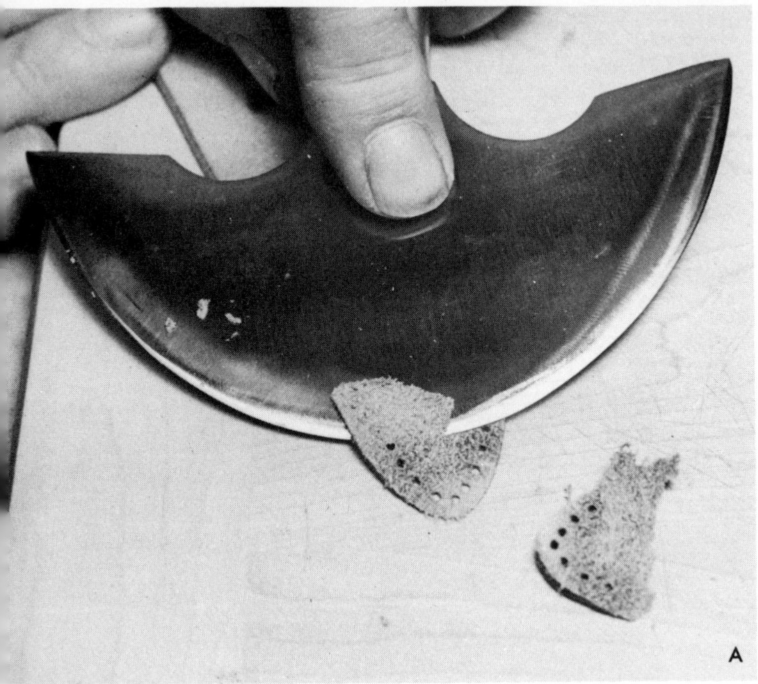

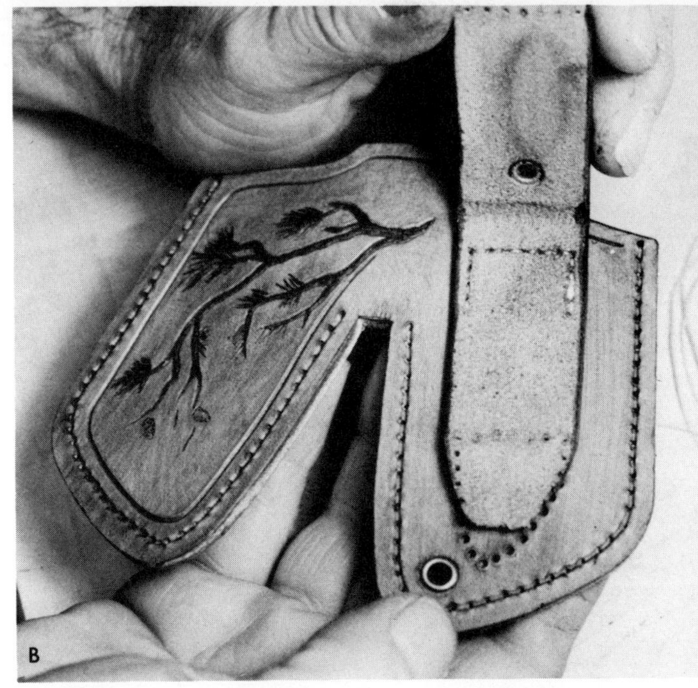

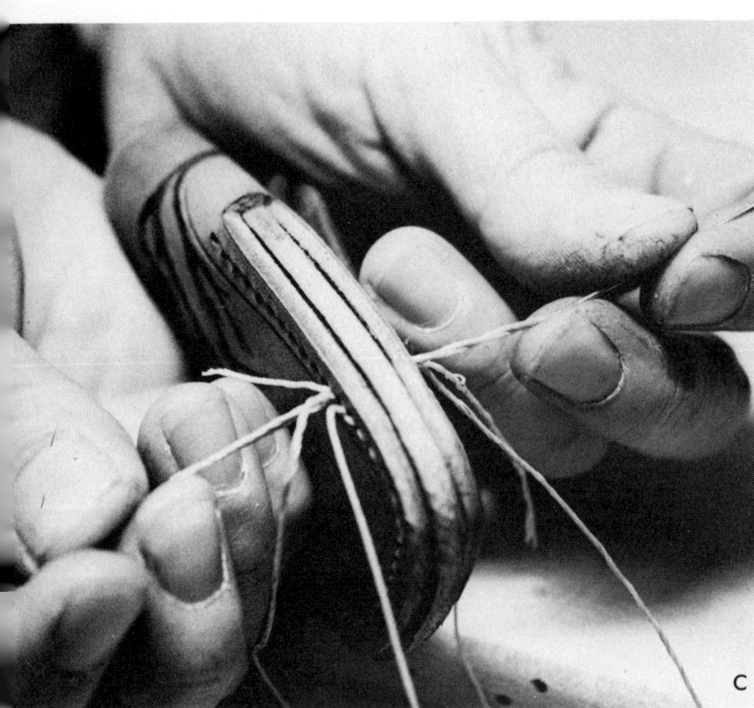

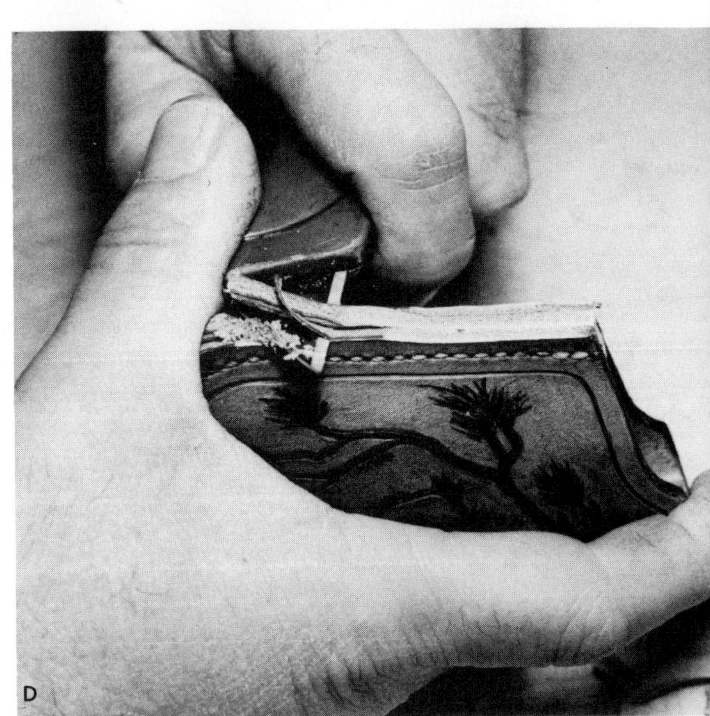

A The edges of the belt loop are skived down with a head knife. This will insure a neat, tight fit.

B Here the brass liners have been set in for the hanger and drain hole. The upper part of the belt loop has been stitched down and all that is now required is to fold the loop down and continue to stitch the bottom part.

C Jack Barnett hand stitches with two needles and pulls tightly with each stitch.

D Once the stitching is finished a sharp knife is used to trim away excess and uneven leather.

Next, mark the stitch line (the STITCH LINE not the stitch itself) with a pair of dividers around the portion that will be sewn. Then the stitch hole is marked, usually about 1/8 inch apart. After this is done, the stitch holes are marked in the pattern on the leather, making certain it is laid on properly for either a right- or left-hand sheath. This is the time to stop and think for a moment. Is the pattern laid on correctly? Will it make the proper sheath for the knife? After making sure of these things, mark the leather around the pattern with a ballpoint pen; use sufficient pressure to indent the leather. The leather can also be moistened and an indentation can be made with a sharp pencil since the slightest mark will show on the leather when it dries. Now, with a small pointed awl, mark the stitch holes in the leather. The holes don't have to go through the leather at this point because the transfer of the pattern is still being done.

At this stage, we've arrived at how the stitching should be done. Barnett prefers hand-stitching and drills the holes in the leather. He uses a drill press, but a Dremel tool or an awl can also be used. Jack advises *not* to try and make the stitch holes by forcing an awl through a number of layers of leather. Bear in mind that three thicknesses of leather around the edge present a pretty formidable obstacle; trying to force an awl or needle through will make for poor stitching holes. Rather, a small bit, approximately the size of the needle or slightly larger, will give a neat row of stitch holes and make the actual stitching that much easier.

The next step is the rounding of the edges of the leather with an edging tool, which will trim neatly and cleanly. Again Jack, as do other instructors, advises practicing on a few scraps of leather. The tool that will work well on the Barnett-style sheath is a No. 2. Do the belt loop and the edge of the sheath prior to stitching. A fine sandpaper, 400- to 600-grit, can burnish the edges down and smooth them off. Now, once the sheath is flat, it's simpler to sand the corners, rather than wait until after the entire sheath is sewn together.

Now we're ready to do the tooling. This is a matter of individual preference. It may be basket stamped, carved, or even initials put on. The leather should not be soaking wet, but merely dampened and then left until it feels almost dry to the touch. Transfer the pattern with a hard lead pencil. Hobby shops have commercially made tools that will also do the job and they are not expensive. The pattern may be done free-hand or any of numerous patterns sold may be used. The pattern is laid over the dampened leather and lightly traced onto it with a pencil or stylus. Once this is done, the leather is allowed to dry in preparation for dyeing. For the ram's head, for example, the color selected is painted over the outline with a small brush and allowed to dry.

Now the sheath is ready for stitching. Barnett prefers using waxed nylon thread with two needles and employs the saddle stitch. The belt loop is put on first and Jack prefers a unique method of fastening it on. First, the long part is stitched on which holds it firmly to the back of the sheath. Then a small hole is punched and brass lined. The latter operation is for hanging the sheath in a gun cabinet and Barnett feels it gives a nice personal touch to the sheath. Once this main part of the stitching is finished, the loop is folded over, shaved down slightly, and stitched to the bottom, making a firm, tight loop.

Before cutting the welt and sewing the sheath together, another hole is punched on the bottom for a drain-hole. Should the careless hunter or fisherman take a spill in a

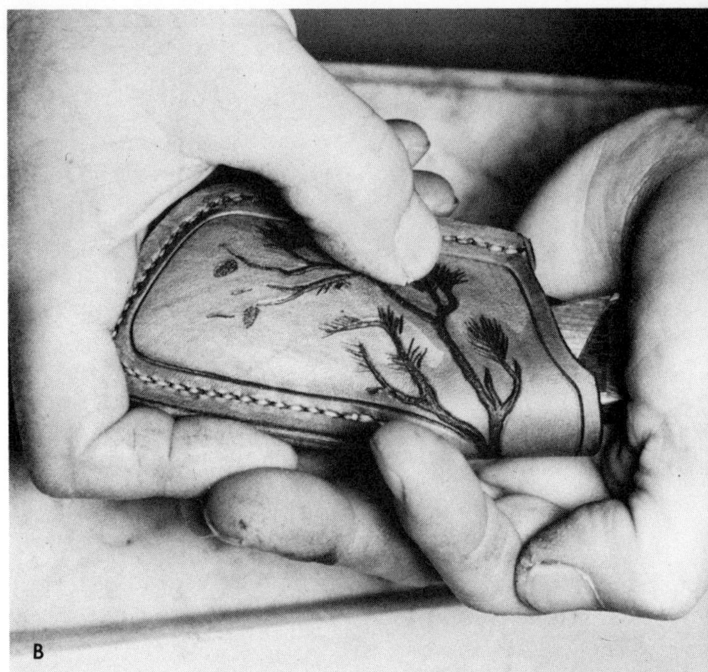

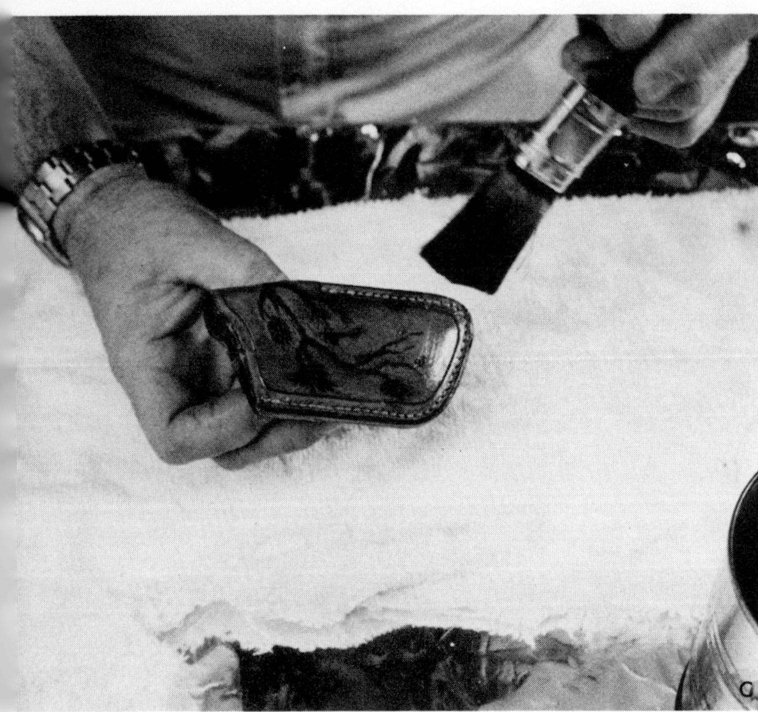

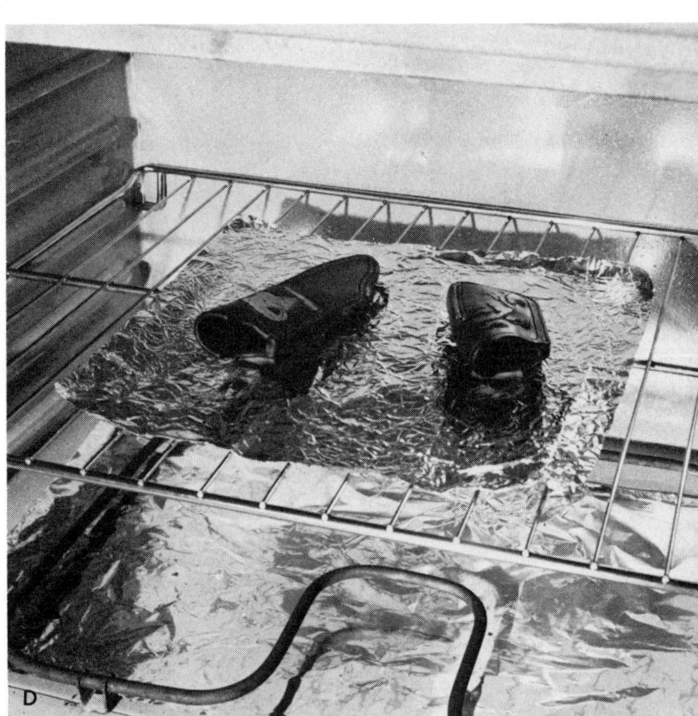

A The edges are sanded to remove any rough spots.

B The final test: Barnett pushes the knife into the slightly dampened sheath for a perfect fit.

C After being allowed to set overnight to dry, the sheath is coated with a mixture of molten paraffin and saddle oil to give protection.

D In the final step, the sheath is set in the oven for 15 minutes at 170°. When removed, it is set aside to cool at room temperature.

Prior to going into the oven, the sheath is set on a stick and slowly turned over a slow flame to allow the mixture to settle into the leather.

stream or get caught in a sudden downpour, this brass-lined hole will allow the water to run out. Waxing the sheath will help waterproof it, but a quick runoff of water will help keep the knife in essentially usable condition.

Once the welt is cut, everything is laid together to ensure a firm fit. There is nothing worse than a knife jiggling about in a custom made sheath—or, indeed, any sheath for that matter. Such looseness only means sloppy work. In any finely crafted knife sheath, a little "hook" in the welt prevents the knife from being forced down into the sheath; it will also grasp the guard firmly once the sheath is sewn together. After the holes have been drilled and the knife fits well, the tooling can be completed. Then the sheath is stained and ready for the sometimes tedious task of stitching. Usually a saddle stitch is used with two needles and each stitch is pulled up firmly before beginning the next one. At the conclusion of the stitching, a few back stitches are taken, the thread is cut, and a light flame is applied to burn the nylon, thus locking it inside the hole.

The small open-topped sheath is for the new Track folder-type knife called the Sun River. It is an excellent all-round knife and, while it comes with a typical snap-top scabbard, we find Jack Barnett's custom job to be more attractive and practical. Although many of the steps in crafting this sheath are the same as the straight-bladed model, there are a couple of little tricks that will aid the craftsman. The most important, as with the regular sheath knife, is to fit the knife securely in the leather before the welt is sewn.

The finishing steps for this sheath are most important to give it a professional appearance, remove any rough edges, and generally dress it up. The picture shows trimming edges with a very sharp knife. Afterward, sandpaper is rubbed along the edges, which first should be slightly dampened. Once the sanding has been done to your satisfaction, a piece of bone, ivory, Micarta, or hardwood can be rubbed along the edge to give a polish.

After the sheath is stitched, it is wet-formed for a tight fit for the knife. Wet the leather—it doesn't have to be soaked but damp enough so contours can be formed with the fingers to the shape of the knife. The knife is then forced into the sheath. Again, be careful not to impress fingernails into the leather or make any other scratches on it since they can't be removed. Set the sheath aside and let it dry overnight. Then it's ready for the finishing wax process.

This final process is what gives the leather its handsome appearance and makes it waterproof. Barnett learned it at a harness company in the Midwest. The old gentleman who ran the outfit took a liking to Jack and told him the process was a baked one that used wax, paraffin, and saddle oil, which is a blend of lanolin and silicon. Roughly the mixture takes about four ounces of molten paraffin, to which is added ¾-ounce liquid measure of saddle oil for body. Don't, however, try the mixture on boots because it will seal the pores in the leather and you might freeze your feet. Mix the ingredients into a can and set on the stove to melt slowly. Care should be exercised at this point because the oils and paraffin are volatile and have a tendency to catch fire. Therefore, keep the flame very low so the mixture melts slowly. Once it's hot, use a brush to coat both the inside and outside of the sheath. Don't, under any circumstances, dip it into the solution since it will absorb too much. It is much better to put on a number of light coats rather than one heavy coat. A stick in the end of the sheath will allow it to be held over the

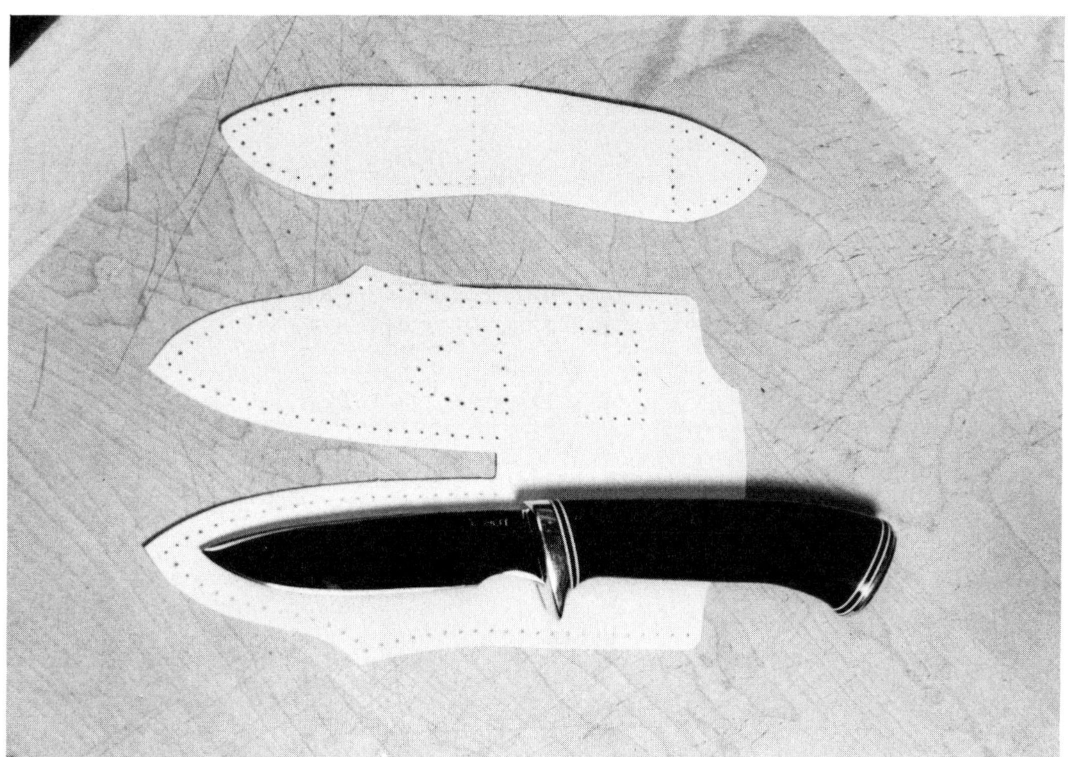

A full pattern is cut from paper and stitching holes indented; it is now ready for transfer to leather.

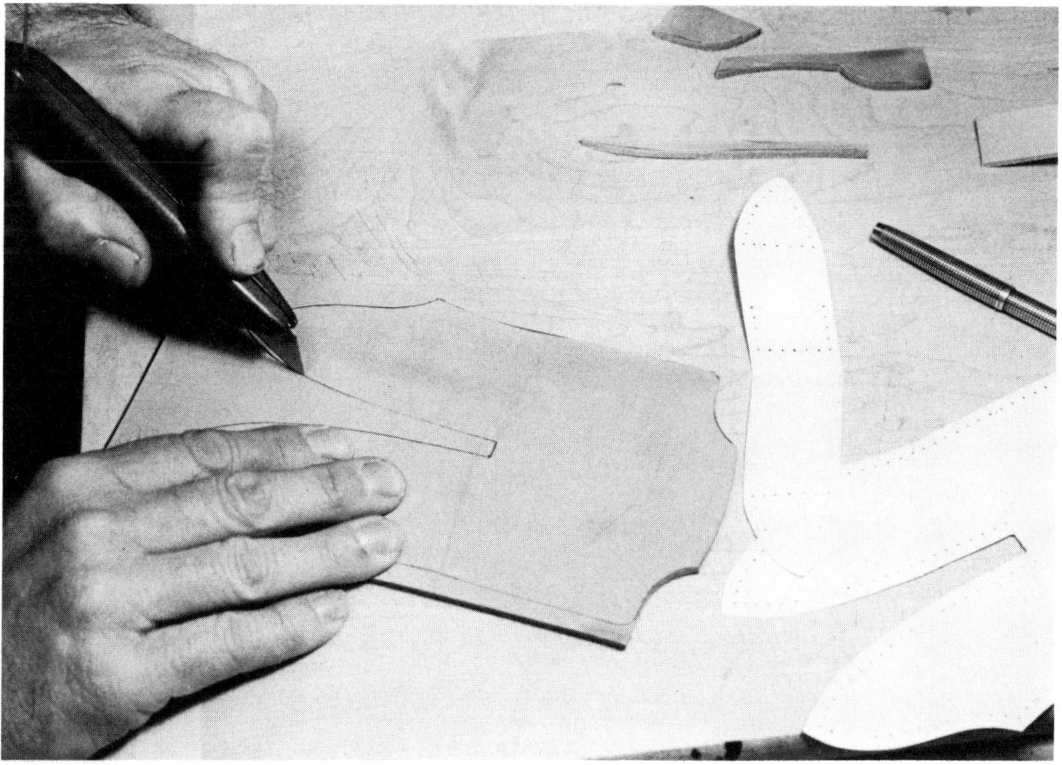

The pattern is drawn on leather, then cut out.

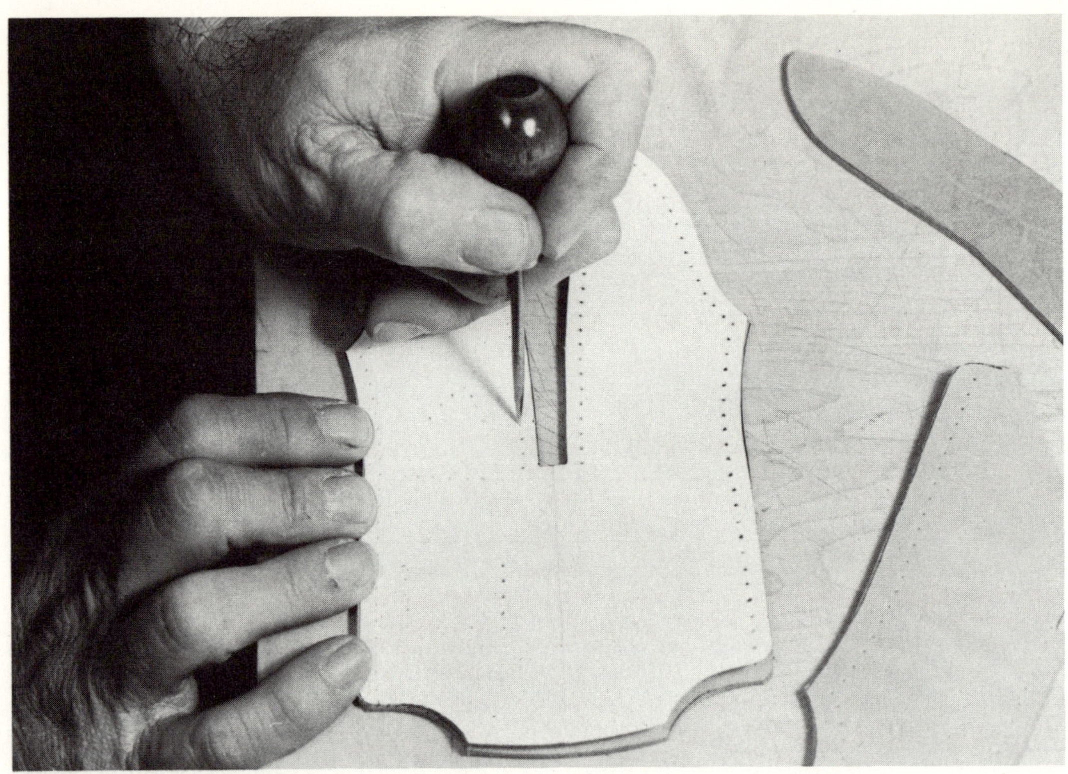

A sharply pointed awl is used to transfer the stitch holes from the pattern to leather.

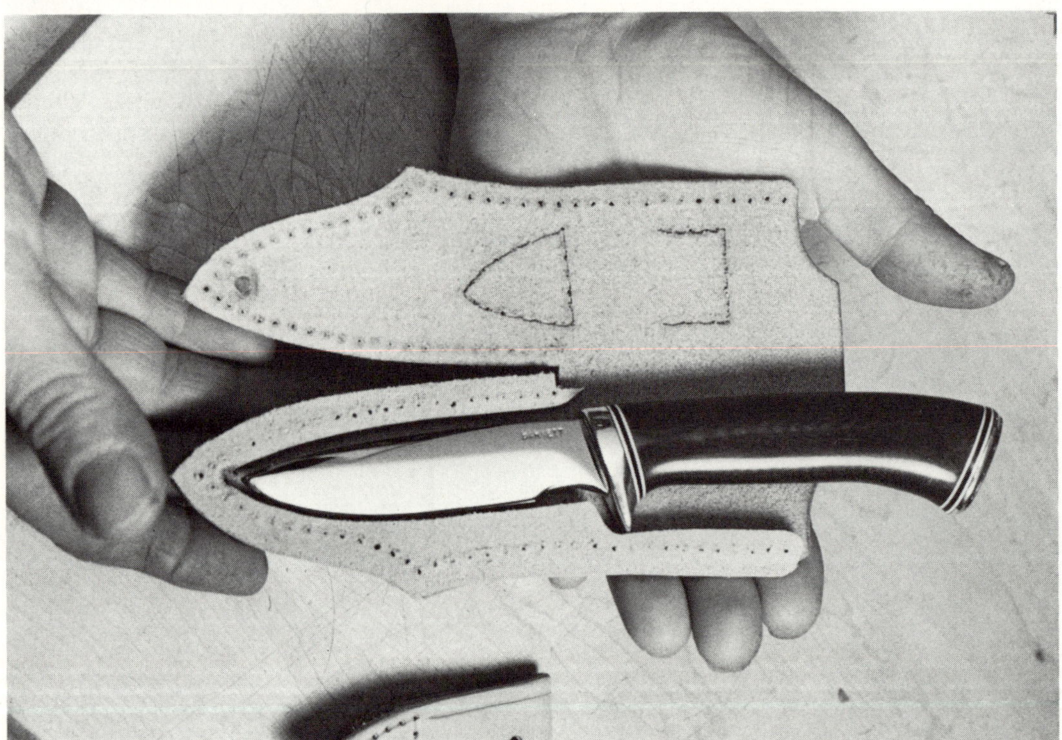

Once the leather and welt are cut, the knife is set in for fit. Note the slight hook where the guard will rest, ensuring that the point won't poke through the bottom of the sheath and cut the welt or threads.

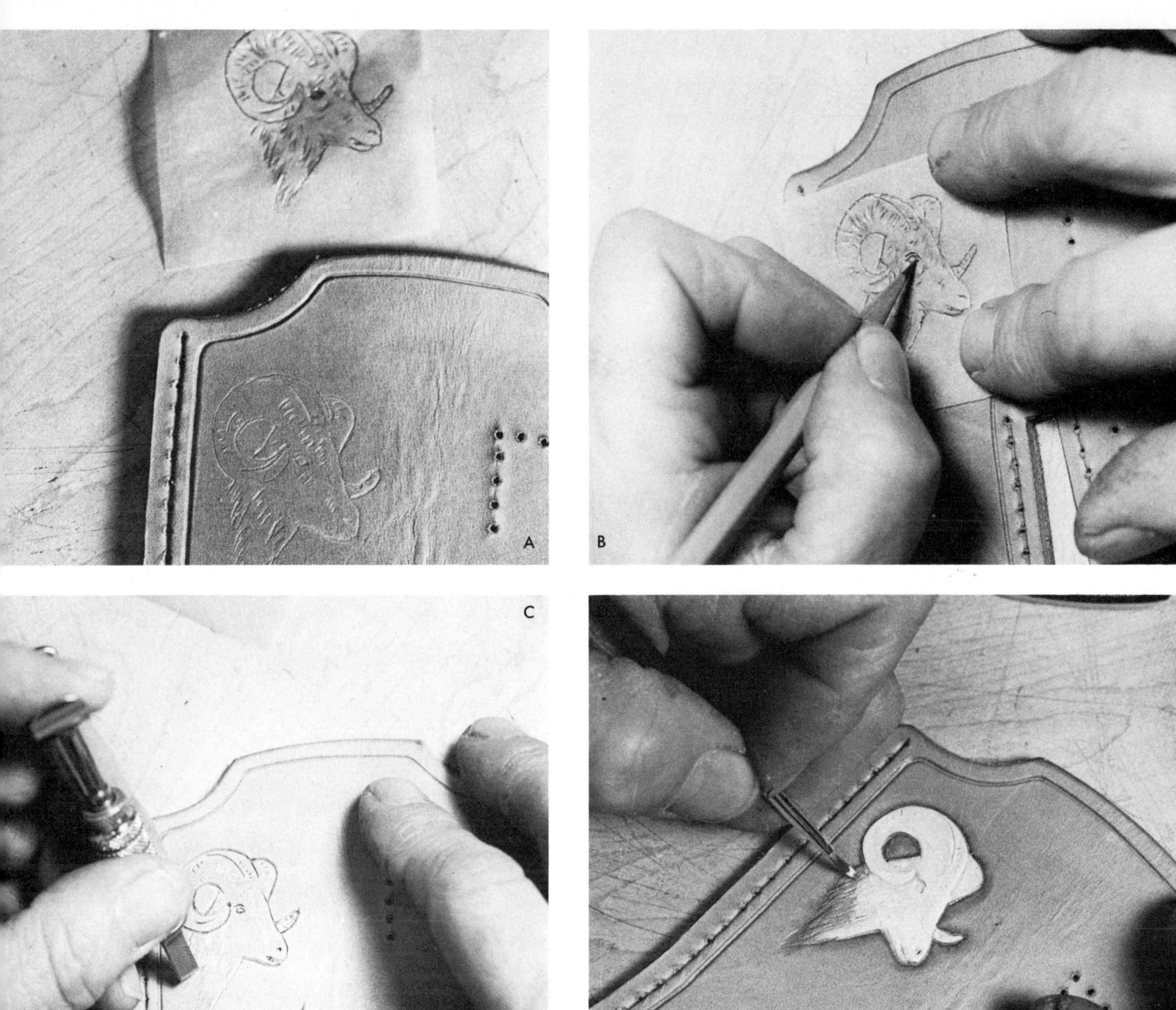

A When the leather is wet, the animal head is transferred with a pencil to the leather.

B Note how well the outline was done with the pencil.

C Now the swivel knife comes into play to carve the head.

D Leather dye is applied with a small brush. Little detail work is done since the stain, to be applied next, will add texture to the head.

A selection of fine sheaths crafted by Jack Barnett.

stove. Rotate it constantly so as not to scorch the leather. The heat will allow the mixture to be drawn into the fibers slowly and thoroughly. Place a piece of foil in the oven and set the sheath on it. With the oven not over 170°, leave it for fifteen or twenty minutes. A knife can now be inserted to ascertain whether the fit is still correct. If it is, set the sheath aside to dry. Incidentally, if there are any blobs of wax, remove them with a toothpick. *Don't* use a knife for this because there is the danger of scratching or scraping the leather. Always clean the knife to remove any moisture. This finish is serviceable and should any marks scratch the surface just use a good paste wax and buff the leather. This will put it back in tip-top condition.

Barnett doesn't claim this is the best type of sheath for every style of knife, but it is certainly the best for him. He likes the convenience of a pouch-type sheath without straps dangling from it. And it is one of the most beautiful scabbards for a working knife we've ever seen.

CHAPTER NINE

Jerry Ashton
"Western Craftsman"

Like many fine leatherworkers, Jerry Ashton was born and bred on a ranch in southwestern Nebraska and, like all ranchers, he soon learned to do his own repair work. His dad, figuring there was never a day so bad where you couldn't do a little saddle repair, gave this chore to young Jerry.

Later, when Ashton moved to Denver, he got into the automobile business. He became such a success he eventually sold out and retired at an age when most men are beginning to worry about their careers.

Asked why he took up leatherwork, Ashton replied, "In self defense." He wasn't kidding, either. "I did leatherwork as therapy, as a relief, as a way of letting down at the end of a day of dealing with the public—who could drive you up the wall at times."

The more Ashton became involved with leatherwork, the more fascinating he found it. "Most of the early requests for my work were from detectives, narcotic agents, and Treasury people," Jerry told me. "They wanted something special in a gun holster and, more important, quality, which they couldn't seem to find in the local hardware store or gun shop." Today, a dozen or so years later, Jerry Ashton is still an amateur at heart, yet one who does professional work. Aside from gun holsters, many finished with Mexican edge-lacing, he does saddlebags, knife sheaths (the latter exclusively for California knifemaker Jess Horn), rifle cases, and just about anything else that can be made of leather.

Ashton is one of those unique people who can pick and choose his customers. Fortunately he doesn't need the work and can be more selective than usual. Jerry won't ever rush a job. He works with great care in a beautifully appointed leather shop in his basement, surrounded by paintings of Indians and regalia of the Old West.

JERRY ASHTON

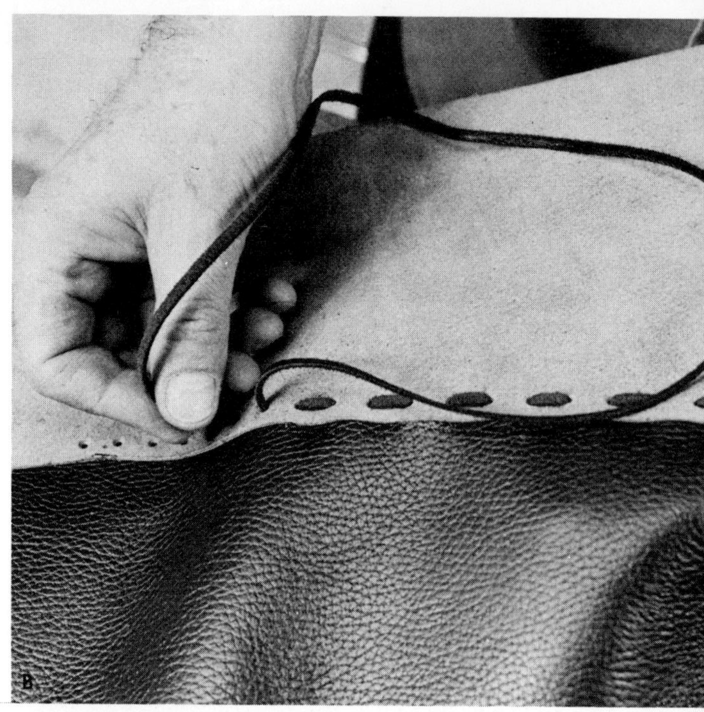

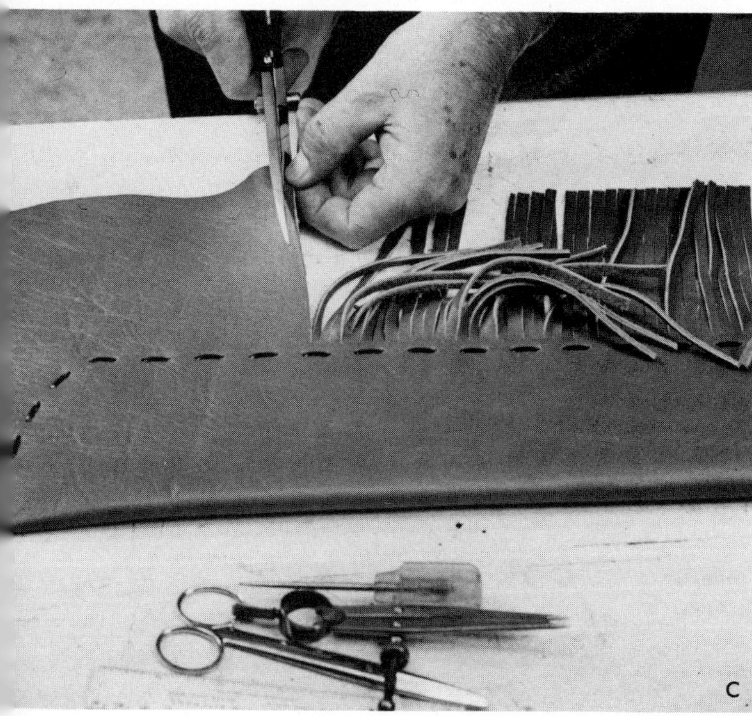

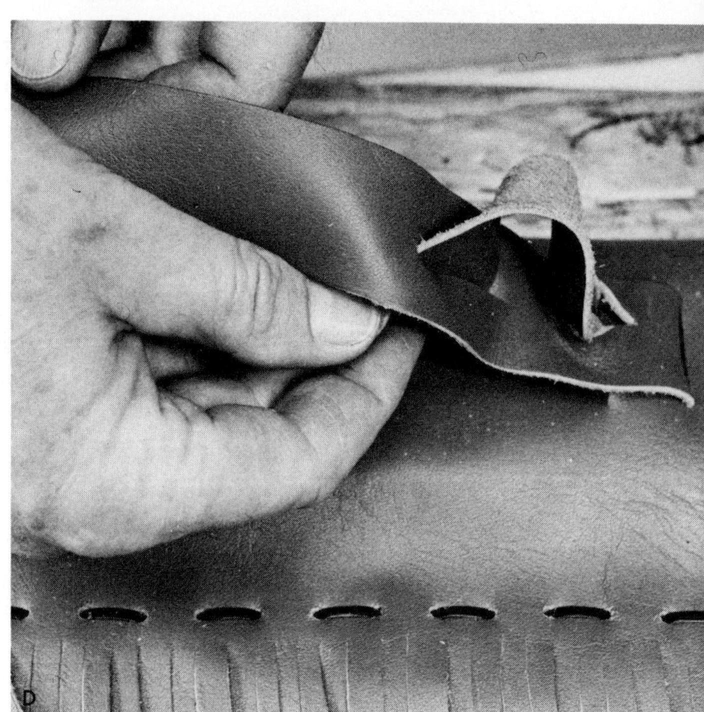

A Ashton, beginning his arrow quiver, measures about 5″ less than the length of the arrows.

B Close-up of the type of stitching used. The lacing thong is goatskin.

C Scissors are used for cutting the fringe.

D The shoulder strap is cut and tied on without additional lacing.

An arrow quiver can be crafted even by the neophyte worker. It's made of chap leather and is a bit softer than normal. Usually the best method of selecting leather is to go to a good leather shop and tell them what you want to make and ask for their suggestions.

A stiffer quiver might have been made from 9/10-ounce hide. It can even be tooled and laced for a fancy job. Although this is a much simpler quiver than others, it will show the aspiring leatherworker the routine in making a basic quiver. The best way to proceed is to lay down an arrow for measuring purposes and make the quiver four or five inches shorter to enable the arrows to be grasped quickly. As with the Indian-type rifle sheath, a buck stitch is used. The shoulder thongs or straps are fastened by cutting two slips and running the strap through. One end of the strap is slit to run the thong back on itself and the other is caught in a left-locking slit. The accompanying pictures are self-explanatory.

Ashton's advice on learning leatherwork is: "There ain't no place to go." By this he means that it is largely self-taught. True, there are leathercraft schools where one may learn the fundamentals of using tools and how to stitch or lace, but when it comes to learning how to make saddle bags, chaps, holsters, knife sheaths, camera cases, tapaderos, or headstalls, it's really a self-taught school of trial and error.

Perhaps the most important thing is to find somebody who is willing to teach these skills, and once the new craftsman has moved beyond wallets or key cases, he will then be able to create his own visions of beauty in leather.

Ashton proudly shows off the completed arrow quiver.

The leather Jerry uses for a gun holster is oak-tanned, not oil-treated. The weight should be a minimum of 9/10-ounce for the weight of the gun shown. The pattern can be made from a shopping bag or a piece of wrapping paper. Solid advice, as always, is to make it slightly larger than may be required because when the leather is dampened and the gun fit, it may be necessary to take it up for a snugger fit. Ashton usually measures his stitch line a quarter inch in from the edge and centers it a quarter of an inch apart. A Speedy Stitcher is used with nylon thread to stitch the wet leather. The gun is worked in until it fits properly, then removed and dried. The stitched holster is set aside to dry until the next morning. Up to this point no welt has been stitched in.

The next morning the holster should be dry and hard. It will give a solid sound when rapped with the fingers and, in fact, should sound like a piece of wood. Next, the stitching is taken out and the welt is cut. The welt is that piece of leather which fits between both edges of the holster. Before anything else is done, the flat holster is turned over and a decision is made as to the proper placement of the belt loop. The angle is important since there are various requirements between professional and amateur gun toters. When the belt loop is fastened, it is usually stitched with a 3/16″ stitch. It should be stitched in from the edge as well, since this seems to make a neat row and holds the loop well. Now the holster is turned over and the welt is cemented in and allowed to dry. Ashton, like Jack Barnett, uses a drill for the holes and selects one that corresponds with the size of the lacing. These holes are drilled, by the way, through the same stitch holes that were used for the form fitting the day before. The stitch used for the holster is called a back stitch. The holes are alternated or skipped and the end result is typical of the Spanish or Mexican lacing so popular in Mexico and the Southwest. The lacing used here is calfskin although other types may be used. In this instance, however, calfskin is a lot tougher and comes in different thicknesses. Once this lacing is done, the holster can be dyed any color.

When the holster is finished, it is treated with Fiebing's oil treatment, which is a combination of lanolin and silicon. It doesn't soften the leather. The worst thing you can do to any piece of leather, Jerry emphasizes strongly, is put too much oil on. After a couple of light applications, a fine wax is used to seal the pores. Jerry says, "I use Johnson's Paste Floor Wax, but anything can be used such as any fine saddle wax." When the holster gets scuffed up, just clean it with a light coat of saddle soap and put another application of wax on it. Use light coats and buff it well. This helps remove scratches from briars and branches and puts it in brand new condition. One additional thing can be put on the holster and this is a hammer thong. A hammer thong covers the hammer of a single action gun to prevent the gun from tumbling out when hunting.

Everyone knows a saddle bag is carried on the rear of the saddle; however, today's modern traveler can use one for a ditty bag. Saddle bags make excellent conversation pieces. Moreover, they are spacious and comfortable to carry over the shoulder because of their design. Those who have been weaned on Western films know that the cowboy carried all his personal items in one of these large bags. I've used them for carrying cameras, film, and lenses in the field. Aboard aircraft, I find that carrying things in my saddle bag leaves both hands free for handling tickets and passports.

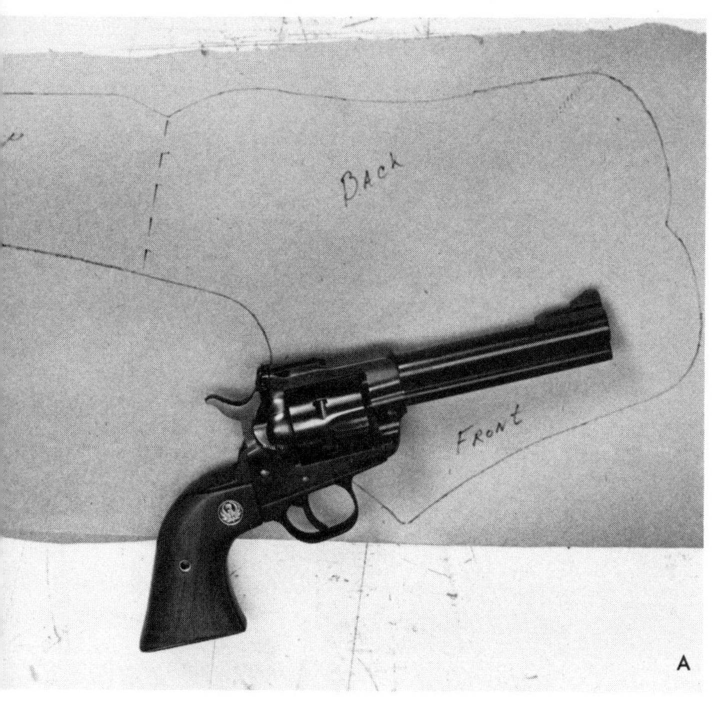

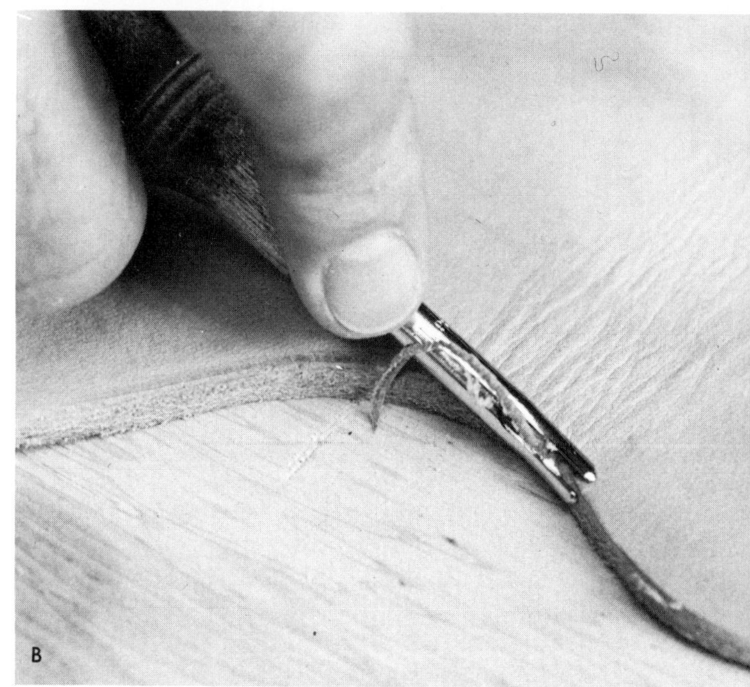

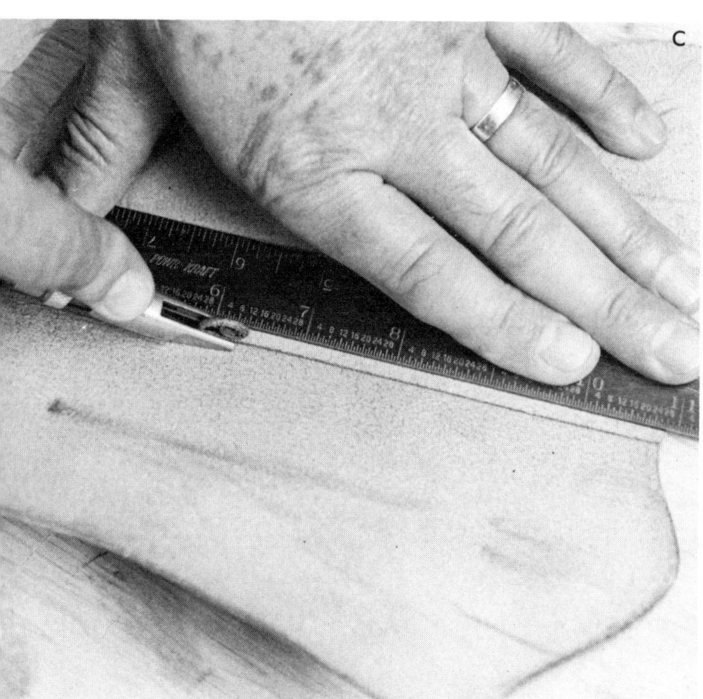

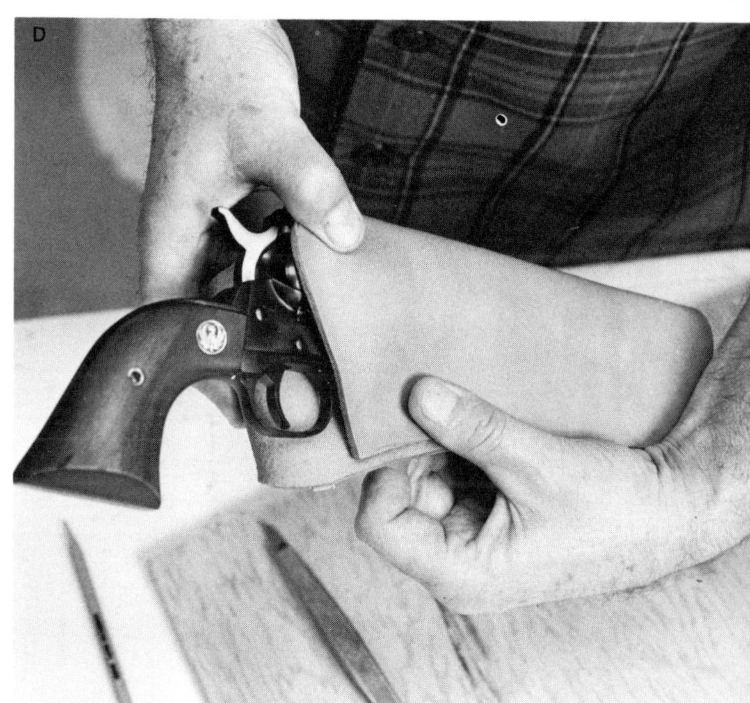

A A drawing of the pattern, showing the parts of the holster that will be cut from one piece of leather.

B A beveler is used to trim all around the exposed edges for a professional appearance.

C The center fold is creased for an easy fold. A steel ruler is used to run a straight line.

D Once the leather is cut and trimmed, the gun is set inside to judge the proper fit. Note that the welt has not been cut or set in.

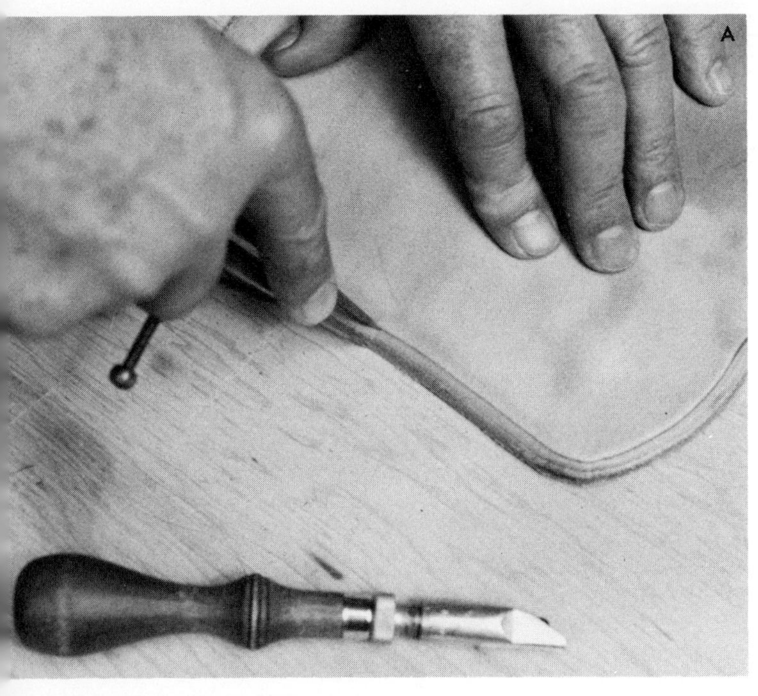

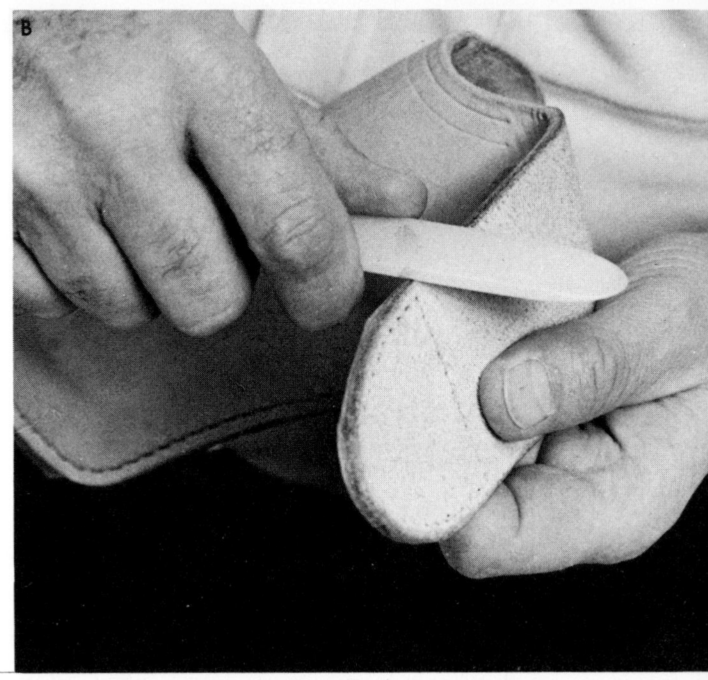

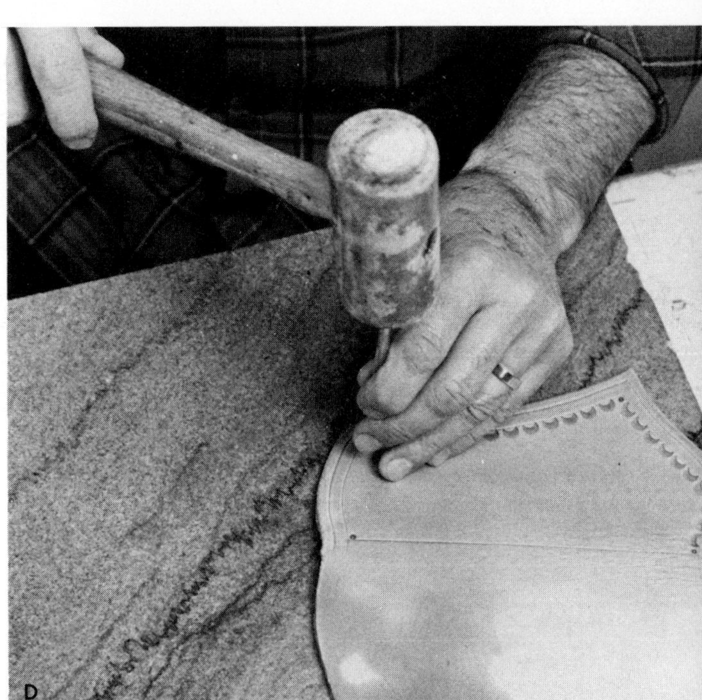

A The divider is again used to mark the stitching line as well as the border for basketstamping.

B Before sewing the belt, loop edges are boned to make them smooth.

C A stitching awl is used to lock stitch the loop to the back.

D The border is next stamped on after dampening the leather.

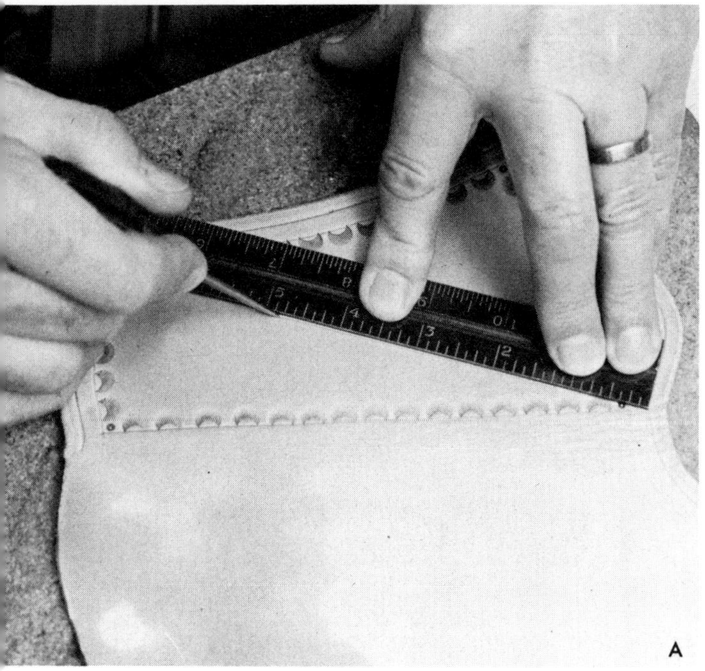

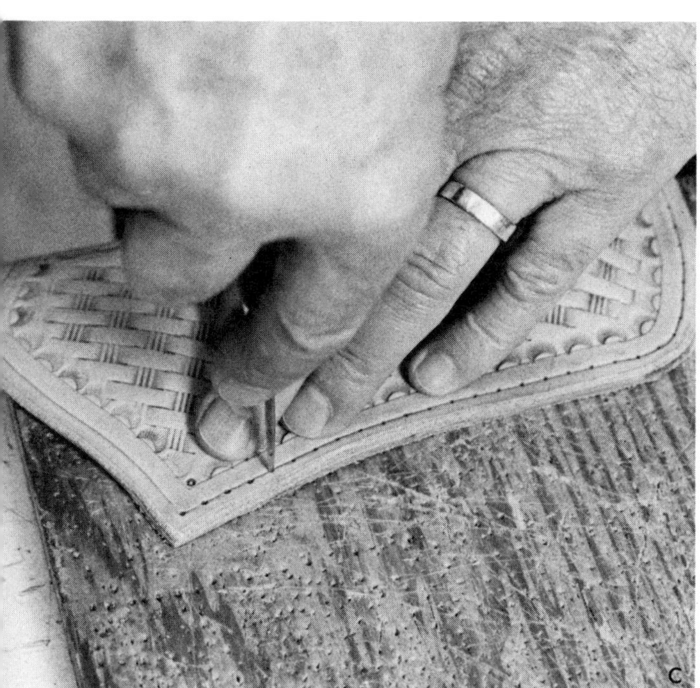

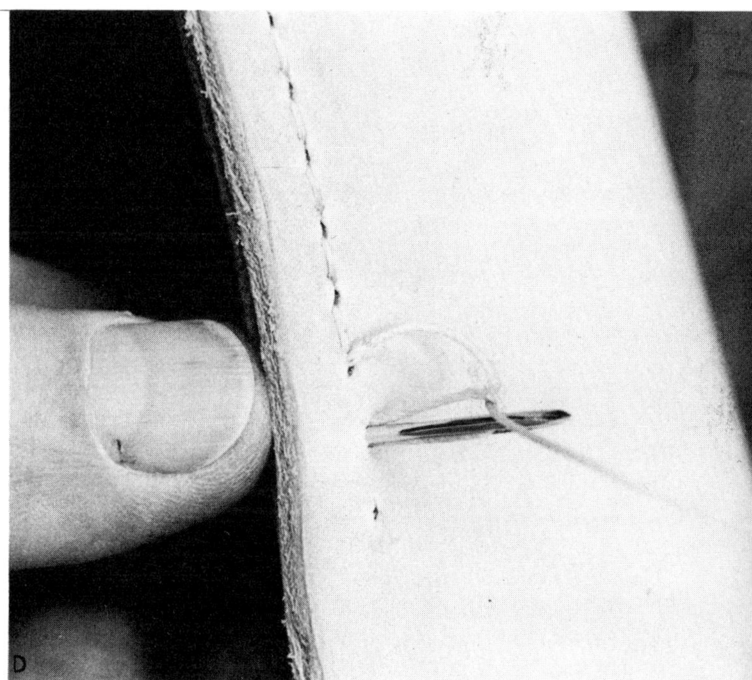

A Again the ruler is used to mark the center angle in order to keep the basketstamping running straight.

B The basketstamping partially completed.

C Once the stamping is done the stitch or lace holes are forced through with an awl.

D Here Ashton departs from the usual technique of crafting a holster. The holster is stitched with thread, without the welt, and the gun is then fit to the wet leather.

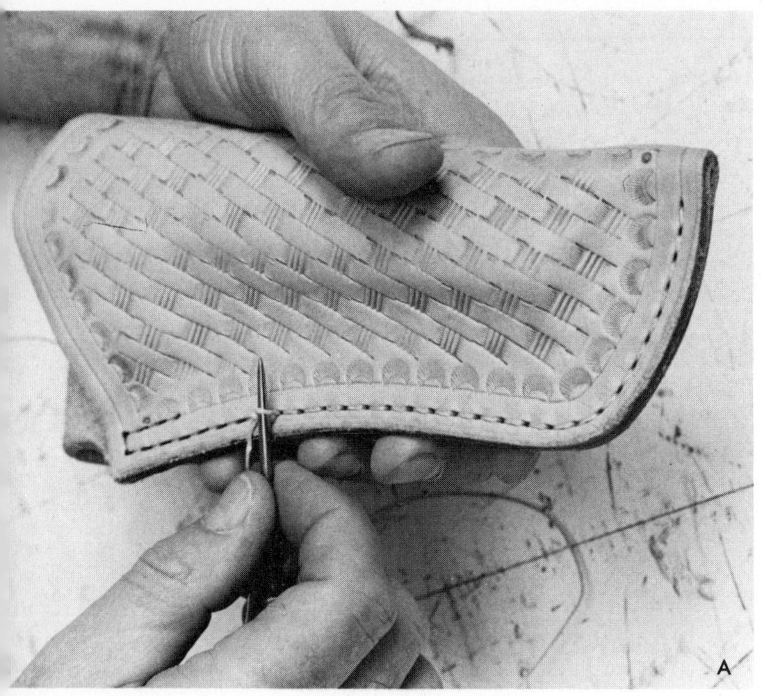
A

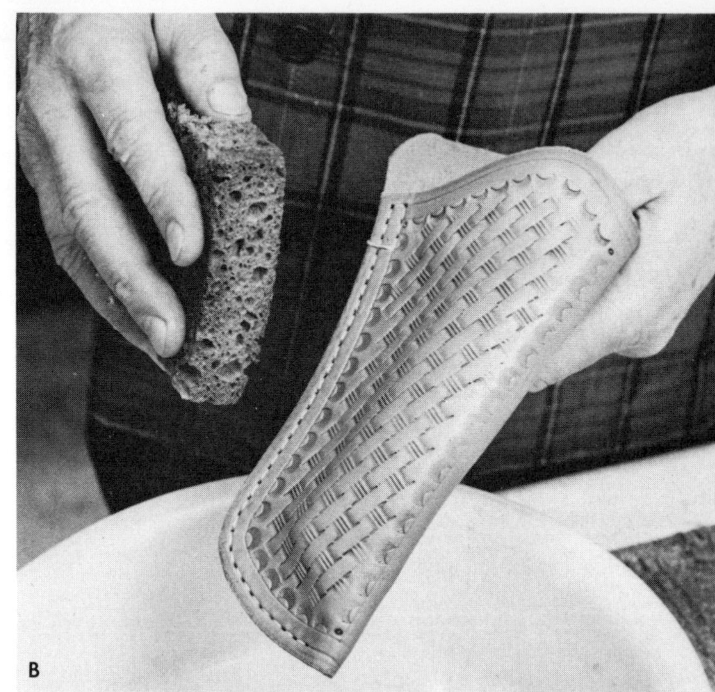
B

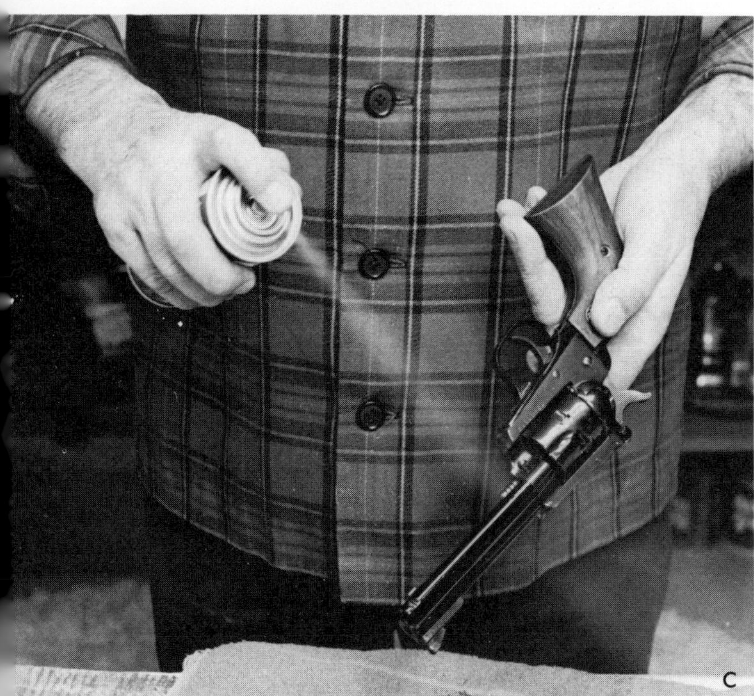
C

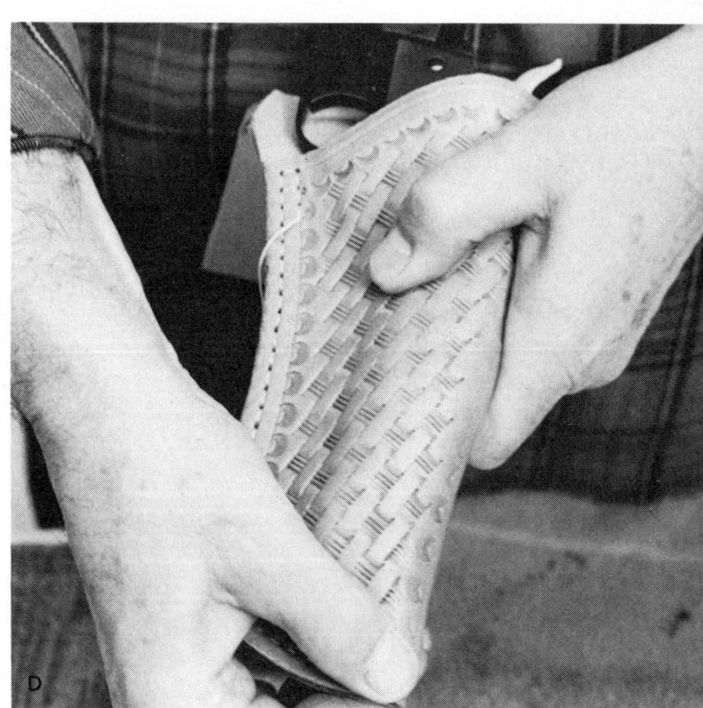
D

A Pulling up the stitches tightly. An awl is best for this operation.

B The holster is thoroughly dampened.

C Then the gun is sprayed with a protective oil.

D With the gun in place, the holster is worked with the fingers and allowed to dry overnight. Incidentally, the gun does not remain in the holster, but is removed and thoroughly dried.

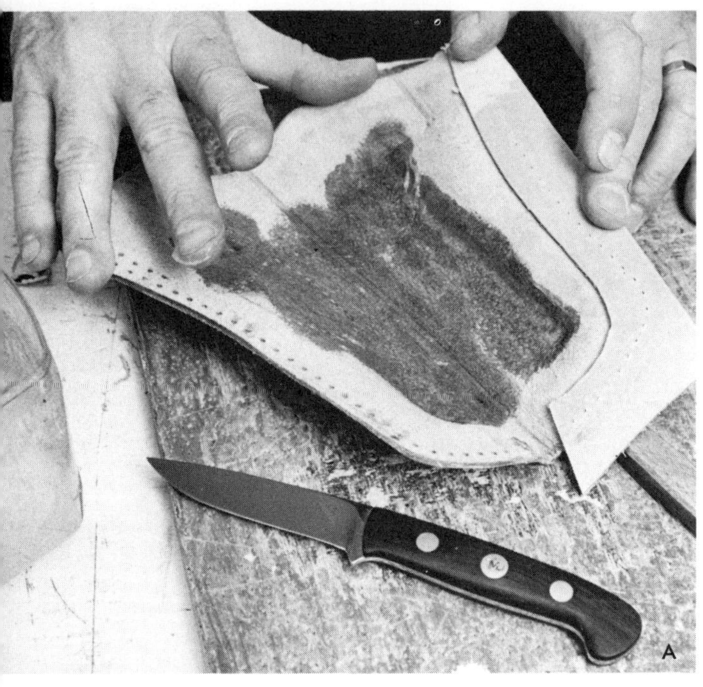

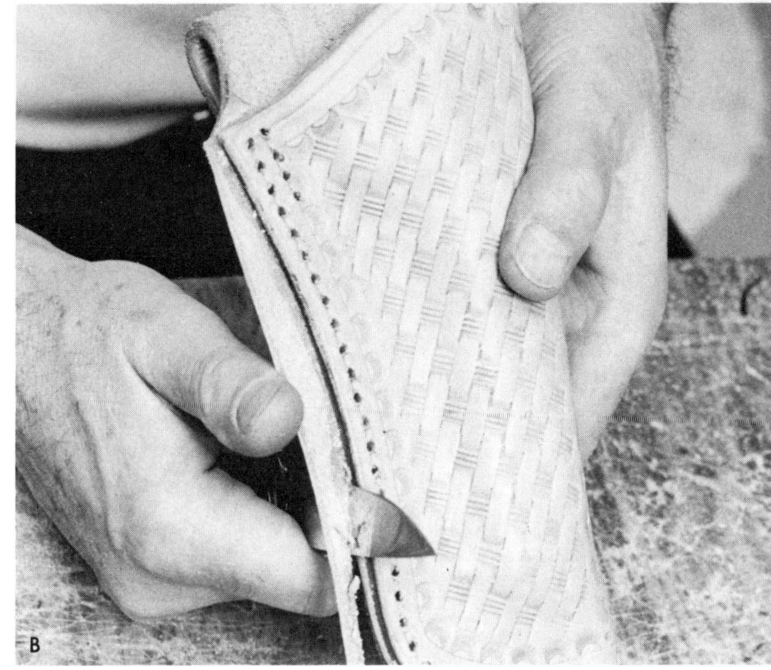

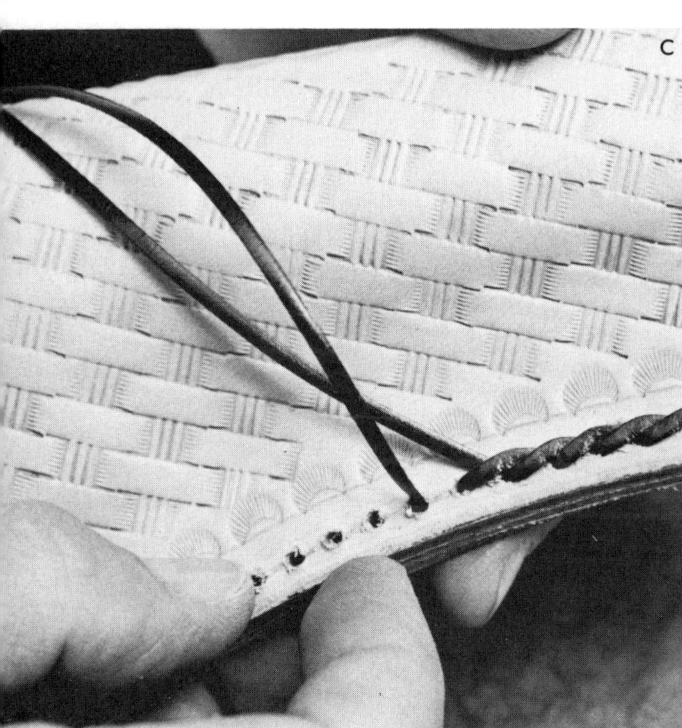

A Next morning, the stitches are removed and the fold area coated with a leather compound to aid the crease in remaining exactly in place. Note the welt, already punched for lacing, is now set in place after being coated with Barge Cement.

B After the welt is set, excess material is trimmed with a very sharp knife.

C Close-up of the lacing showing the reverse type of lace used.

D End the lacing on back by running under a few loops.

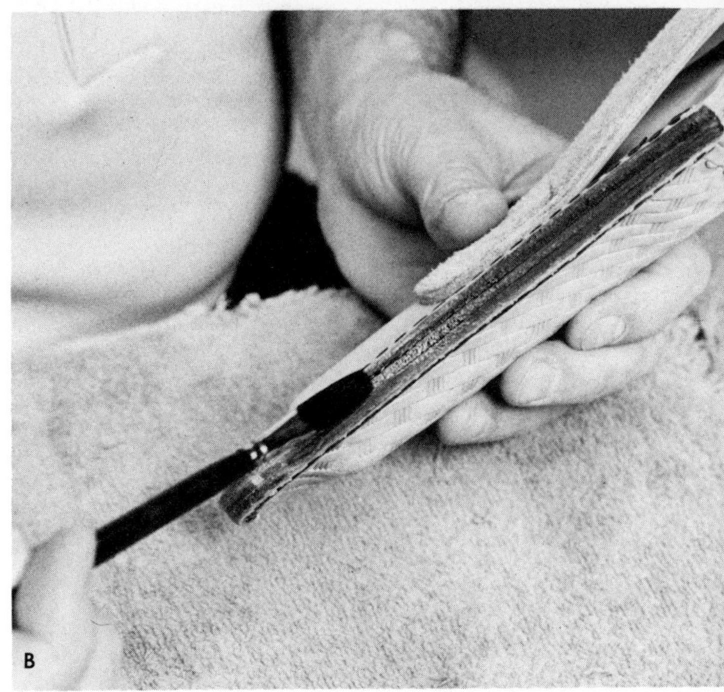

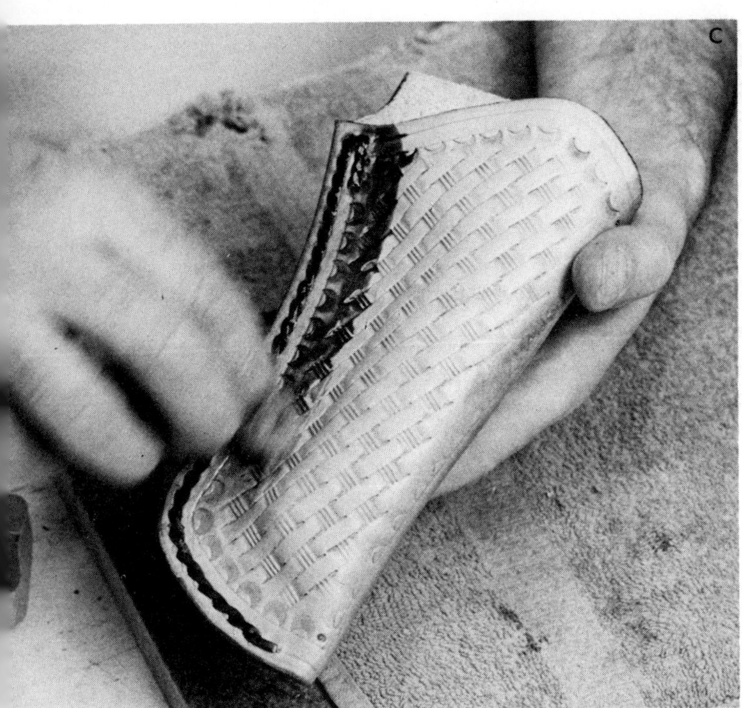

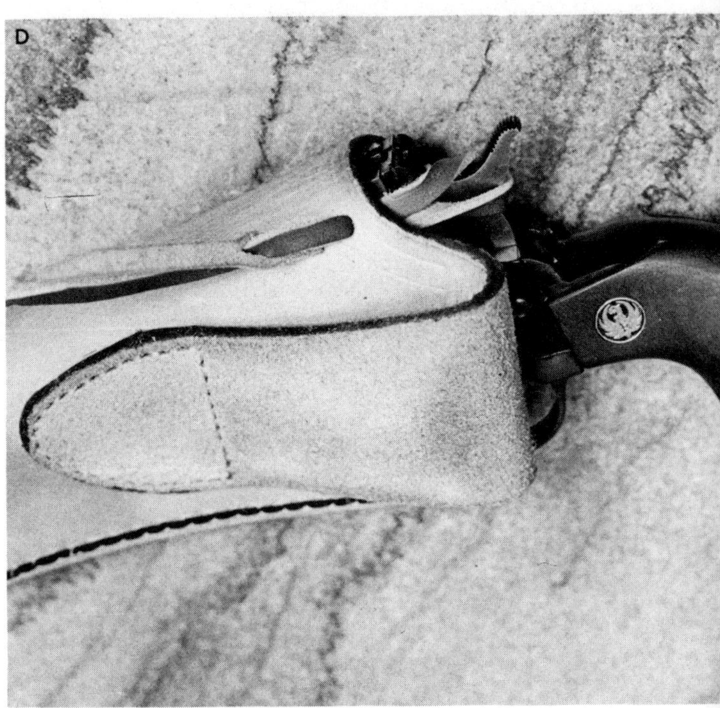

A Once the lacing is done, pound the edge to make it flat and also to make certain the cement is adhering properly.

B Dark dye is brushed along the edge for contrast.

C Wax is rubbed over the entire holster. As it is rubbed in, it will lighten the color and give protection.

D The final step is to place a thong onto the holster to tie over the hammer. This prevents the gun from being pulled out or falling out while riding or running.

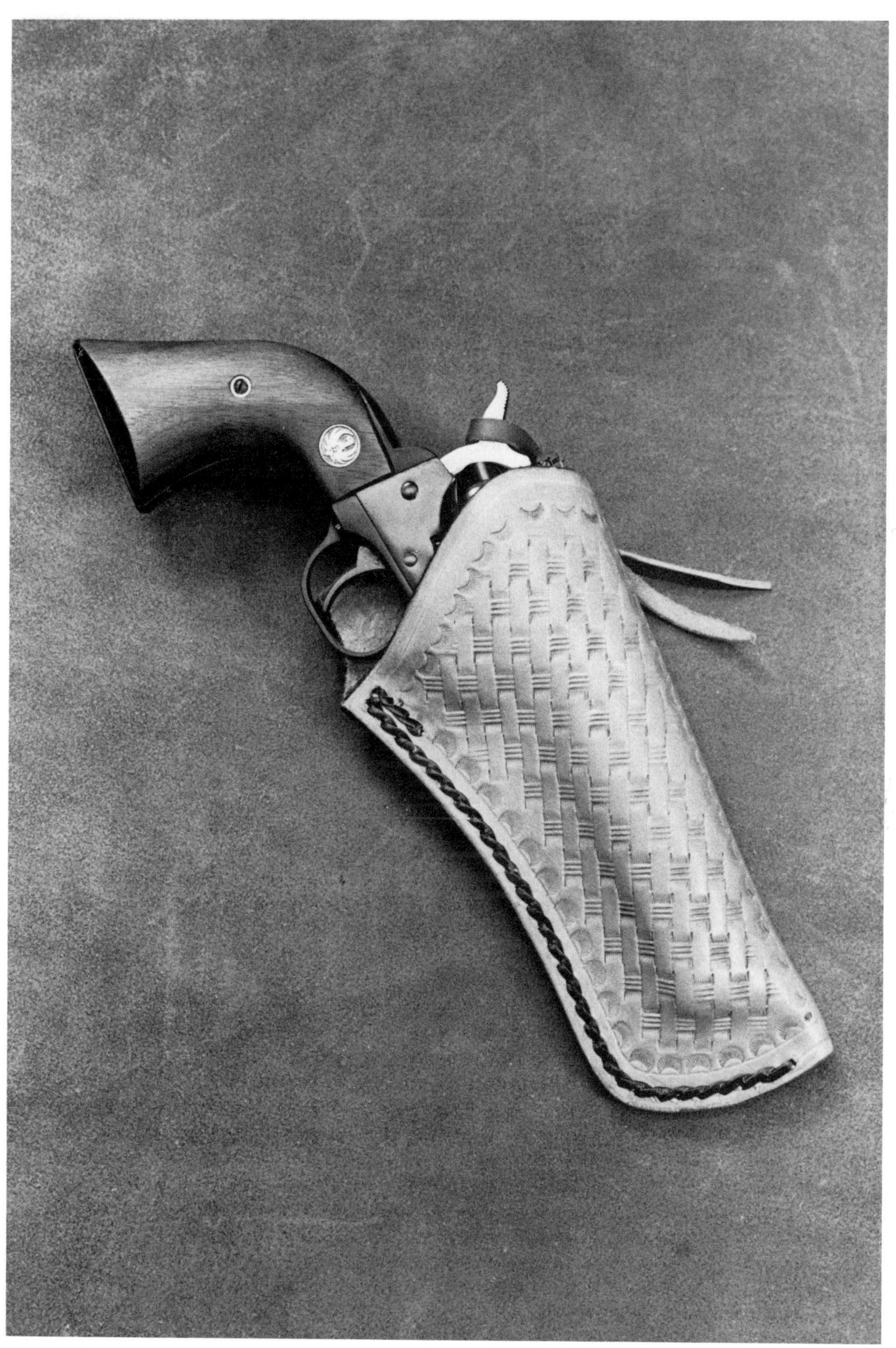

The finished holster with gun in place.

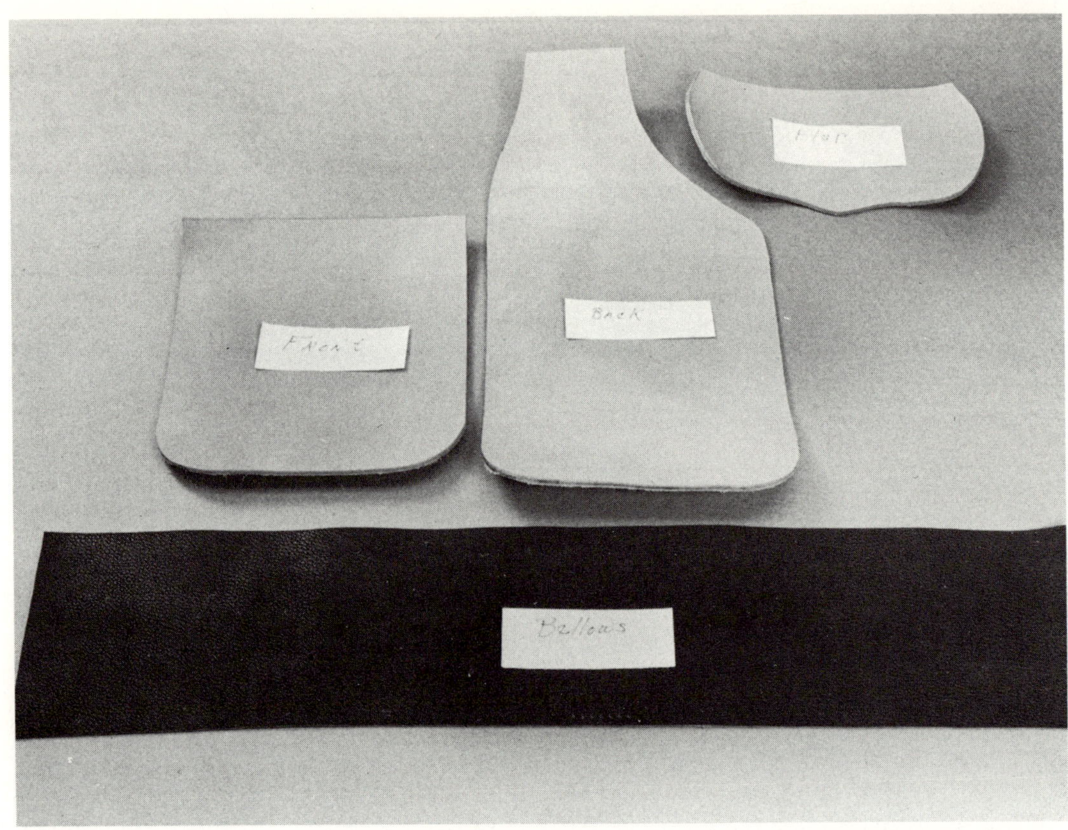

The saddle bag requires a few pieces, but demands considerable patience with both basketstamping and Mexican edge-lacing.

Crafting a Saddle Bag

The bags crafted by Jerry Ashton are simply made from three pieces—the back, the bellows, and the flap. The back is cut of one piece of $^{8}/_{9}$-ounce leather. The bellows—that piece which opens up to receive all those odds and ends—is usually crafted from a piece of latigo leather. It is very flexible and light in weight. The saddle bags are laced together with calfskin thongs and usually Spanish lace is used. This type of lace does two things: it binds the two pieces of leather together (the back to the bellows), and it also finishes the edge.

The bag is tooled with a small basket stamp. Although it is an extremely tedious task, a smaller size of stamp looks more attractive on a saddle bag than a larger one. The finish is again lanolin and silicon. Note, however, that these particular saddle bags are *not* treated with wax. The reason for this being that these bags are not intended for use on a horse. If so treated and swung over the shoulder, the oil would soil one's clothing. Ashton's suggestion is to leave them perfectly natural and use some sort of a waterproofing spray like Rain and Stain. If they are not so treated, every smudge and stain would discolor the leather.

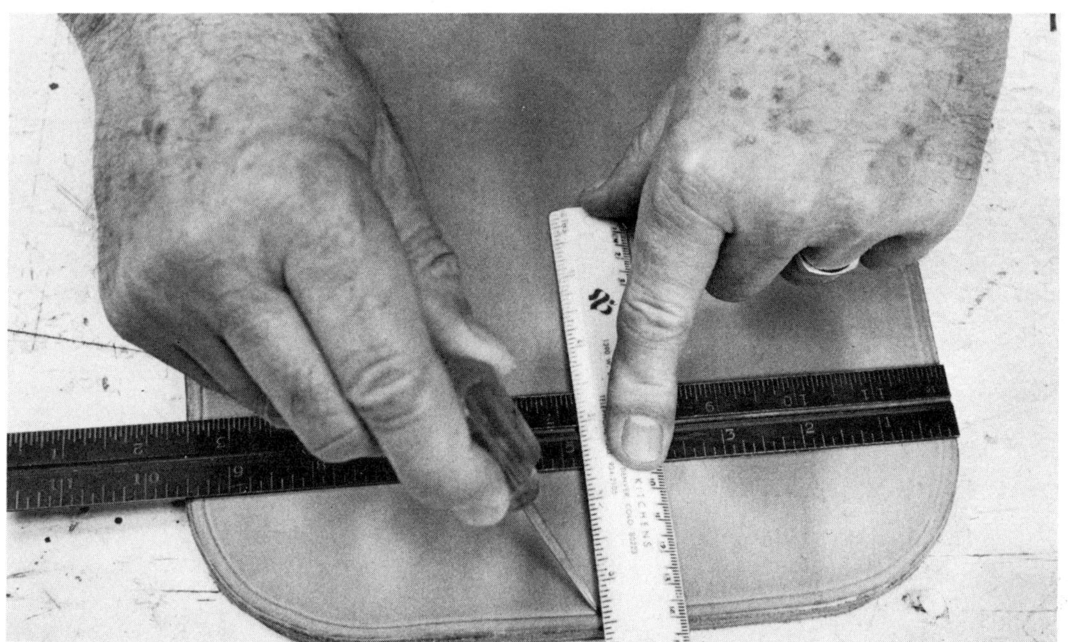

As with Walter Kneubuhler's possible bag, the exact center must be marked. Note the stitching line already put on with dividers.

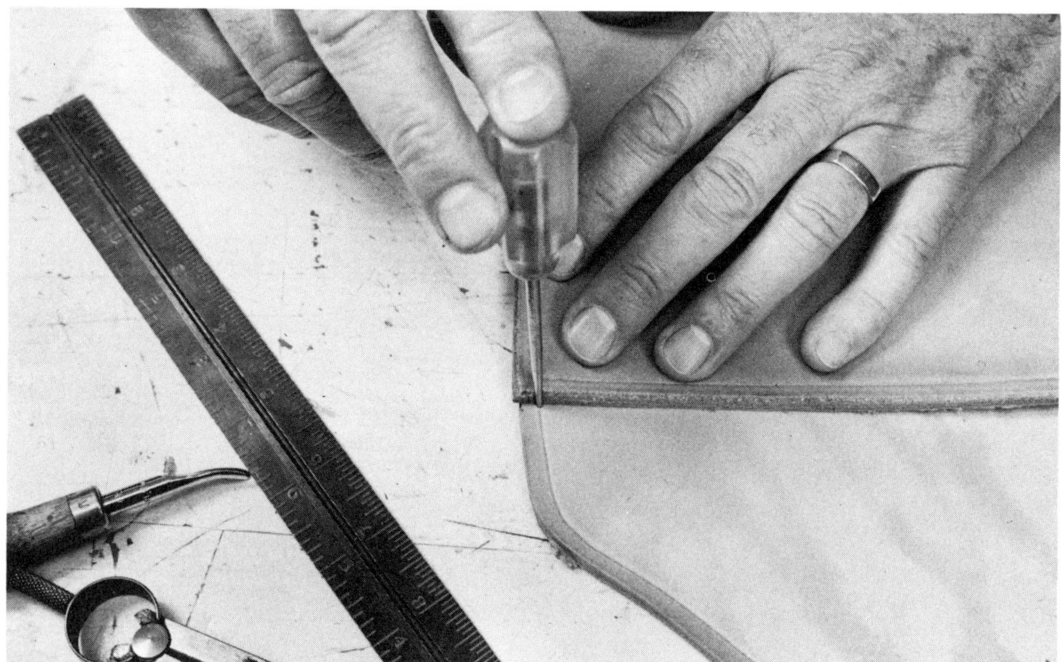

A small awl is being used to bring the line even with the pouch.

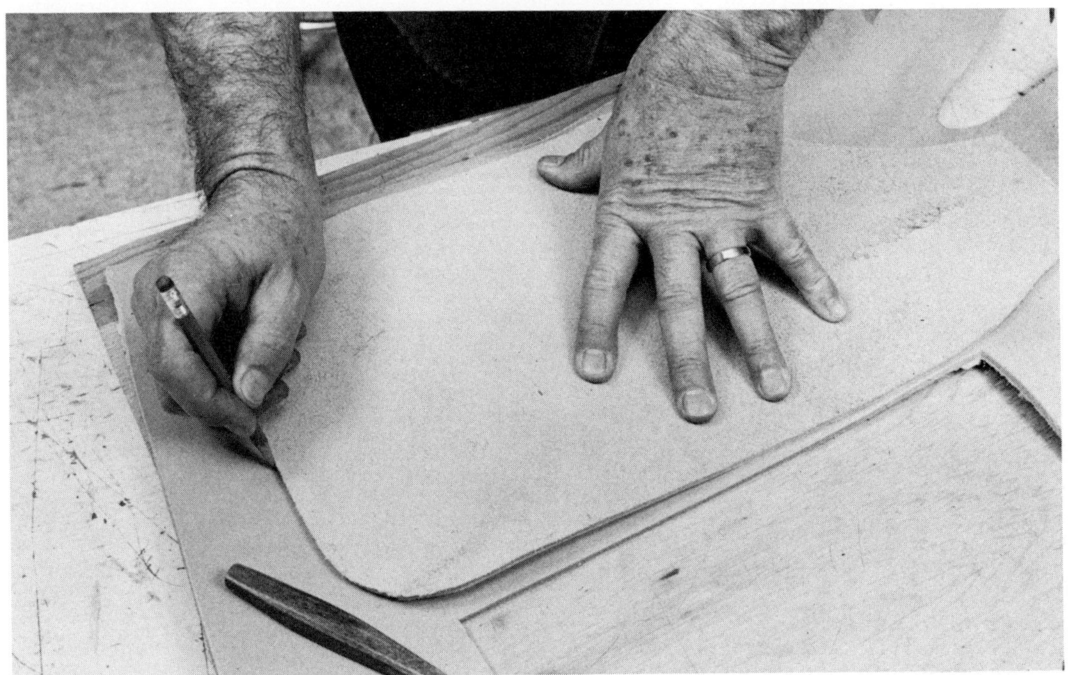

Before assembly, a matching piece is cut and the outline is already being drawn for the opposite side.

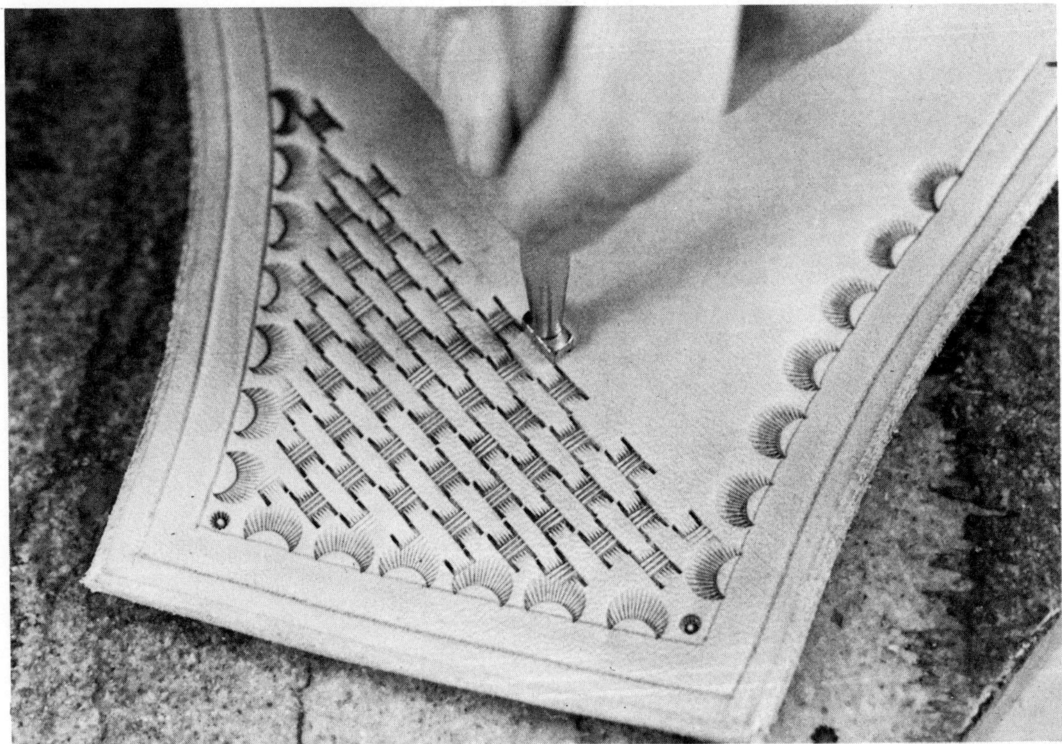

Basketstamping is begun. Although a larger size stamp is being used here, a smaller stamp will prove to be more attractive.

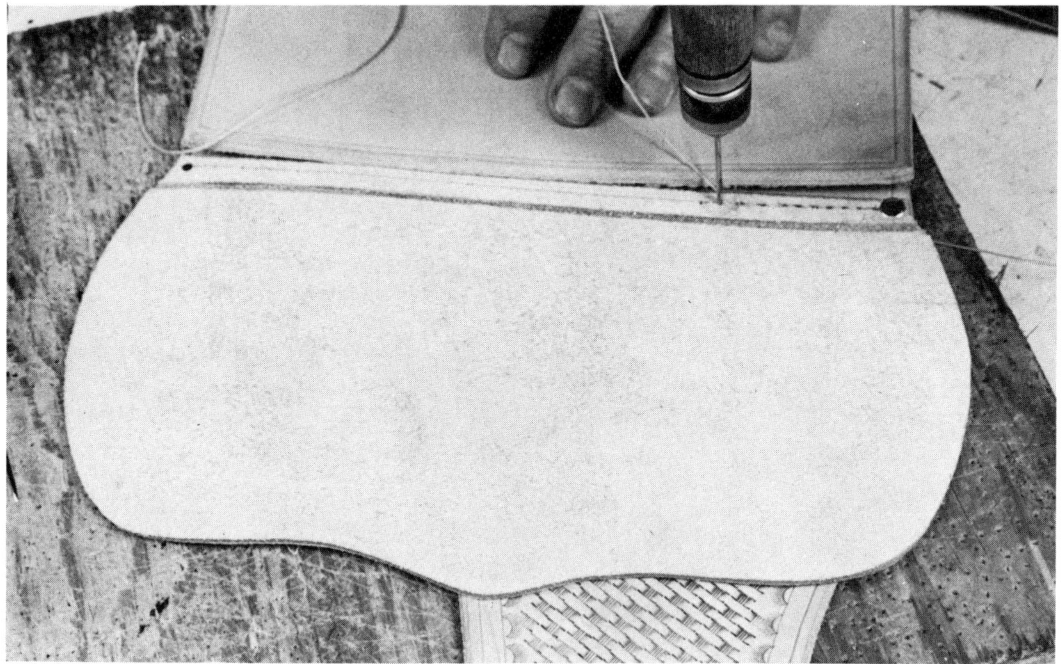

Here the sewing is done to fasten the two backs together. Notice the wooden board to allow forcing the stitching awl through the leather.

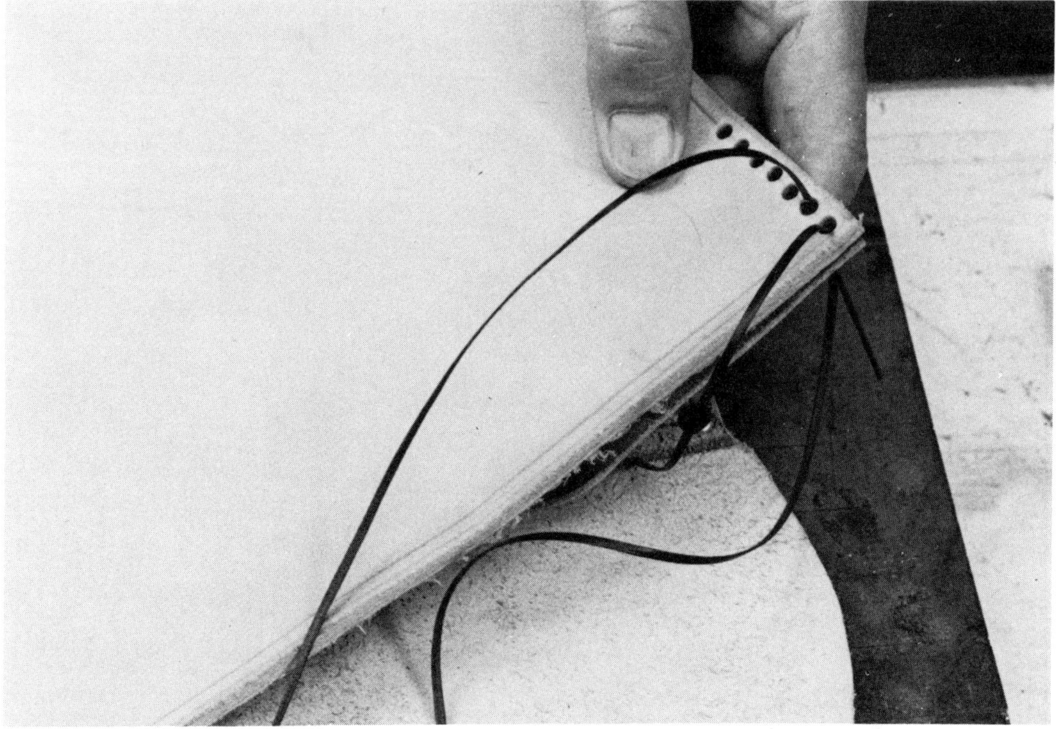

The Mexican style edge lacing is begun. It will not only fasten the leather sides and bellows together, but will also finish the edge without additional work.

Close-up of the technique used in this type of lacing.

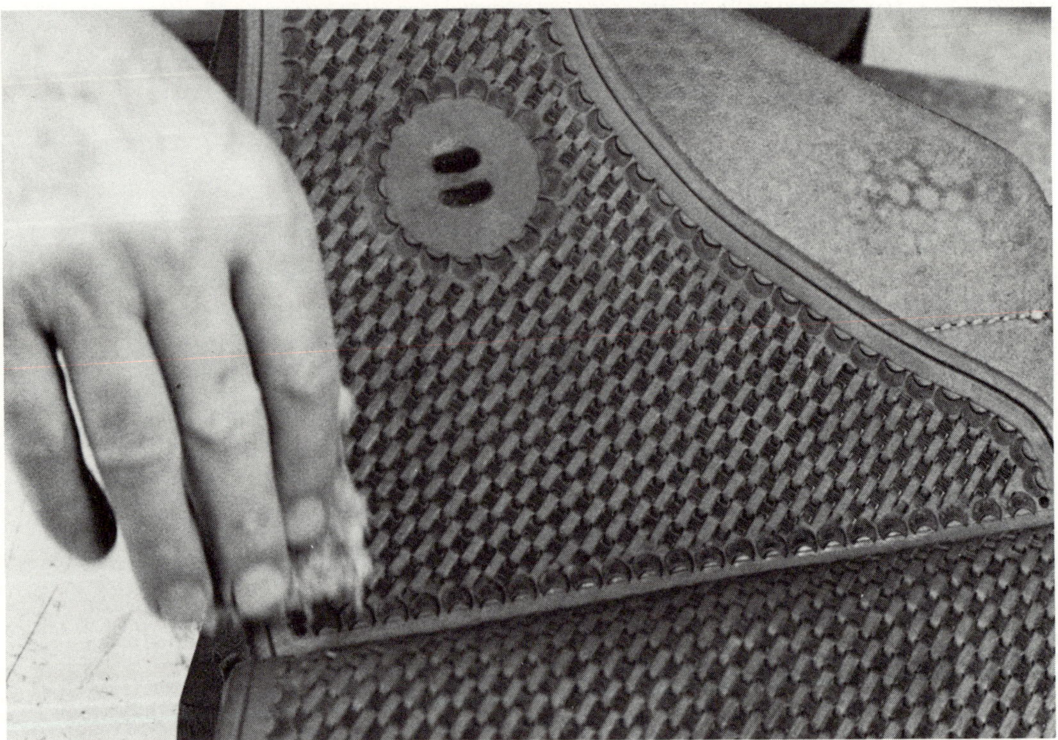

The completed saddle bag being touched up with a finishing wax. The tie strap is placed through a cut slot and then fastened with a rivet. The upper rosette in the leather can be used for either a silver concha or thongs to tie to the saddle.

Making a Rifle Sheath

Rifle sheaths, particularly those made to cover old powder-burners or Winchesters, were highly desirable items. The old Indian-style sheaths, decorated as they were with beadwork, eagle feathers, and dangling fringe, can scarcely be found in the West any more. Even if one were found in some small trading post, the price would be prohibitive and it would be classed as an antique—too expensive to carry any gun to a shooting match.

The rifle cover crafted by Jerry Ashton is a replica of a Plains Indian sheath and was made of a heavy weight latigo-type leather. It would probably fall into a 4/5-ounce weight. It is really quite an easy sheath to make. The rifle is laid on the pattern as shown in the accompanying photograph. The stitch is probably the easiest of all the various methods of fastening leather. It is called a buck stitch and simply runs in and out the length of the scabbard, turns slightly upward toward the end, and is then fastened with a back stitch to lock it in place. For purposes of beauty, fringing should be added—in this case the longer the more attractive. The fringe shown is about ¼″ wide and 6 inches long. The beaded rosettes are Indian-made from Arizona. They are affixed by cutting two slits on the sheath and laced through. The lacing then goes through two slits cut in the back of the rosettes. For additional decor, imitation eagle feathers, purchased at Tandy's, are wrapped with a leather thong and fastened in the same manner.

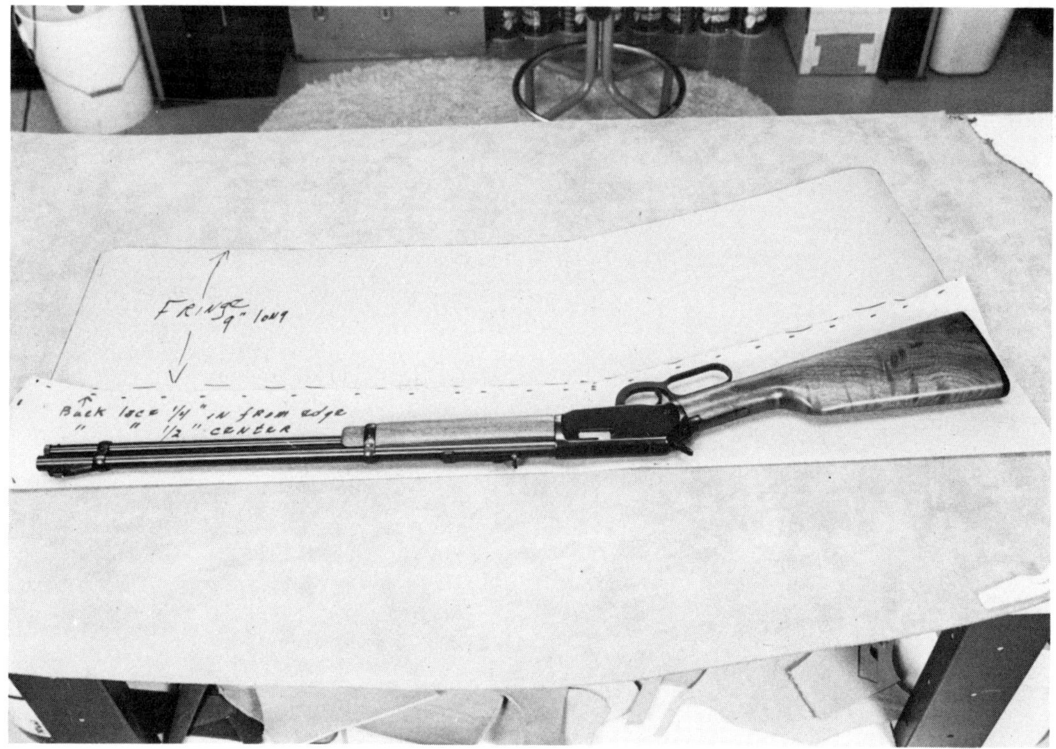

Picture shows pattern drawn on leather. Rifle is set in for comparison; however, this type sheath may be crafted for any length weapon.

This type of rifle scabbard was primarily used by both the Indians and Mountain Men to cover the gun and protect it in inclement weather. It was not made to tie to the saddle, as the true boot scabbard we've all seen in Western films. It was carried across the crook of the arm or across the shoulder and did nothing more than protect the weapon inside.

This simply constructed old-time scabbard makes an excellent den decoration for those who have an affinity for the Old West. It will also dress up those black-powder shooters in the full regalia of the period. For those who want to make more elaborate rifle scabbards, such as those crafted by the Cheyenne, Blackfoot, or Crow Indians, a trip to a museum will amaze the viewer with the beauty of these items. Many are fully covered with beadwork, twelve inch fringe, and the softest and most fragile buckskin.

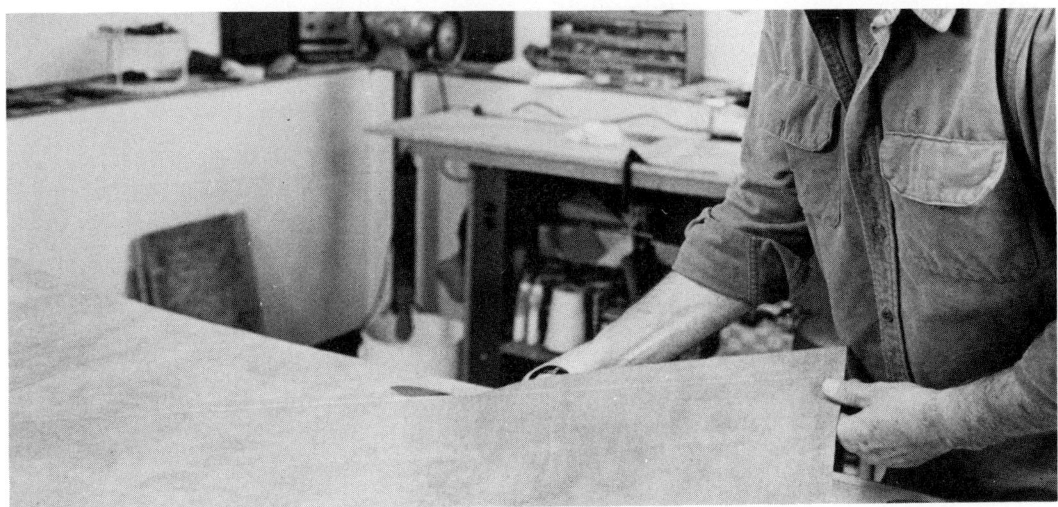

Because of the soft leather, Jerry Ashton uses shears to cut the leather to size.

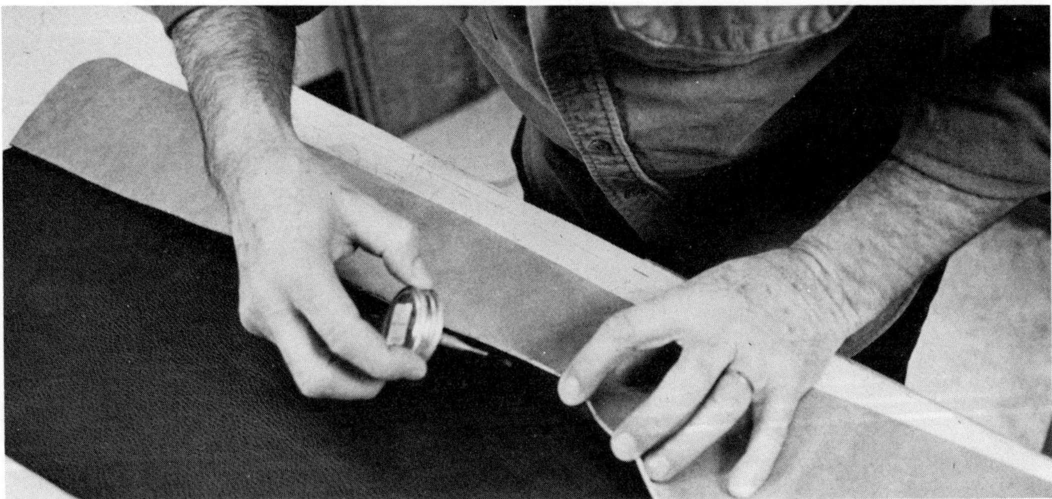

Barge Cement is used to fasten the edges together for lacing.

Ashton uses a steel ruler to measure the holes for buck stitching.

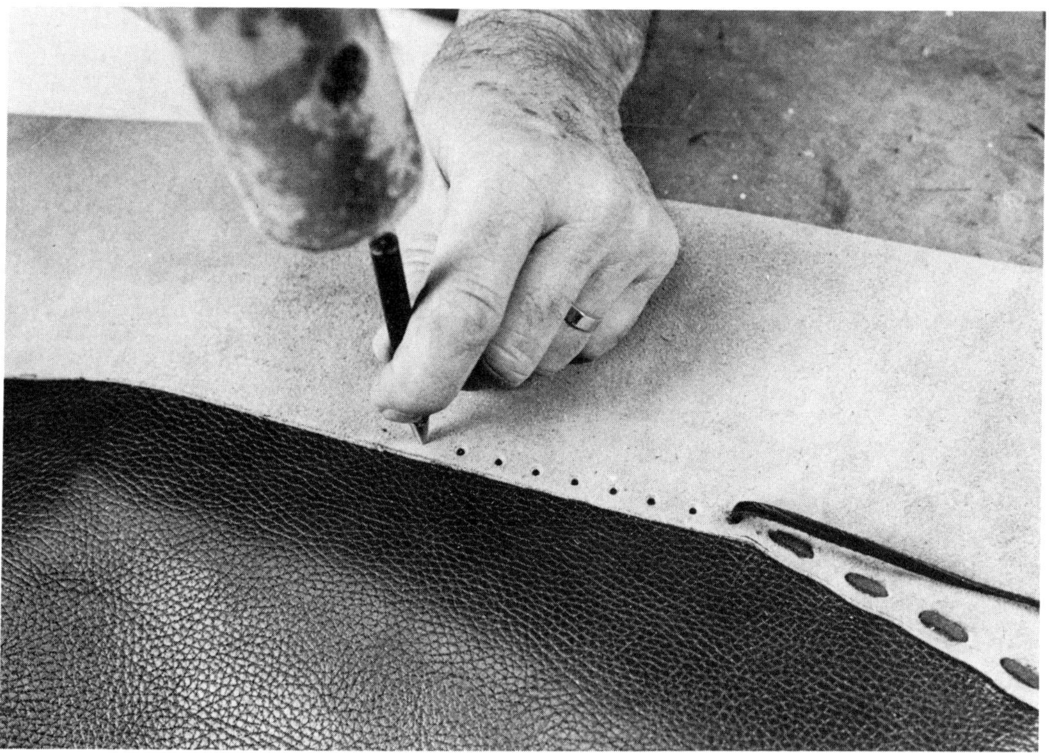

Using a small punch and hammer, Ashton punches holes for stitching.

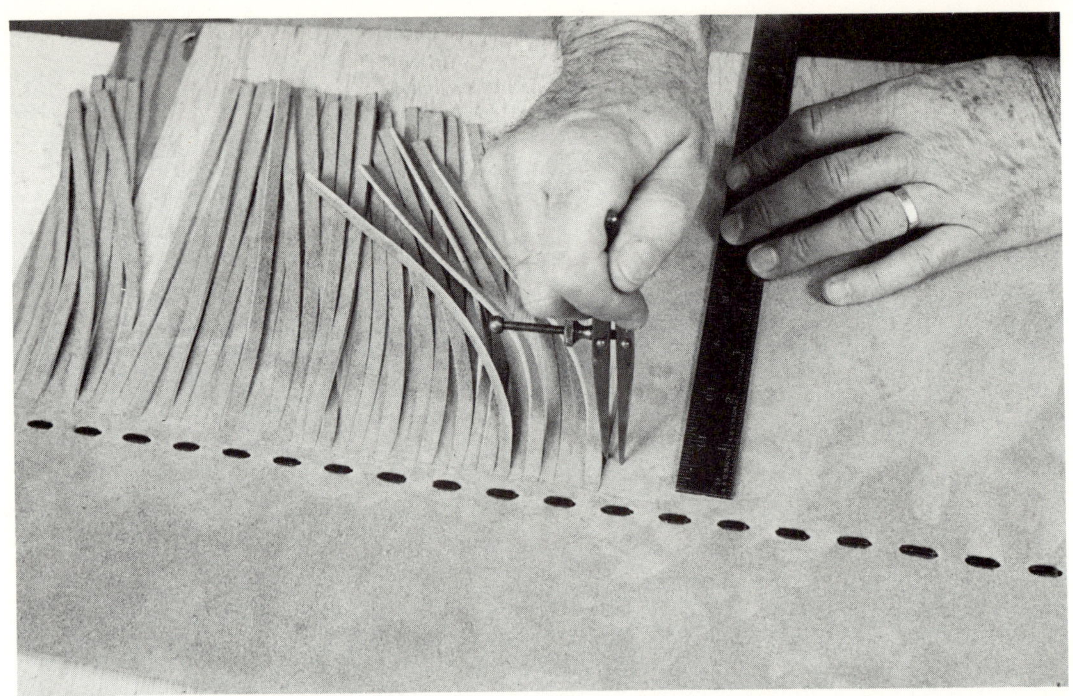

A divider is used to mark the fringe.

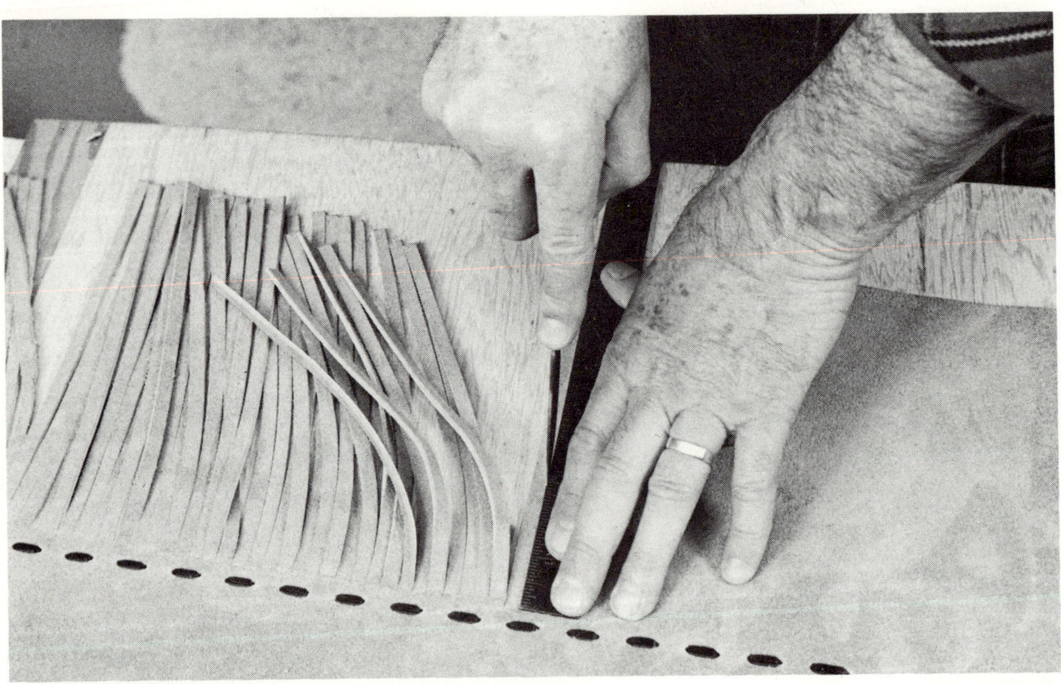

With a steel rule as a guide and a sharp knife the fringe is cut.

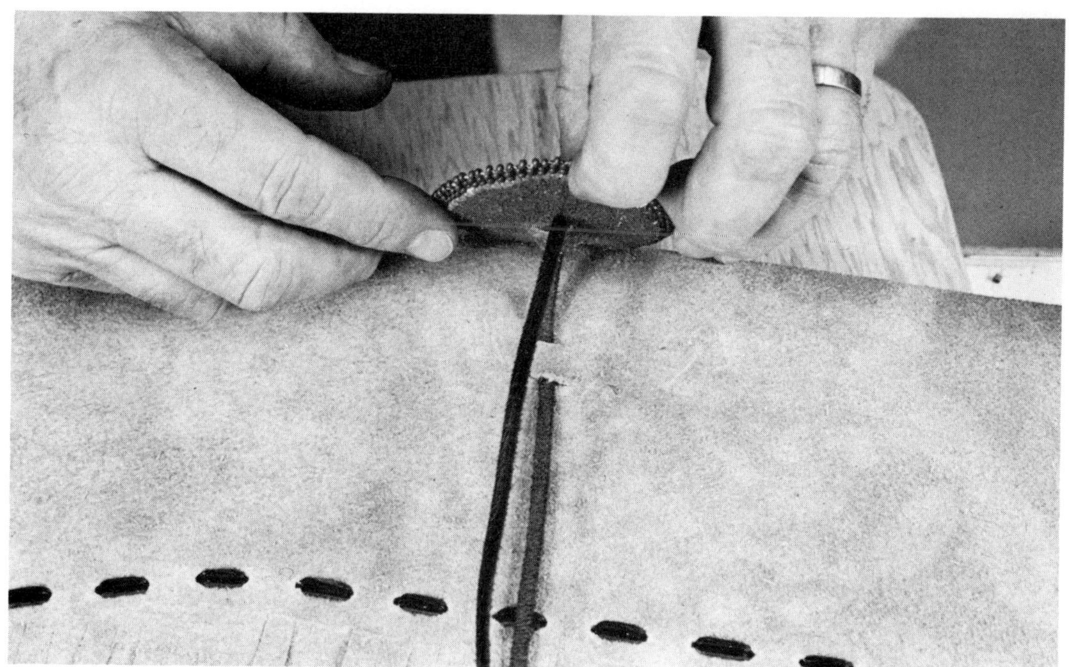

Beaded Indian rosettes are fastened for decor.

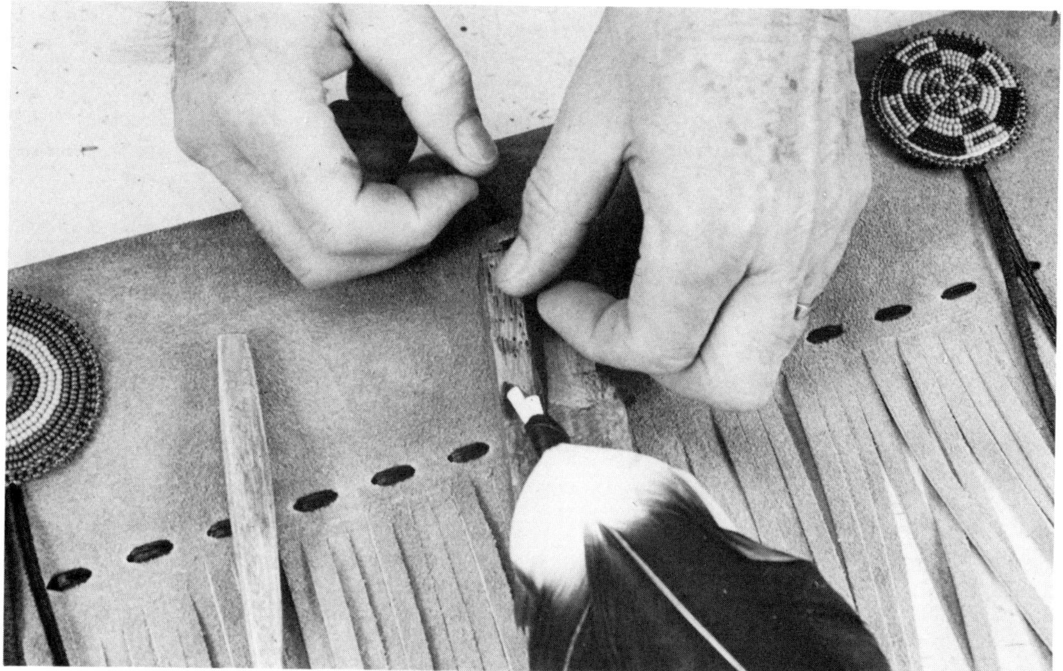

Eagle feathers are tied with a buckskin thong and added for an Indian flavor.

Chapter Ten

The Sweetfield Leather Company "The Modern Craftsman"

River Street in old Savannah, Georgia, is a mixture of pubs, fine restaurants, and some superb craftshops. The Sweetfield Leather Company, run by Sam Lynah, can be found at 109 East River Street and has some of the best leatherwork to be seen anywhere. Lynah has made custom-crafted camera cases for many *National Geographic* photographers; belts, hats, and leather bags for movie star Burt Reynolds and his film crew while on location in the historic old town; and a pair of sandals for many tourists who have visited his shop.

The street has gained a national reputation for high quality craftwork and Sweetfield has become one of the best known. Lynah and his co-workers opened their doors about five years ago and quickly gained fame with their classical leatherworking techniques, natural finish materials, and hand stitching of modern-style leather goods. Although vegetable-tanned leather is used for most work, Lynah has also worked in zebra, fox, bear, kangaroo, elk, deer, and various snakeskins from the lowland marsh country of the area. In addition to creating original custom-designed leather goods, the shop also reconditions old leather items. Sam Lynah says that vegetable-tanned leather that has been hand-sewn will last as long as one hundred years if it is properly cared for. He adds, "We've had some original officers' leather articles from the Civil War brought in for reconditioning and found them to be still in serviceable shape."

Now only thirty years old, Lynah didn't start out to be a leatherworker. He studied engineering at Southern Tech and then switched to an English major. He picked up leatherworking as a hobby in the beginning and liked it so much he began doing it full time just a few years ago. His first shop was in the rear of a boutique and he became so successful that he moved to his present location about three years ago. Although the

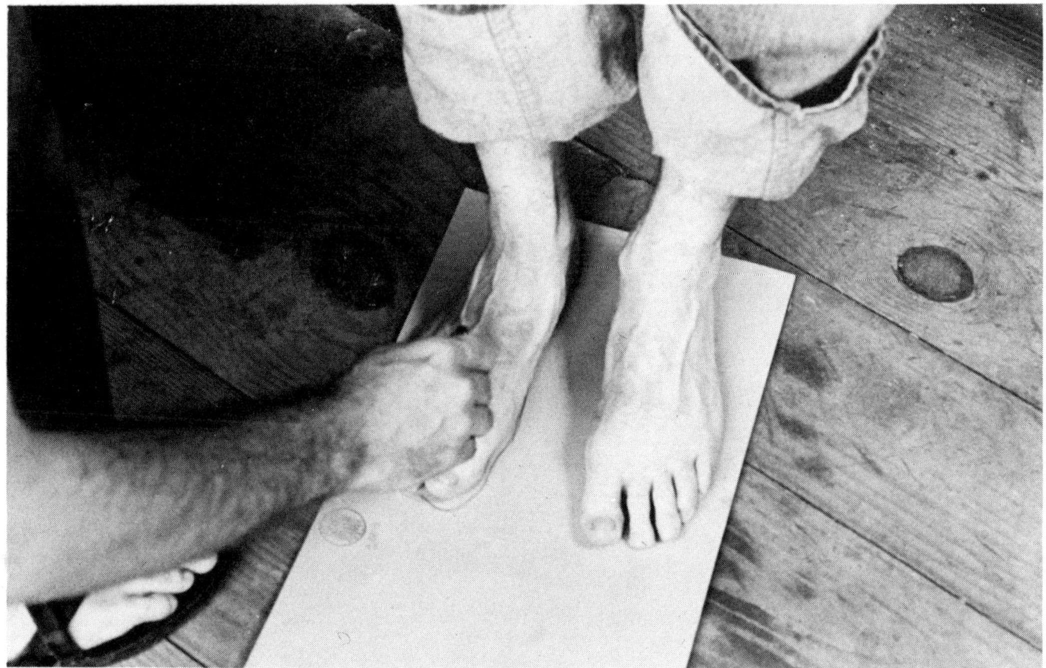

The foot outline is drawn directly onto the leather.

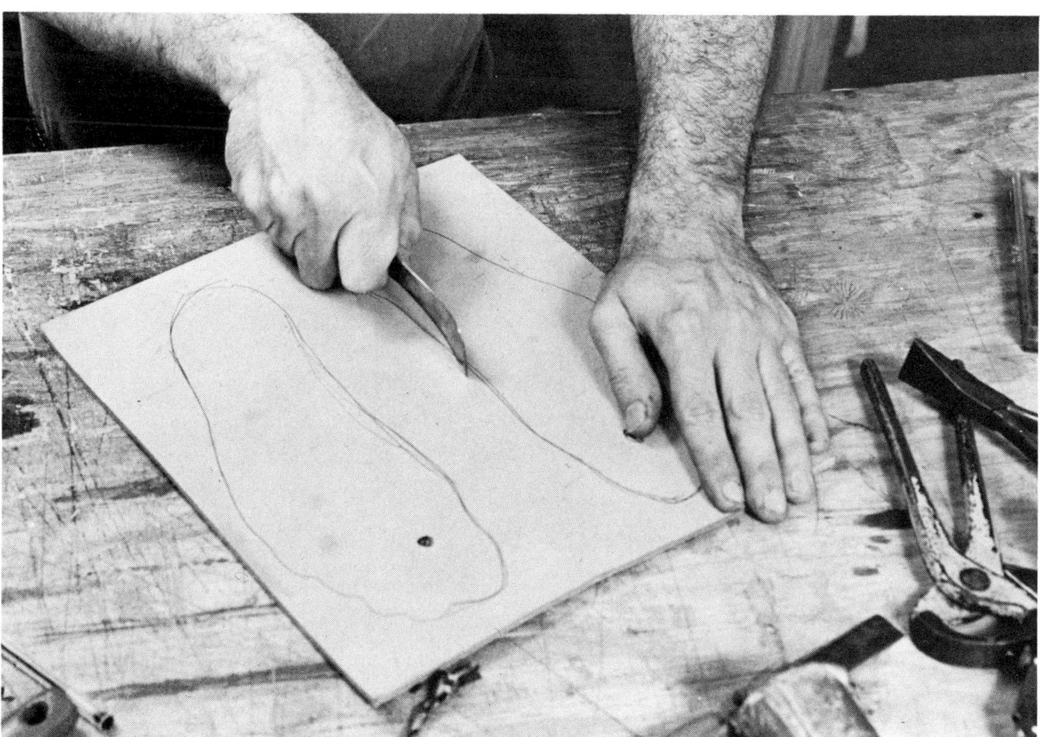

A knife is used to cut the pattern.

company deals in the usual run of leatherwork, Sam admits a lot of time is taken up with special-order items. Their most famous items are sandals and a number of other leathercraftsmen frequently stop by to see how Sweetfield makes them. Let us see how Lynah crafts his sandals.

Crafting Sandals

In making sandals, Lynah uses four pieces of leather: top sole, bottom sole, heel, and straps. For the top sole, Lynah uses eight-inch iron shoe leather, for the bottom sole twelve-inch or fourteen-inch iron chrome-tanned leather, and the strap is 6/7-ounce chrome-tanned dressed leather. (Dressed leather is leather that is simply waxed and oiled at the tannery.) The strap is generally four and a half feet in length for a man's sandal and roughly six inches less for a woman's. The back or keeper strap on the back of the sandal is usually eleven inches in length and 5/8″ wide. The top sole is perhaps the most important part of the sandal. It will give both support and comfort to the wearer.

Drawing the bare foot right on the leather can be done with a ballpoint pen since the dye will cover the ink lines later. Once the leather is cut, the slots are punched for the straps. An important point here is to bevel the edges of the underside of the slots; this will prevent the sharp edges of the leather from wearing out the strap. After the slots are cut and beveled, the top sole is dyed. It is then dipped in a bucket of oil containing a mixture of neatsfoot, Lexol, and some mink oil thrown in. Exact measurements? You don't need them. Lynah just says, "We throw in a batch of this, a glob of that, stir the mess up, and it works." The top of the sandal soaks for about five minutes. This puts enough oil in the vegetable-tanned leather to prevent it from drying and cracking. It also keeps the leather pliable. With this treatment, many of Lynah's sandals have gone five years without attention.

After the top has dried, it is worked with the hands to mold the arch for a proper fit. The straps are run through at this point and Barge Cement is used to coat the underneath of the top sole everywhere *except* where the strap runs across. The bottom sole is completely covered with cement and when the two pieces are put together the straps can still be pulled free to adjust and fit properly. Once both top and bottom are allowed to dry for about fifteen minutes, the two pieces are put together and hammered down all over to ensure that the glue adheres well.

After this, a sharp knife is used to trim the excess from the bottom sole; then the cobble work is done all around the sandal. This can be a bit tricky. Except for the nails coming through from the top to ensure that the strap won't be nailed, all the other nails are put through from the bottom. At this point the cobble work can be taken to a local shoeshop and they'll know exactly what to do. However, if the craftsman wants to attempt the work himself, a small anvil or other piece of steel can be used for a hammering base. The proper-size cobbling nails (their length is shown in picture B, page 156) can be obtained and an ordinary hammer used. It would be advisable to practice hammering a few nails through some scrap leather since a precise tap is necessary to hit the nail through the leather and *ball* the end as it comes through. Bent nails can, of course, be pulled out with a pair of pliers. Lynah uses brass nails because they are in a salt air area and many of his sandals are worn on boats or at the beach. But iron nails will work as well and the choice depends on the craftsman's own climate and geographical locale.

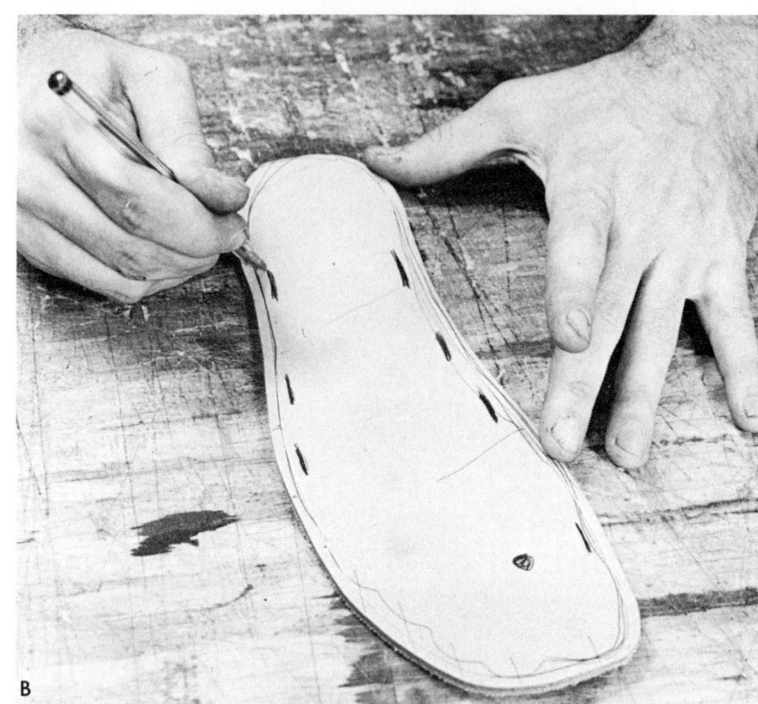

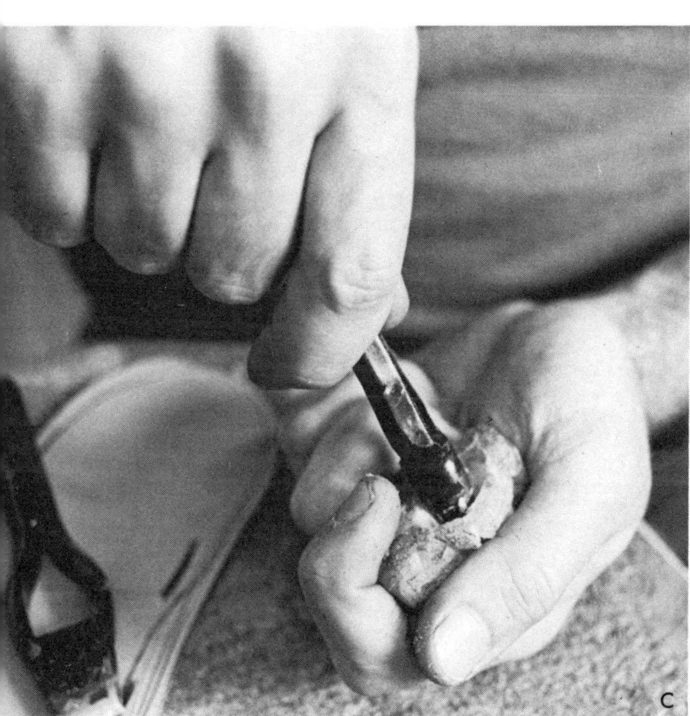

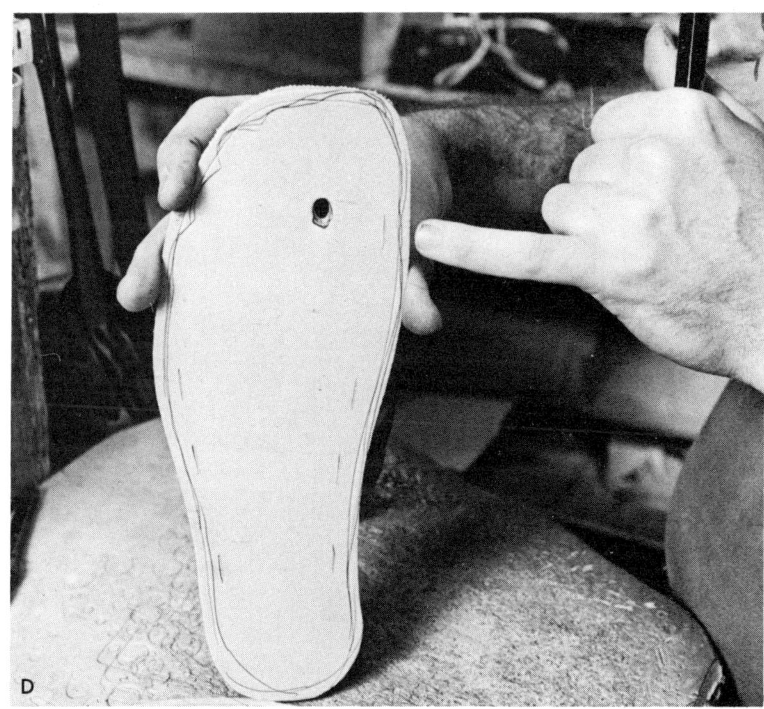

A Edges are trimmed with an edge-beveler.

B Thong slots are carefully drawn for proper placement and comfortable fit. Circle in front is for toe thong.

C Before cutting the thong holes, the die is coated with beeswax to ensure sharp and even cuts.

D One foot has the thong holes cut while Lynah points out the care in placement of the other slots so they won't bind or rub on bones of the foot.

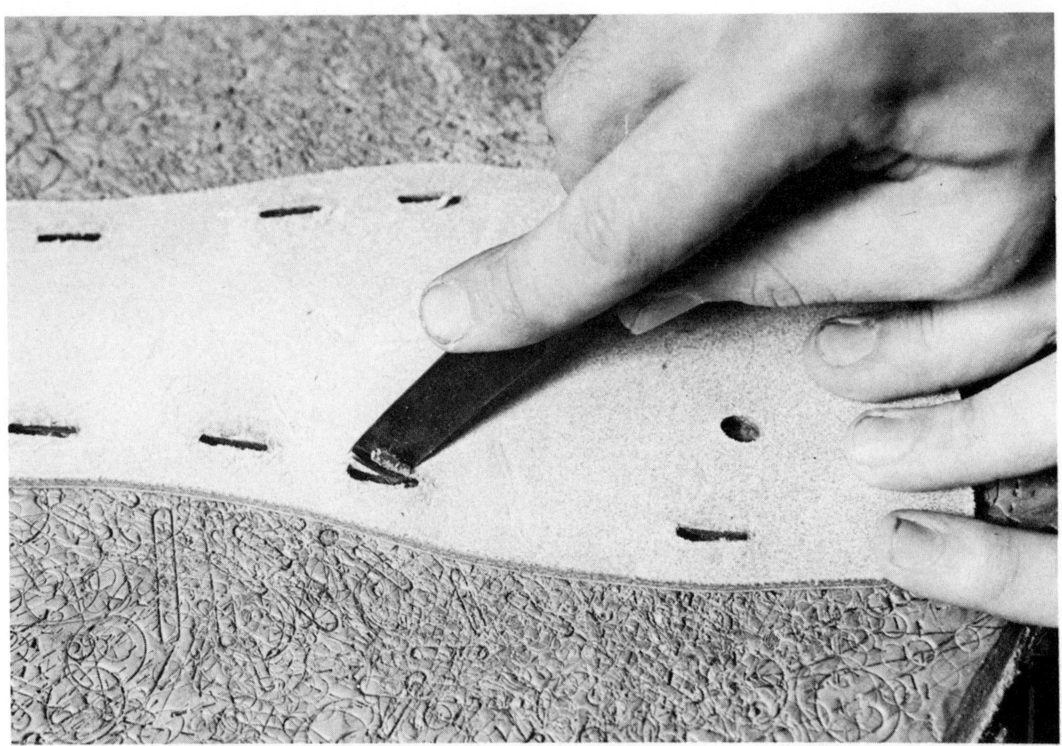

A seemingly trivial but important point is to round the edges *of the bottoms* of the thong slots so the sharp edges won't wear the tie thong.

Sam Lynah begins to dye the upper part of the sandals.

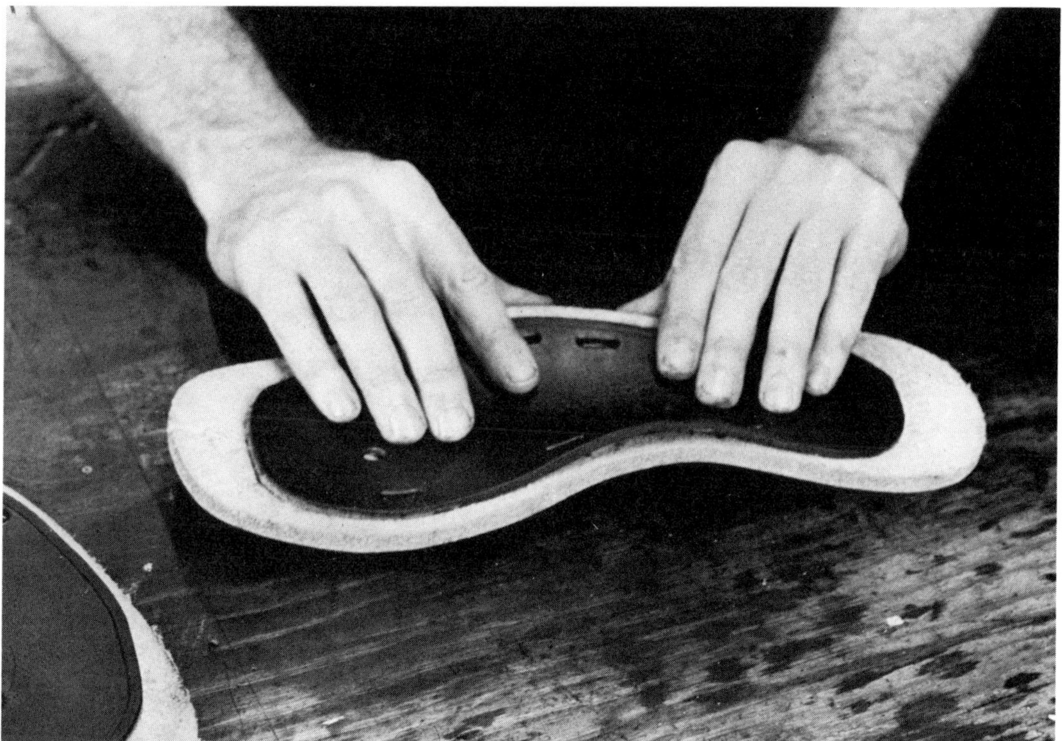

The bottom sole is measured and then cut to size.

Thongs are cut and placed through the slots.

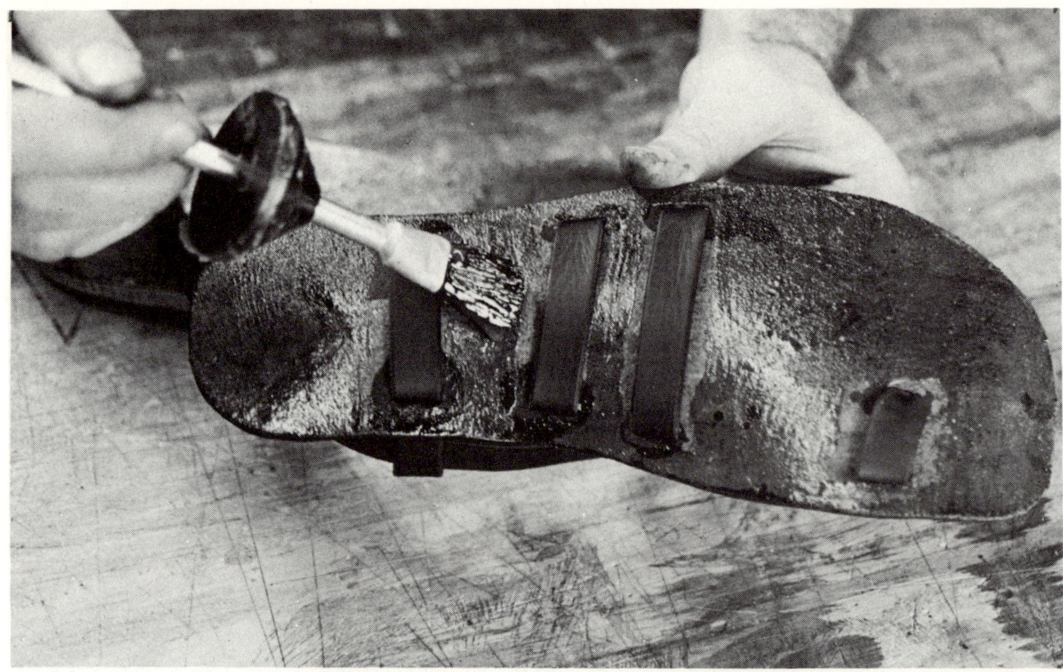

Once the thongs are laced in, the bottom of the sole is coated with Barge Cement *except where the thongs cross the bottom*. This will allow them to be pulled and tugged for proper fit once the bottom sole is fastened on.

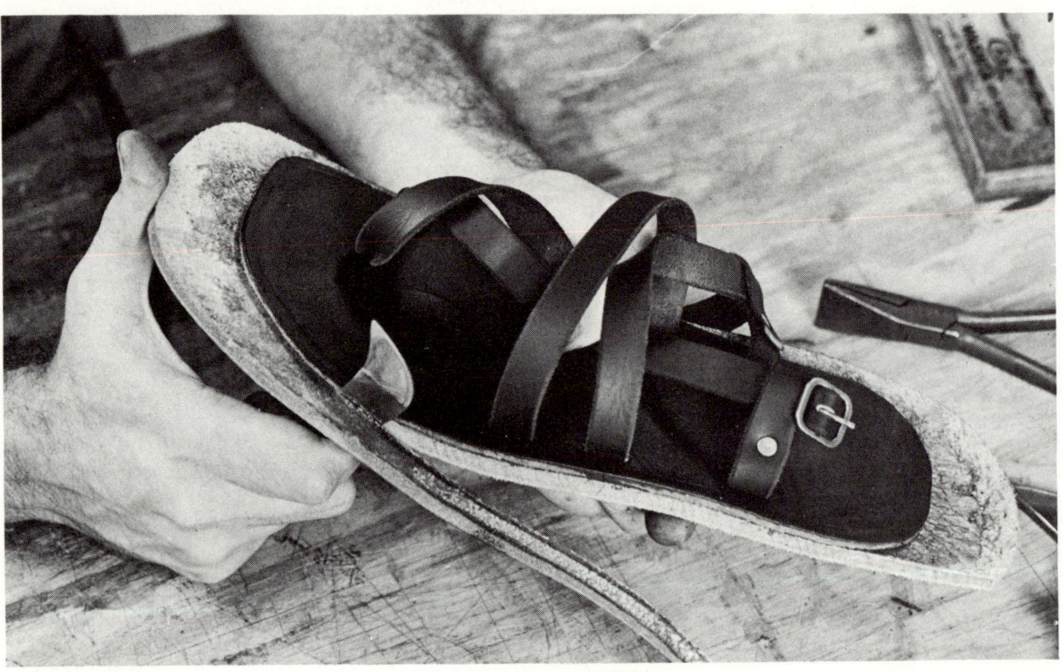

After the bottom sole is cemented on, excess material is cut away.

Brass cobbler's nails are hammered in. Except for those nails showing by the thongs, all other nails are hammered in from the bottom.

After the tacks are hammered in, an edge-beveler is run around the top side for a smooth finish.

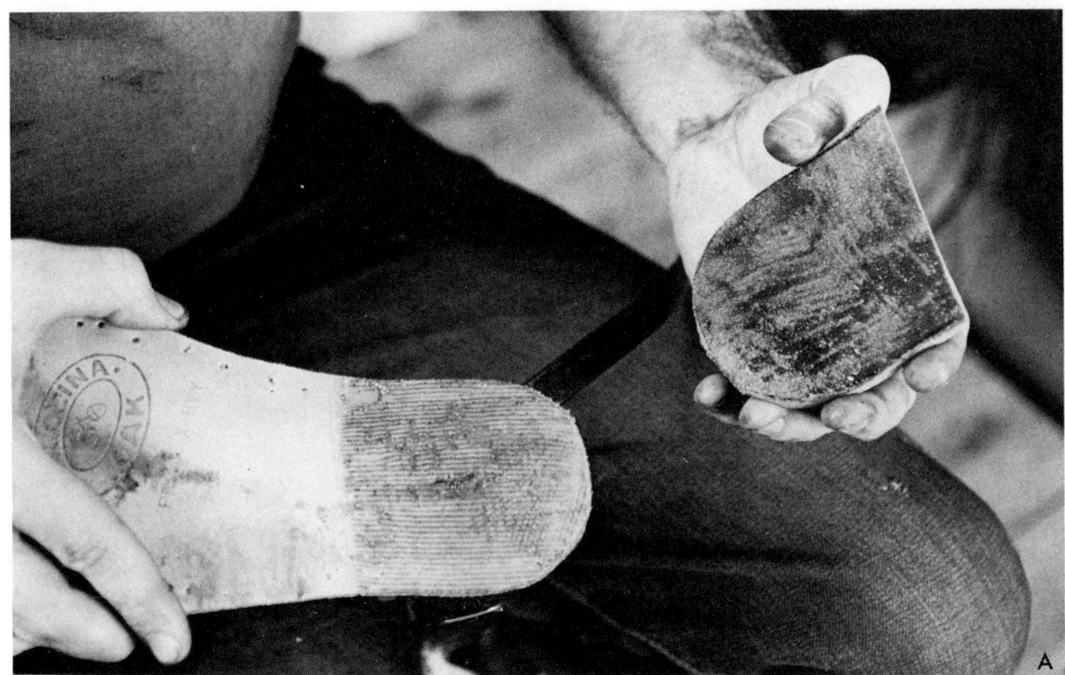

Leather or rubber may be used for the heel and cemented down with Barge Cement.

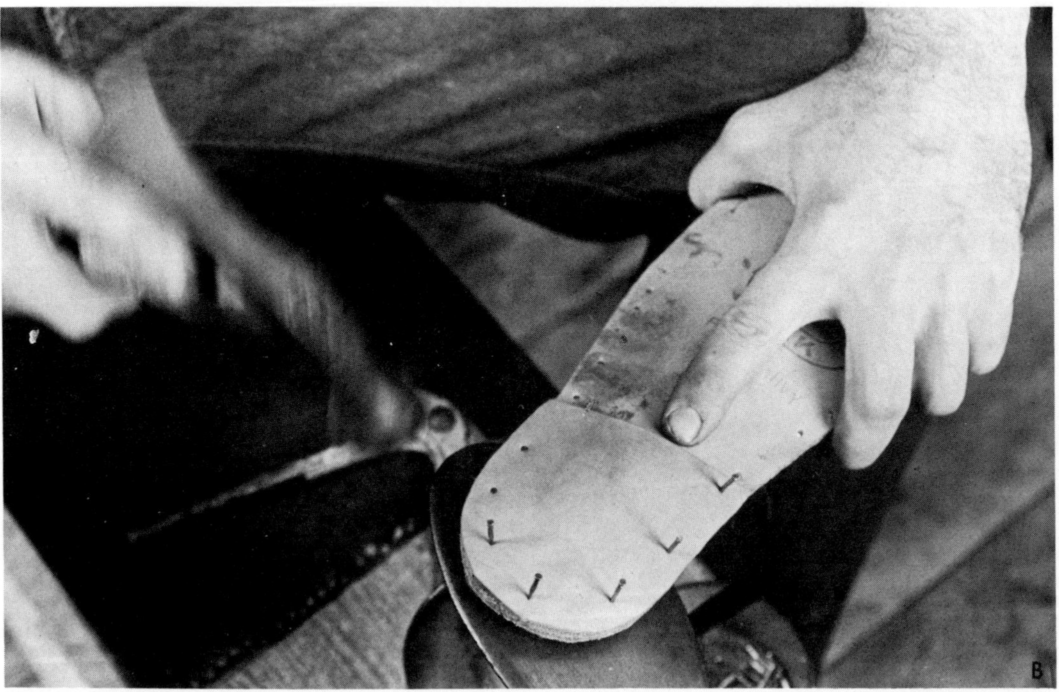

When the cement has dried, brass nails are hammered in. Note that it is important to have a steel or iron base to "ball" the nail as it comes through the leather. The small balling is what keeps the upper and lower sole together, plus the cement.

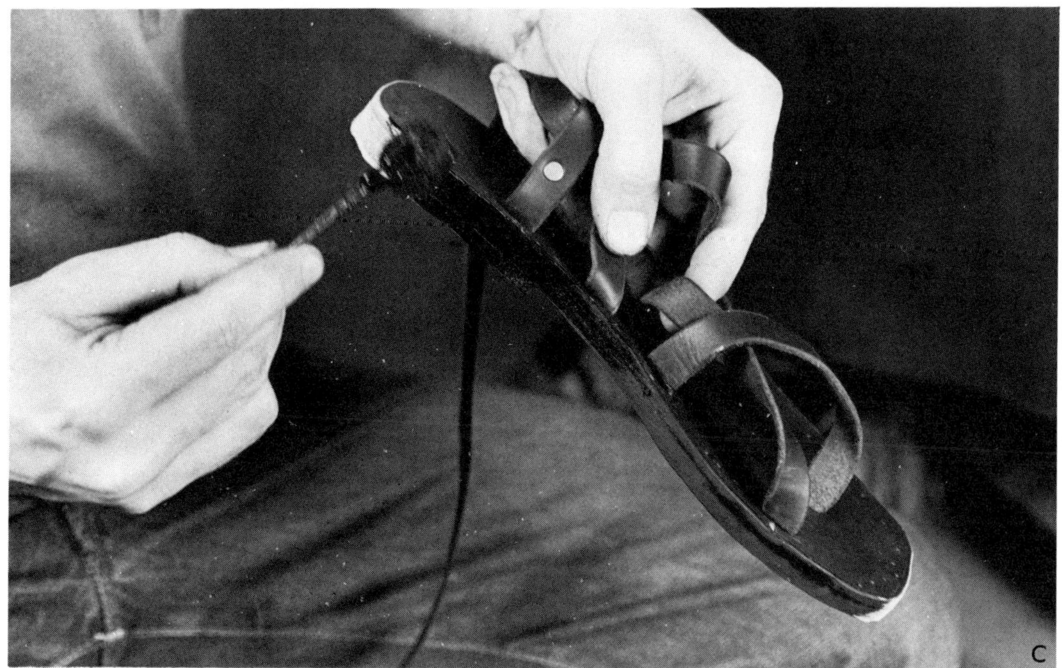

A small brush is used to dye the unfinished edges after rubbing with sandpaper to obtain smoothness.

Fitting the sandals. The thongs will run freely, with some fair amount of pulling and tugging, and can be properly adjusted to the foot. After fastening buckles, holes are punched and excess thong cut away.

Once this work is done the edges are sanded. Again, this can be done by a shoemaker if the craftsman wishes. Next, the heel is placed on with Barge Cement and nails. Then dye is rubbed around the finished and sanded edge. Finally, the sandal is placed on the foot and the straps are pulled and tugged until there is a proper fit. Although crafting sandals may sound fairly complicated, they are really quite easy to make and some of Lynah's craftsmen can turn out a dozen pairs a day with ease.

The completed sandals by Sam Lynah.

Making a Leather Hat

Leather hats are also quite easy to make and there is little wastage of leather. The hats can be quite dashing, can complement a Western outfit, and they are excellent for outdoor wear particularly when treated with Rain & Stain. Actually, a hat is formed from three pieces of leather: the brim, the gusset (that piece which forms the upright portion of the hat), and the top.

The most important piece is the brim. To make a pattern for it, an oval is drawn for the head on cardboard. Then cut out the oval, discard it, and try the other piece over your head. If it doesn't fit properly, keep cutting more out until the brim hole fits comfortably over the head. Once the brim fits well the pattern is transferred to 4/5-ounce latigo leather and cut out. The center piece is set aside and will be used for the top. The gusset can be taken from any part of the hide that doesn't have flaws or holes.

Basically, all that is done to the leather is to cut out the three pieces. After that, you punch stitching holes, dye it the desired color, run a little oil over the hat, and it is

After proper center or head measurement is obtained, a cardboard pattern is then transferred to leather. The cut-out center piece will become the top of the crown.

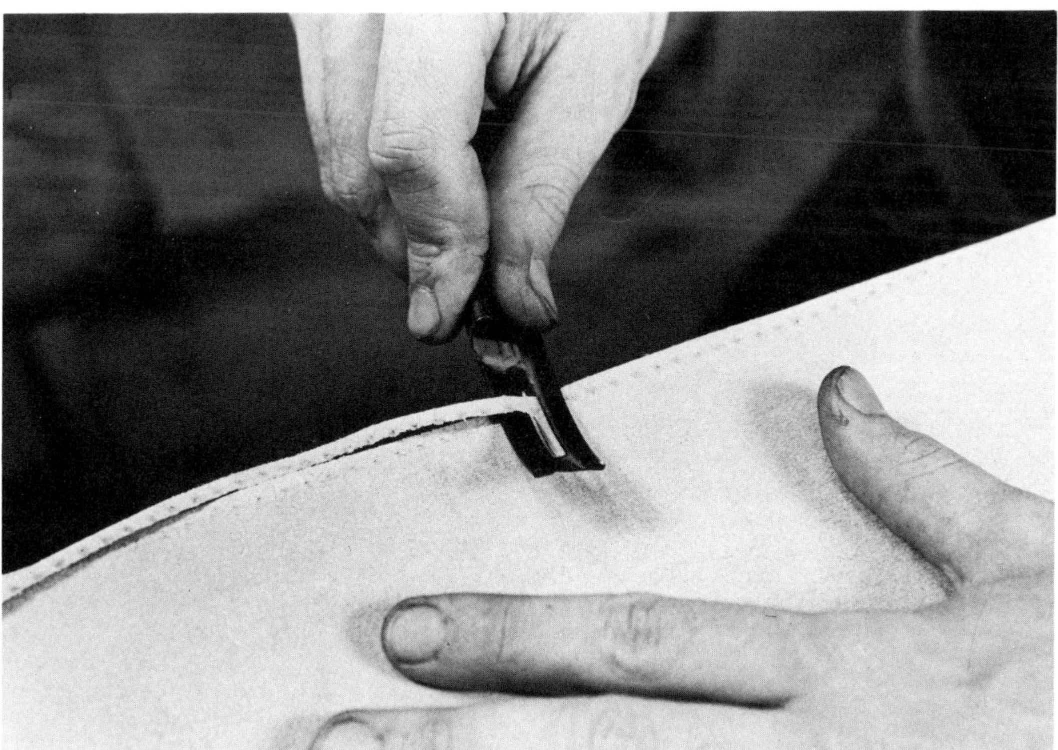

After stitch holes are punched with a small awl, the edges are slightly shaved down with a skife. Used here is a type of knife that allows razor blades to be held for fine work.

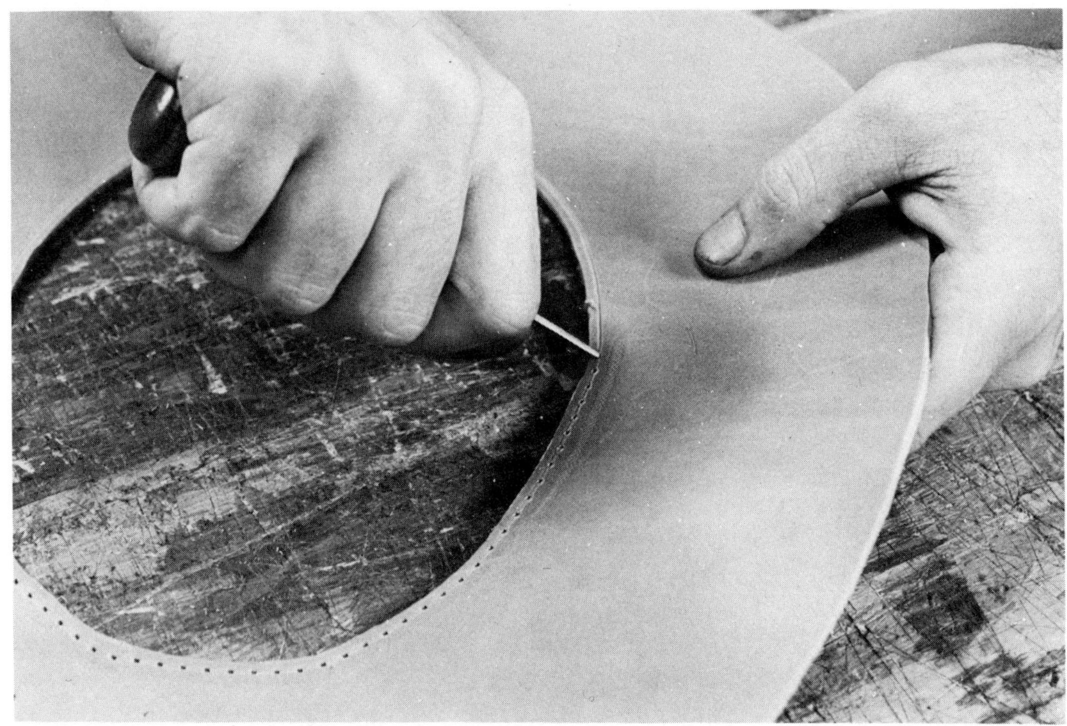

Punching holes in the center of the brim. An awl is used for this step since the leather is thin. Again note the board below to protect table tops.

Fiebing's Leather Dye is rubbed onto the leather before assembly.

Needle and thread are used to assemble the three pieces.

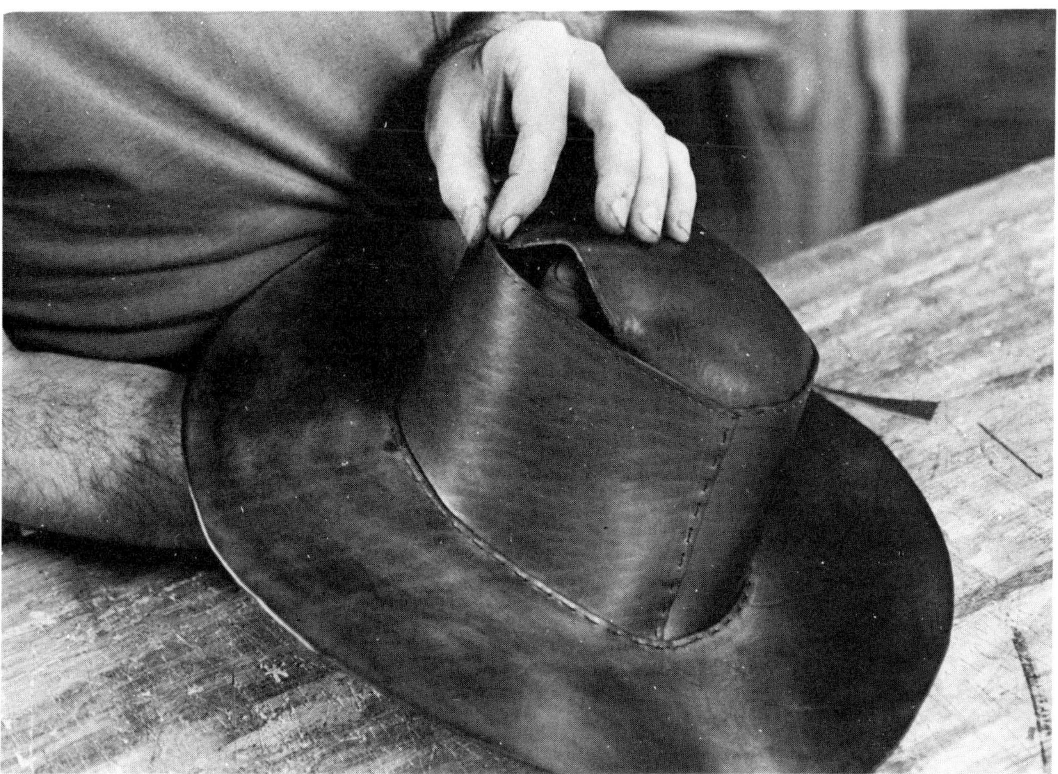

Almost completed, the top is then sewed on.

A dashing Western-type hat with snakeskin hat band tied on for a touch of color.

ready to be assembled. When the stitching is completed Lynah likes to run a coat of Fiebing's Resolene over the leather for protection. Resolene is a resin-type finish that is easy to apply and won't change the underlying color. It also acts as a preservative and imparts a soft, satiny finish. The hat shown in the photo was topped off with a snakeskin band to add some color.

Making a Gun Case

Gun cases are used by almost every sportsman to carry sporting arms into the field. They are excellent protection for the gun, preventing knocks and other harm coming to the weapon when it may be bouncing around in cars and boats. Depending upon the style of case made, either of soft or hard leather, some of these cases can even be used to ship a gun by air. Such a case was designed by Sam Lynah in a technique not shown before in this book.

Sam uses a molded, or formed, wet-leather method. This is exactly what the name implies: the wet leather is formed over a wooden mold and allowed to dry. The leather will then retain its shape. If a plywood liner is used, as it was in this case, it will give excellent protection to the gun inside. To add a central piece of decoration, Lynah had a Texas Lone Star cut from pine and glued to the top of the wooden form. As the wet leather was worked around the star, it would slowly begin to take the same shape and retain it on the completed case.

Basically, what we end up with is a leather box that can be lined with part of the plywood form for added strength, and then sheepskin placed over it for protection of the gun.

Molding of leather is done over forms. Here Lynah cements down a Texas star in the center of the case. The prepared mold has been cut and finished and is ready to be covered with leather.

A hand stapler is used to fasten the leather, although nails may also be used. It's necessary to get the leather as tight as possible over the form.

This same technique can be used for any type of gun case. Even breakdown shotguns and small cases for hand guns can be crafted using this method. The first step is to lay the gun down on a piece of paper or directly on the wood and make the measurements. The case shown here was made for a favorite well-used Winchester Model 94 and the measurements were taken with the gun laid on a piece of ¼-inch pine. Allow sufficient room all around for the top to close over the bottom. This ¼-inch piece is glued atop another piece of pine for greater thickness and the cutout star is glued exactly in the center of the lid.

The leather used for this case was six-ounce vegetable-tanned leather. Leather with a good tight back should be used. It is soaked for about twenty minutes and removed from the water and allowed to dry for a few minutes. Next, it is pulled and stretched over the mold. A staple gun is used to staple one row along one edge. The leather is pulled as tightly as possible and then stapled down the other side. Once this is completed return to the first side, remove one staple, and continue to stretch at that point. Then re-staple. Do this all along the edge and if necessary re-staple along the opposite side. This will pull the leather as tightly as possible and give a good fit over all the edges and angles of the box.

Once the leather fits tightly, it can be worked with the hands along the edges and pressed into any recesses, corners, and around sharp angles or edges. All these different recesses will give the case character and variations will add to the completed appearance. After this is done to both the top and bottom sections of the case, they are set aside and allowed to partially dry for an hour or two. Now go over the case with dye thinner. It will soak in and make the leather a bit brittle which will help it keep its shape. On small cases, the thinner won't matter too much, but on larger cases it will help them maintain a rigid shape.

At this point, it is necessary to work around the star on top with the fingers pushing and pressing the leather down and stretching it more and more until it begins to take shape. Once the case has set and hardened overnight, it is trimmed as shown with a *sharp* knife. Then the mold is removed and separated with the thinner top piece plus star re-glued into the top of the gun case for support. If the craftsman prefers a slightly lighter case, shoe or sole leather may be used. It is sufficiently rigid, will give good protection, and may be used instead of the wood. This is done to both the top and bottom sections of the box and then it is dyed. After the dye has dried, use a mixture of neatsfoot compound and pure neatsfoot and beeswax. Melt it all together and run into the leather thoroughly. This will not only help protect the leather but also give it character.

After all the fairly dirty work of dyeing and oiling is completed, the bench is cleaned and cleared and the sheepskin liner is inserted. This is done by simply cutting a piece of sheepskin to fit exactly into the box. The wood for the inside form, previously glued into the box, is coated with Barge Cement, as is the inside or hide side of the sheepskin. Again allow it to dry for a few moments, then begin to set the sheepskin into the box. It's best to start at one end and press down firmly with the hands as the skin adheres to the box. While the cement is drying, begin to cut the straps. To make it easy to open and close the case, saddle-type cinch rings and a stud were used. The cinch is sewn on one end and the pin inserted into a hole. With this type of strap, there is no feeling or

The corners are cut for an even fit. Then they will be stapled down.

Lamb's wool has already been cut and set onto the bottom of the case at the right. Lynah is coating the cover with Barge Cement in order to fasten the pine mold into the top.

Trimming the leather off. All excess must be cut neatly.

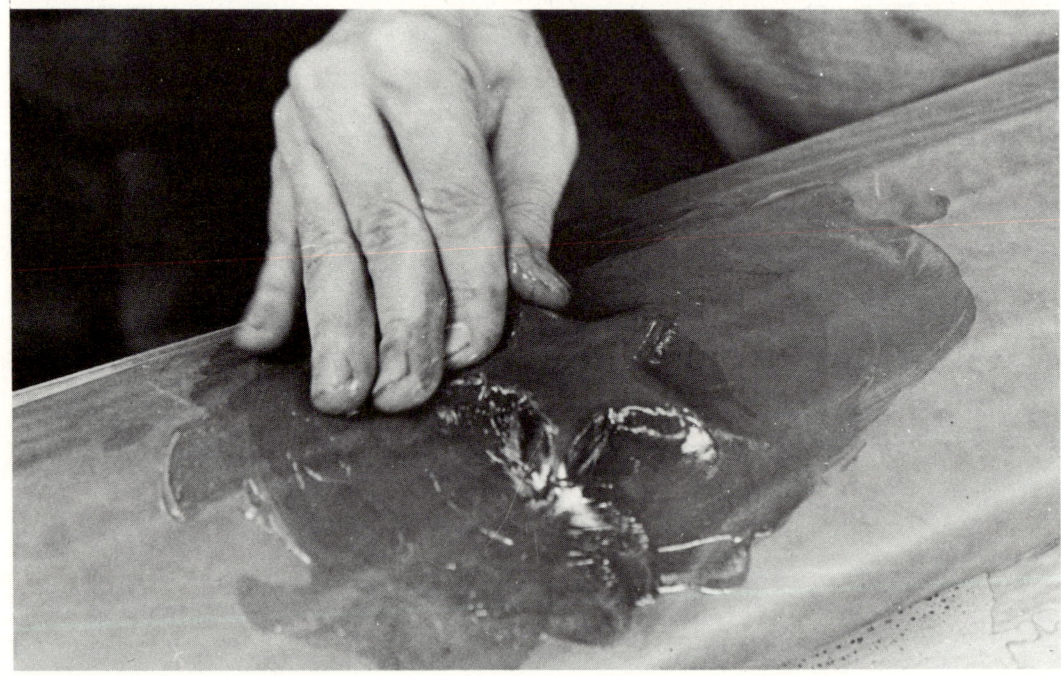

Warm Lexol and wax is rubbed in and around the star and worked with the fingers to insure its proper form.

Inside base is coated with Barge Cement as is the inside of the lamb's wool, which is neatly set in and pressed down.

Lynah dyeing the keeper straps. No straps are used inside the case since it is a tight fit and the rifle won't move about once the case is closed.

An unusual and attractive rifle case of molded leather by Sam Lynah.

searching for more than one hole. The stud stands upright and the strap is pulled tight until the single hole snaps over the stud. A slightly longer strap is then sewn between these two wrap-around straps for slinging over the shoulder and the case is completed.

With this type of case, hinges could be put on the back or leather thongs used. Certainly the craftsman can use his imagination and ability to craft and embellish almost any type of case he desires.

Here are a few tips on wet-forming leather. Pine makes the best mold since it is soft and can be carved if necessary; or a couple of different thicknesses can be easily nailed together. If a staple gun isn't handy, nails may be used to nail the wet leather over the mold, but they should be rustproof. Another important tip is that vegetable-tanned leathers *only* should be used for this type of forming because they absorb moisture and will retain their shape when dry. Chrome-tanned leathers will just spring back and won't retain creases or folds.

Many creative and imaginative leatherworkers are using this technique to form masks, boxes, replicas of Indian war shields, and even free-standing bits of sculpture. Don't let the fact that Sam Lynah is a professional leathercraftsman deter the reader from trying many of his techniques shown here. Remember that Lynah was an amateur himself just a few years ago and readily admits that his first sandals and camera cases were a far cry from the skilled work he performs today.

Every object he crafts from leather will add to the skills and knowledge of the beginning leatherworker. And soon, very soon, some of these seemingly tough tasks will be accomplished without thought or effort. Even his first tooled belt or carved gun holster can give the novice a feeling of pride in crafting something that he can wear proudly and show off to friends. There are few limits to what can be done with leather. The only restriction I have heard from any of these craftsmen is simply that leather should *look* like leather, retain its essential character, and not try to imitate any other material. That's good advice, too, because the beauty of leather is sufficient in itself and, aside from tasteful decor to enhance the individual article, leather should *never* be subjected to anything else.

CHAPTER ELEVEN

The Fringed Jacket

We've purposely left the fringed jacket for last because it is the most difficult leather project in this book. It entails considerable skill, because it involves the ability to use a sewing machine; some knowledge in reading and making patterns; experience in cutting leather without making costly mistakes; and a tremendous amount of patience in assembling all the small, strange, and odd-looking pieces of leather so that they eventually form a jacket of the proper size and fit.

Gaile Bachand, the young woman who cut and crafted this jacket, is a skilled garmentmaker and is one of the top professional leatherworkers in the United States. At one time in her career, she was also a custom couturière.

To give some idea of the time involved, Gaile selected the skins and cut and crafted the whole jacket in one day. In fact, she began at 9:00 AM and—amazingly—the finished jacket was ready to be photographed around 4:00 PM. This, of course, isn't intended to set the normal time for crafting a jacket as complicated as this. Indeed, Gaile Bachand advises that the inexperienced craftsman should allow at least three days for this project.

The first step for the beginner is to make a pattern of cotton, muslin, or some other inexpensive fabric, and then to make certain the garment fits before actually cutting the skins. The hides used for this jacket were cowhides; however, deerskins may be used. Deer does present a problem, however. Since it takes roughly seven to nine hides, depending upon the size of the animals, it isn't easy for the sportsman to match size and finish, particularly if he has collected hides over a number of years. Unfortunately, if hides are finished at different tanneries there will be a glaring difference in their finish, texture, and even color. The best advice at this stage is to try and trade the skins to a

Leather craftsman Jerry Ashton (left) and Jerry Rush of Jerry's Leather Goods discuss skins for a fringed jacket.

Gaile Bachand notes measurements taken by Jerry Rush.

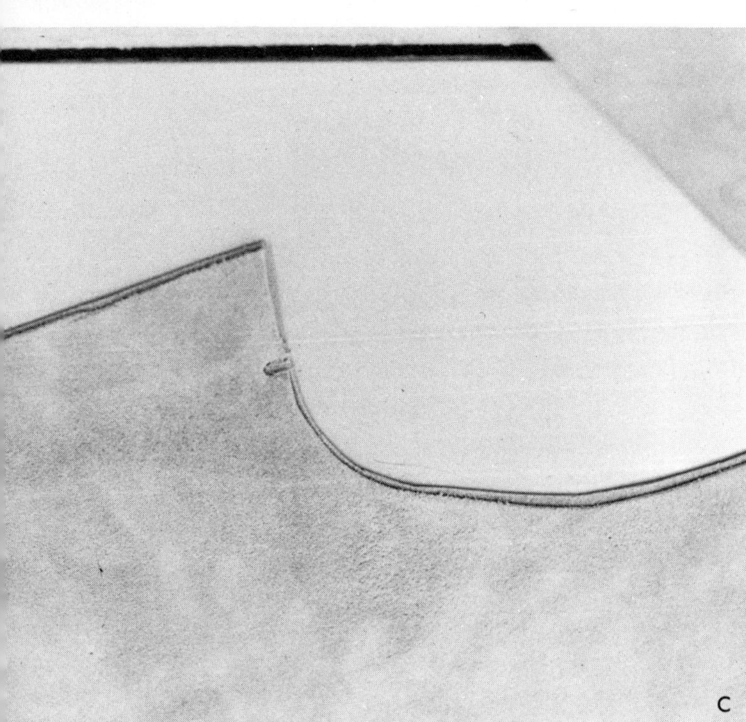

A In a professional craft shop, sufficient skins are on hand to obtain a perfect match. For a good-looking jacket this first step is very important.

B Crafting hundreds of fringed jackets a year, the shop has various fiberboard patterns. Here the sleeve is being marked for cutting.

C As with many leather sections that must match, two tiny notches are cut in for proper fit and match.

D This is what a fringed jacket looks like before being assembled.

tannery for an equal amount so the color and quality will be consistent.

Jerry Rush, owner of Jerry's Leather Goods, advises that it takes about forty-four square feet for an average-size jacket (38 to 40) plus another 50 percent for the fringe. If seven to ten hides seems a great deal, remember that fringing takes a lot of skins. Remember, too, the longer the fringe the more striking the jacket will be.

The tools required for crafting the jacket are very few. They include scissors, pinking machine or pinking shears to trim certain edges, a sewing machine that will take leather needles, a can or tube of Barge Cement, and some spring clips to hold various pieces together when sewing. A word of caution at this point: don't ever use Scotch tape because it will stain and mark the suede finish. Modern tapes of this type are too sticky and gummy; if they are placed on brightly colored suedes it will be impossible to get the residue off completely. Also, don't use pins because the pin holes will show.

Earlier mention was made of the time involved in crafting a full-fringed jacket—roughly three days. However, if a sewing machine isn't available the jacket can be put together with buck stitching (as was done in making the fringed rifle scabbard or arrow quiver). Naturally, this will take longer since all the holes must be punched. However, it will result in more of a frontier or Western appearance. A number of expert leather-workers judge that a buck-stitched garment would take about two weeks to make. This doesn't mean putting in a full eight-hour day, but working, say, three or four hours an evening.

It is most important in beginning this project to take careful measurements. First, determine the normal suit size, then height, weight, chest, and hips. Next, measure from the inside back of the collar to the hips for proper length. Also measure across the back of the shoulders and from neck to waist. Finally, the outer sleeve length and around the waist should be measured. Lining should definitely be considered since it will make it much easier to slip the jacket on and off and it will cover the inside seams and stitching. In this project, perhaps the most important ingredient is patience. Move slowly and think about every step before rushing to put the knife or scissors to a piece of leather.

After the pattern is made and sewn or pinned together, try it on for size. Remember that a jacket of this type doesn't have to fit exactly and a medium or loose fit is best. The jacket made for this book has a twelve-inch fringe across the back, down the sleeves, and in the front. The pockets and bottom have a shorter fringe of about five inches. After making the pattern, the most important step is to select the skins to be used. They should match each other in quality, weight, and color. The next step is to disassemble the cloth pattern and lay it over the skins for cutting. Since Jerry's Leather Goods makes fringed jackets for stock, they use regular patterns of various sizes; this enables them to select the size and begin to cut without the preliminary step of making a cloth pattern. They will, however, devote considerable time discussing with a customer the type of leather to be used and take careful measurements. The selection of matching skins is left to the worker who will make the jacket. A jacket of this type may be crafted of practically any type of hide, with the exception of pigskin and sheepskin. They are not strong enough and the fringe won't hang well. With the exception of those two skins, almost any other type will work well, particularly deerskin or split cowhide.

Once the skins have been selected, the pattern is laid over them and the cutting

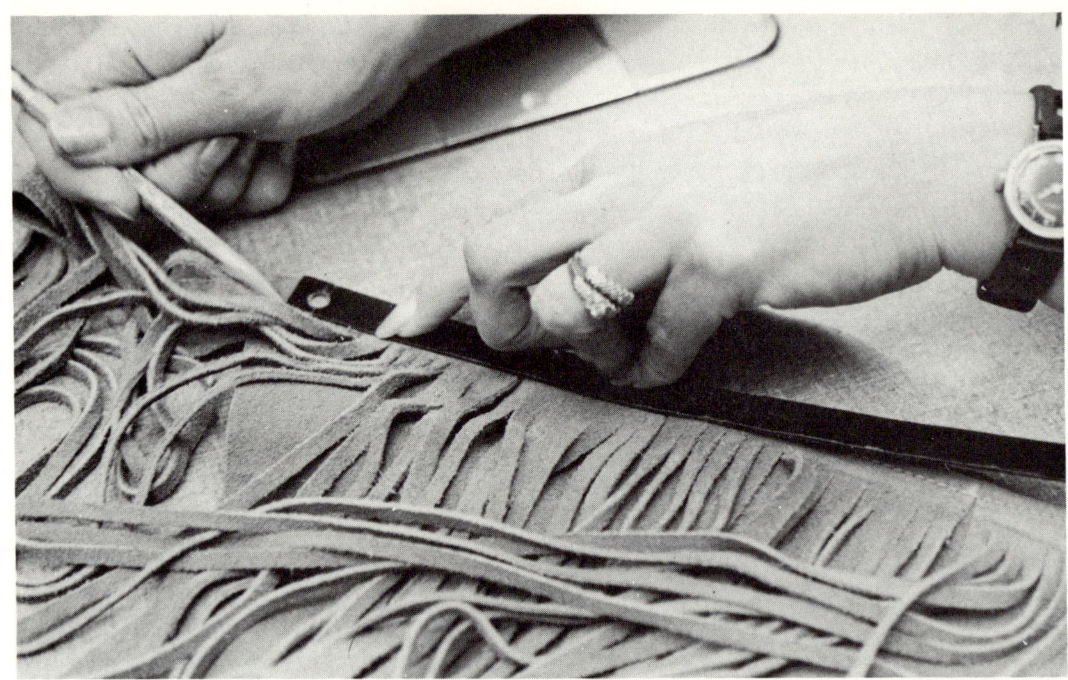

Careful measurements are made to count each section of fringe.

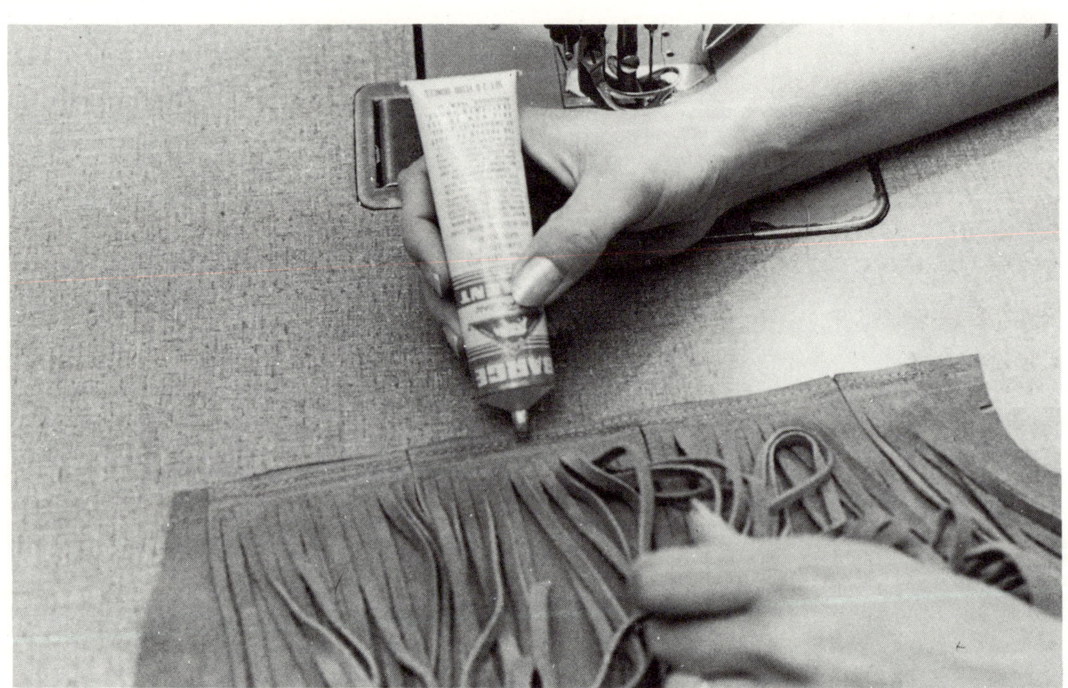

The usual Barge Cement is coated along the edge to hold the covering section. Note how the fringe is sewn on in short pieces.

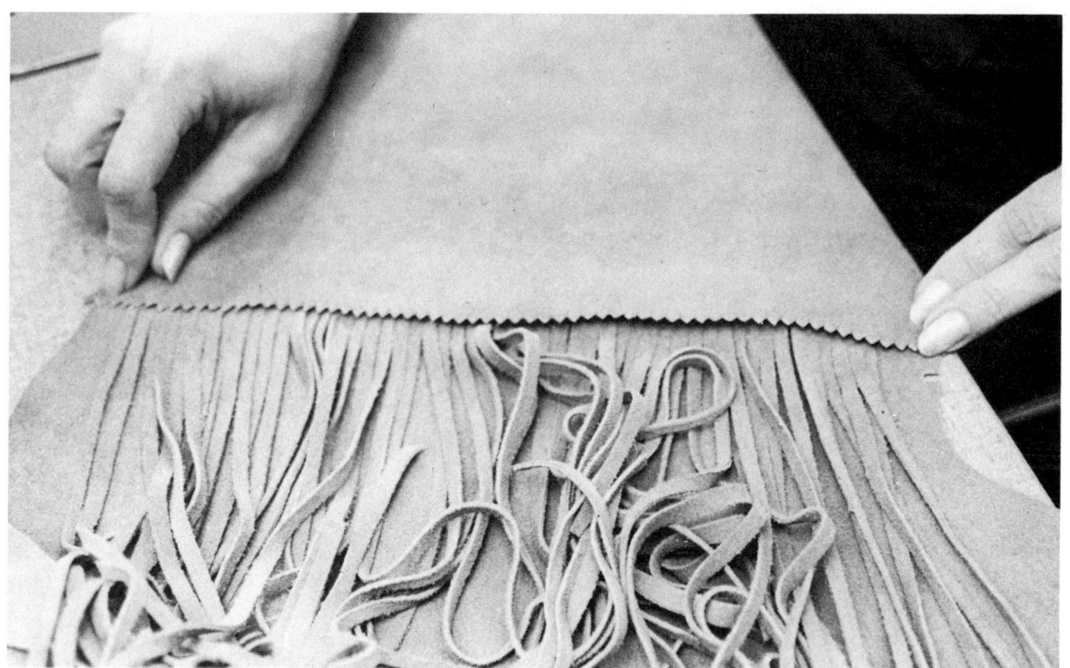

Next the yoke (back) is set over and pressed down before sewing.

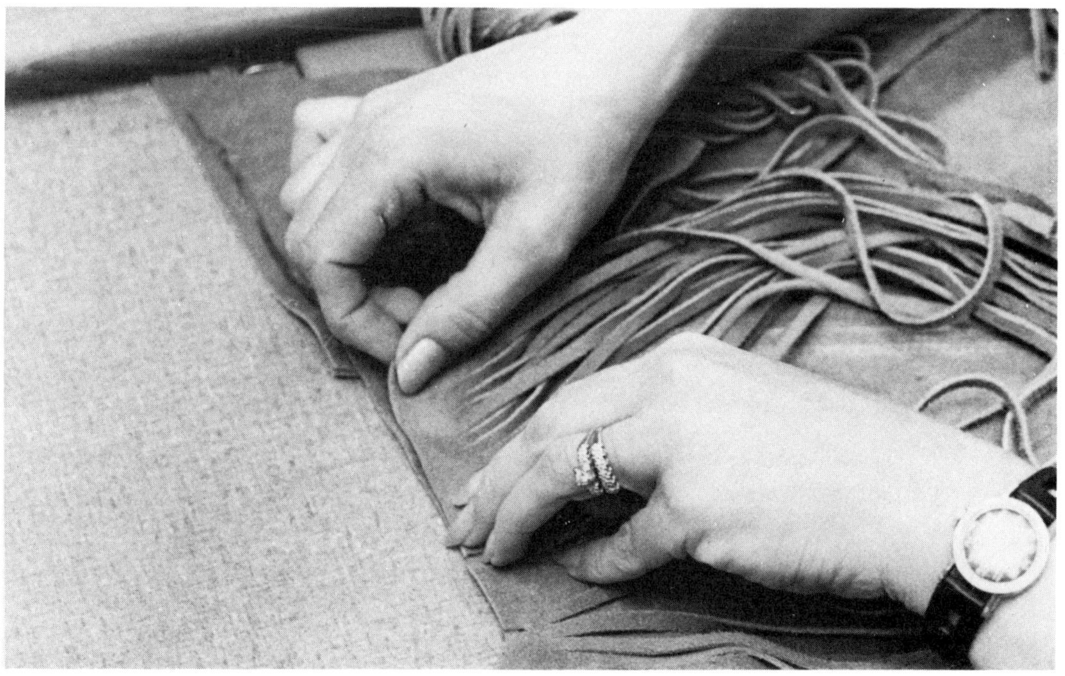

Note carefully how the small notches are lined up before glueing for correct match and fit.

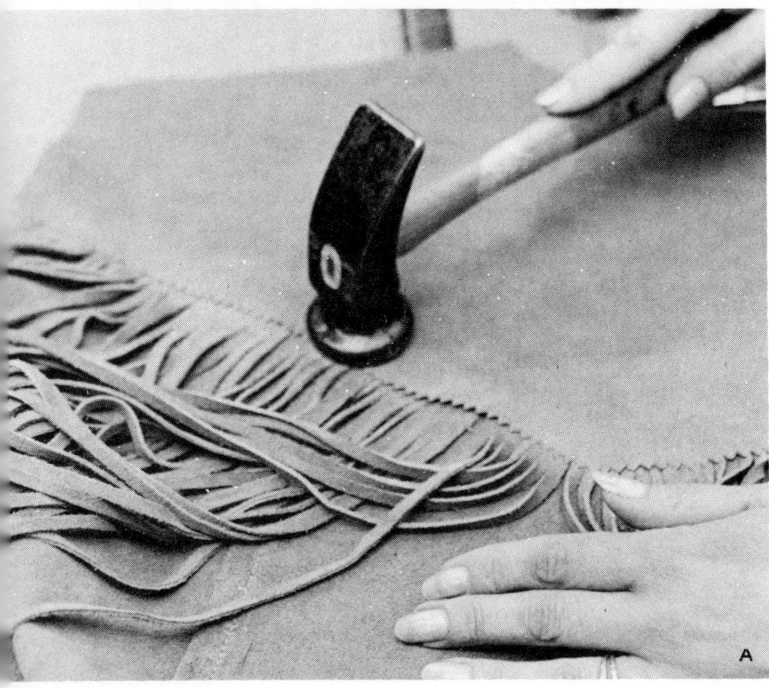

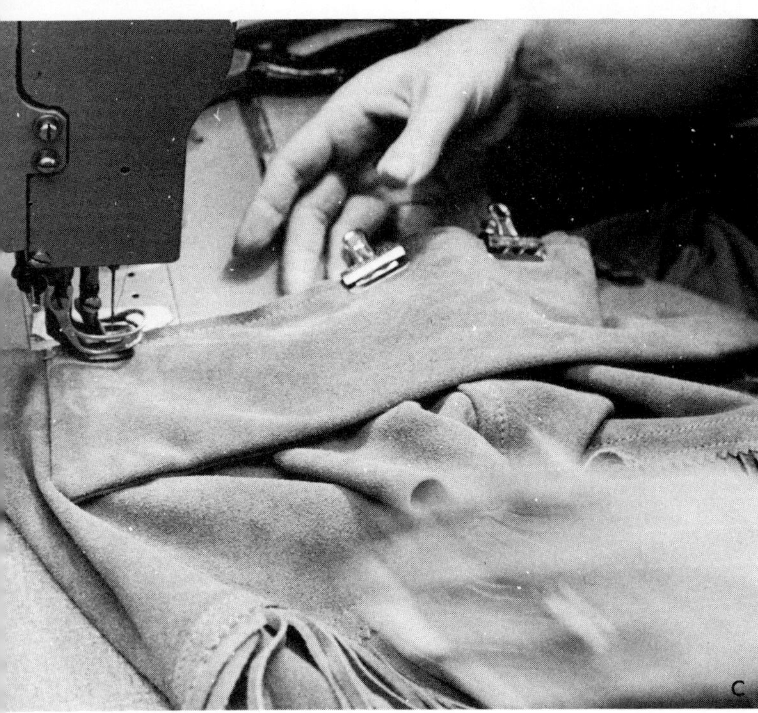

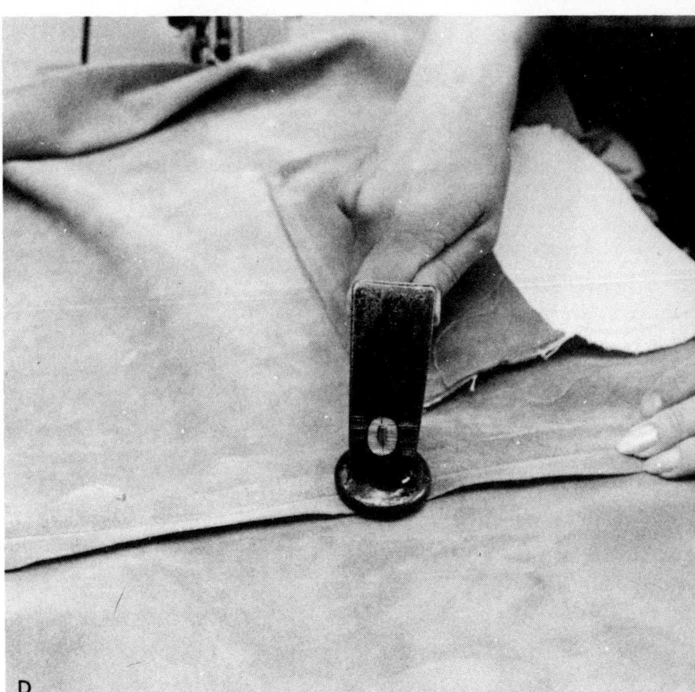

A A hammer is always used after cementing to pound the glue line and ensure a tight fit that will hold firmly before stitching. Barge Cement will not harm or stain suede.

B Bottom fringe is glued on.

C Spring clips are used to hold the leather pieces together for sewing. Caution: don't ever use any of the various cellophanes on the market. They will stain, make marks, and it is impossible to remove the residue.

D The center stitches are hammered down for a smooth fit before lining is put in. While the jacket may be made without lining, it will be easier to take on and off *with* a lining.

begins. Since these skins are soft and reasonably thin, a scissors, a razor blade, or a very sharp knife may be used at this stage. In the illustration, Gaile Bachand is using the regular shop patterns; however, once the cloth pattern is taken apart the various sections will resemble the same cutouts made from fiberboard.

After cutting skins and fringe, the entire pile of bits and pieces is ready to be sewn. The craftsman may notice in the accompanying picture that the various fringes aren't very wide and may well wonder as to the technique of getting a long, single piece of fringe across the back of the jacket. The answer is very simple—the fringe is sewn on in sections covered by the overlying seam hiding the point where they meet. On page 172C is shown a closeup of two small notches in the leather. This is done so that the various pieces meet exactly and is a great aid in assembly.

The next step is to lay each cut piece over its pattern section to check its size and to see how the different pieces shape up for sewing. The various pieces of fringe are measured after stitching to ensure they match before the shawl back is put on. Barge Cement is run along the edge. Then the top back skin is pressed on and hammered to ensure firm adherence before it goes to the sewing machine. Matching the notches will guarantee a proper fit in the completed garment. Here shorter fringed pieces are being set around the bottom of the jacket.

When sewing large sections, after Barge Cement is used to hold the pieces together, spring clips will grasp the pieces firmly and won't work loose as the skin is fed into the machine. Again cement is used to hold down the inner seams for stitching. Be sure to pound them with the hammer so they adhere well.

Keep in mind when crafting a jacket of this type that many small bits of leather have to be fastened to larger sections; then the bigger pieces are finally sewn together to complete the jacket. What it all takes is time and patience. At this point, let's discuss a few tricky areas that may confuse the reader—pockets for one. Those on this jacket are inset; that is, a slit is made and the pocket is sewn on the inside. Naturally, a stitch is taken across the top with a fold of skin to protect the edge. If the craftsman finds this too difficult, a patch pocket may be made and it will look just as well. Don't forget to fold over the top a bit so that a finished edge will protect the pocket, make it stiffer, and prevent it from sagging. Buttonholes may also present a problem and a neighborhood tailor can always be called upon to make them. Buttons should be of a type to match the jacket and could be of bone or antler. They will add to the rustic appearance and give character to the finished jacket. The fringe is always a problem because it takes so long to cut by hand. Jerry's Stripper, shown in Chapter 3, is an excellent piece of equipment, particularly if the craftsman intends to cut a lot of fringe. It will certainly make the project easier and give the craftsman instant fringe.

For those sportsmen who may have hides on hand, here are some figures supplied by Jerry's Leather Goods as to the number of skins it will take to craft a jacket. For an average size man whose suit size is 38 to 40, it will take six mule deer, eight whitetails, or two and a half elk to make a fringed jacket. Remember that a jacket of this type will have less wastage than any other type of garment because scraps and ends are used for the fringe.

I'll close now with these hints for the craftsman. First, spray the completed jacket with Rain & Stain so it may be worn outdoors in rainy weather. Second, don't ever store

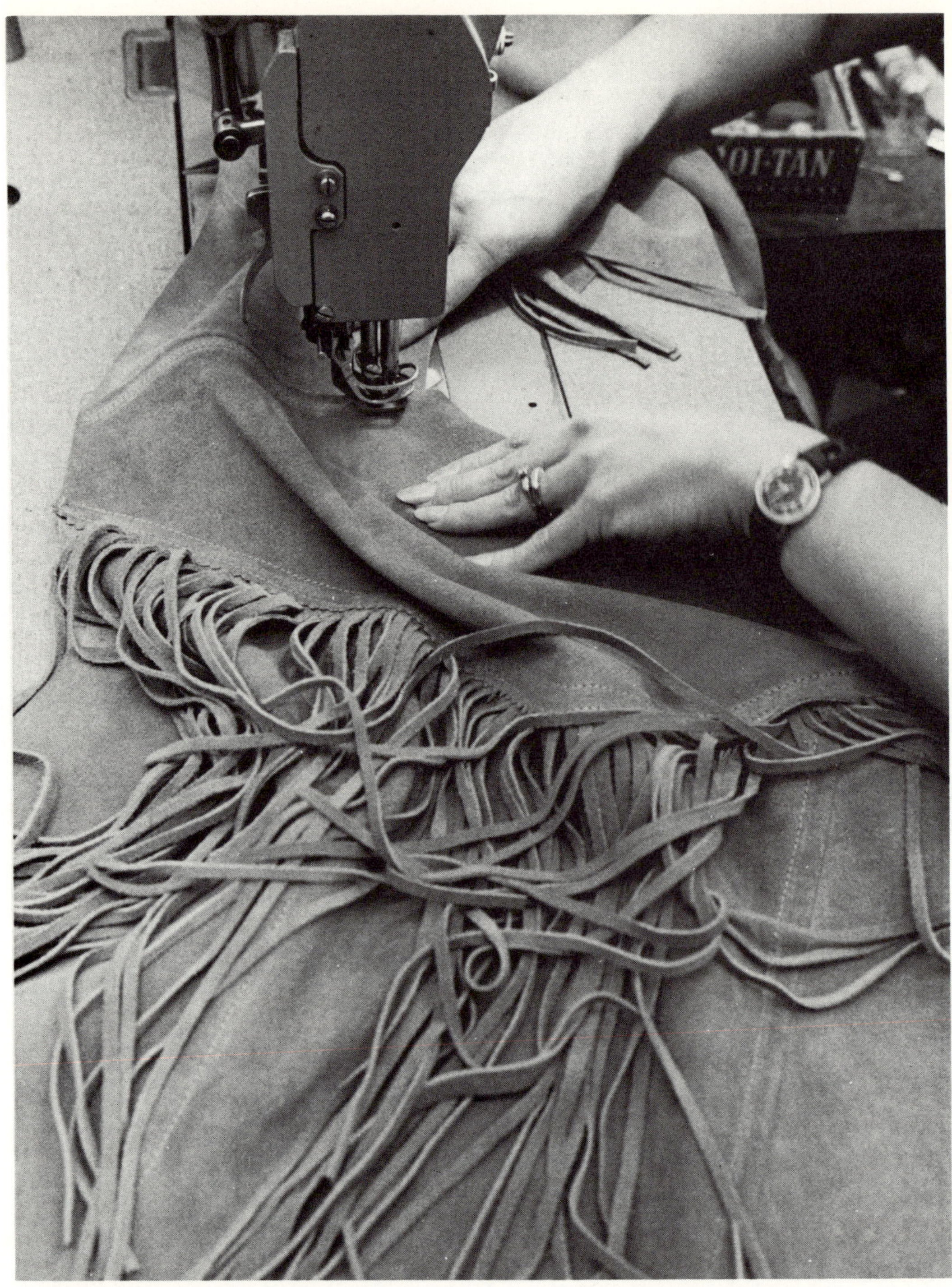

The jacket is almost finished and the sleeve is being sewn on.

leather garments in those plastic bags used by commercial cleaners. They will prevent the leather from breathing and the garment will quickly begin to discolor. Last, if you have any problems, don't call me. Write Jerry Rush, 4965 South Broadway, Englewood, Colorado. His outfit made the superb jacket shown here and he can answer any technical questions. Good Luck!

Front and back view of the completed jacket.

INDEX

Boldface numbers refer to illustrations